"I'm not into serious bondage, [...]t a B&D-er. No Japanese rope tricks. I can take it or leave it. This is something I do for women. Women really get off on bondage. Have you ever read a romantic novel? They like you to overcome their resistance. I'm an erotic game player. Bondage is a game."

"I believe this is something you're more likely to get into if you have money. I've lived extensively in Europe and more recently in both Manhattan and L.A. The people I know who play around with S/M on any level have money. It's not a poor person's game."

"I've always wanted to find a man who was man enough to do this to me," she said. "My first whipping was a revelation."

"You either get it or you don't. It's as simple as that. If you get it, it's part of you, like faith in God."

*St. Martin's Paperbacks Titles
by Susan Crain Bakos*

WHAT MEN REALLY WANT
SEXUAL PLEASURES
KINK

VC-Lost

Kink

THE
HIDDEN SEX LIVES
OF AMERICANS

Susan Crain Bakos

St. Martin's Paperbacks

With the exception of the experts, the people who appear in the following pages have been assigned different names and identifying characteristics. This was done to safeguard their privacy.

The author would like to thank Race Bannon for permission to reprint material from his book *Learning the Ropes*.

KINK: THE HIDDEN SEX LIVES OF AMERICANS

Copyright © 1995 by Susan Crain Bakos.

Cover photograph by Herman Estévez.

ISBN 0-312-95684-3

Printed in the United States of America

St. Martin's Press hardcover edition/March 1995
St. Martin's Paperbacks edition/December 1995

10 9 8 7 6 5 4

To Jack Kaplan and Jack Heidenry, my best friends

Acknowledgments

I am grateful to the following people for their help:

Eric Wybenga, who helped shape and edit *Kink*—and asked the right questions in the margins. Master George and Mistress Zena, who brought so much passion, humor, and enthusiasm to the project of educating me. Isadora Alman and Fred Berlin, for their time and patience. Peggy Cone, performance artist extraordinaire, for making the East Village scene accessible to me. V. K. McCarty, for her guidance, glasses of champagne, and always wise journalism advice.

I also wish to thank the many people who consented to be interviewed, most of whom did not make it into print for space reasons.

Contents

Introduction:
What Are Your Neighbors' Sexual Secrets?

"Slomo," a San Francisco "leather dyke" (a lesbian sado-masochism devotee), gave her mother, a Midwestern grade-school teacher, a whip for Christmas—and not the kind of whip horsewomen use on their steeds. The gift was a red deer suede flogger, which Slomo had handcrafted.

"Mom's not into using it on her boyfriend," Slomo says. "She hung it on the hallway wall, where she displays the best family photos, hung it right next to the framed Mother's Day card I made for her when I was six. She isn't ashamed or anything."

In the recent film *Exit to Eden*, Dana Delaney, who played that nice nurse on TV's *China Beach*, commanded the role of sex goddess/dominatrix. Macho actors Wesley Snipes and Patrick Swayze can be seen in a movie about crossdressers, *To Wong Foo, Thanks for Everything, Julie Newmar*, in which the actors look and act the parts of transvestites, not men dressing as women to get a job or to be close to their offspring like most characters who have masqueraded as women in mainstream films. In *Philadelphia* magazine's "first ever" survey of sex in the city, editor Carol Saline reported "something surprising": 20 percent of the respondents "gave high marks to bondage and discipline." Once shrouded in secrecy—like the dresses that purportedly hung in J. Edgar Hoover's closet—kink is visible now.

In Los Angeles, I attended a party in the mansion of a film star. The distinct sadomasochistic (S/M) overtones that evening included conversational innuendo and clothing cues—a lot of black, a lot of leather, a lot of black leather, very high heels on the women and crossdressing men, and heavy concentrations of metal inserted through skin. No "scenes" were staged. A young man had come directly from the now-defunct S/M club Fuck!, since raided and closed by Hollywood Vice. He described the closing as "a form of rape of the S/M community." Giving him the same benign respect they would accord an animal rights activist, people nodded politely.

A young woman in her early twenties, dressed in a black leather bra, hot pants, and thigh-high boots with five-inch heels, surveyed the guests and complained that "the normal people are taking over S/M." The tiny golden rings piercing the outlines of her ears and the flesh beneath her eyebrows glittered as she moved her head. The bar through her tongue glistened while she talked. Her nipples and labia were pierced too, she told me. She had grown up in Philadelphia, where her parents still lived—or "stagnated," in her estimation. I wanted to ask her: Doesn't this body mutilation break your mother's heart?

"It's scary," she said, indicating the assemblage of beautiful people with a sweep of her hand, incredibly long nails painted a red so deep it was almost black. "It's scary to see these people taking over our things. They don't know how to do it. Someone could get hurt."

"Most of them probably don't do it," I told her in a

reassuring voice. "They want to look like they do."

I thought about the article in *Philadelphia* magazine. She was wrong when she said there was no action in her hometown. What would she think of the suburban wife quoted as saying she liked hanging from the attic rafters while her husband whipped her with his belt?

A few weeks after that party, I was in Baltimore, conservative *Baltimore,* drawn there by the revelations in "Kinky Sex," a January 1993 cover article in *City Paper,* a free weekly. The piece described both homosexual and heterosexual forms of kinky sex as practiced by a group of people who consented to be named and photographed, meaning they were part of the inner circle of a group known as The Scene—whipmakers, bar owners, political activists, and others whose lives and livelihoods are defined by S/M. Their hobbies include heavy whipping, branding, cutting, scarring, and the piercing of penises, labia, nipples, navels, and tongues. One of the men interviewed, a self-described "master" and "true sadist," explained how he liked to perform his favorite activity, piercing, on a slave: by inserting needles every half inch around the prone perimeter of the slave's body, then tying the needles with a cord to nails he'd nailed eighteen inches away from the body. His goal, he said, was to be "creative" with S/M.

His candor in a publication read by many mainstream Baltimore residents surprised me. His inventiveness did not. For several years, I wrote sex-advice columns for *Penthouse Forum* and *Penthouse Letters,* where I was the "Superlady of Sex." I heard from men, and more than a few women, who were foot fetishists, S/M devotees, crossdressers, spankers or spankees, rubber enthusiasts, and practitioners of various other forms of kinky sex, the sort of behaviors labeled "paraphilias," or perversions, by the psychological establishment. Many of these writers had devised fiendishly clever ways of sexually tormenting themselves or their partners. They were largely articulate, intelligent, sometimes witty, and often upper middle class. My correspondents were, in fact, typical upscale city magazine readers.

When I researched my previous two books, *What Men Really Want* and *Sexual Pleasures,* I interviewed many men and women who were at least dabbling in alternative forms of sexual expression, including a few who only had "sex" in extreme ways most of us don't consider sexual. They no longer had intercourse at all—and might not experience orgasm often either. Instead, they found erotic stimulation and satisfaction through the playing of complicated mind games involving humiliation and control, the giving or receiving of pain, for example, or the worship of feet.

In my research as a magazine writer and author, I found a direct correlation between socioeconomic standing and kink. Poor people seem to do it far less often than the rich. According to the Kinsey Institute, more than one-third of American men engage in sexual practices outside the "norm" (foreplay, intercourse, and oral sex). These practices include heterosexual anal intercourse, exhibitionism, fetishism, travestitism, S/M and bondage, and others. The higher up the socioeconomic ladder one goes, some researchers report, the more prevalent kinky practices become—which either suggests that people higher up the scale respond more frequently to surveys or participate more readily in research studies, or that they actually feel less social pressure to conform to the sexual "norm" in their lives.

I remember telling a beautifully dressed, coiffed, and groomed acquaintance over an expensive lunch at a Park Avenue bistro in Manhattan, "There are many levels of kinky behavior, beginning with heterosexual anal sex, and there are more practitioners on all levels among the middle and upper classes than you think."

Her reply? "I'm glad to hear it. My husband likes to wear my lingerie, and sometimes I wonder if that is very odd."

It may be very odd in the mind of a "vanilla" person who has failed to pick up on the subtle signals sent by certain friends, neighbors, relatives, and professional associates and who believes "perverts" are those guys with their hands in their raincoats at peep shows. "Vanilla" is the designation the hardcore S/M players assign to the rest of us when they're talking about us behind our backs. These "heavy players," as they often call themselves, *are* "The Scene," several notches on the kink scale above the more casual players who stage "scenes"—S/M tableaux that involve more costume drama than pain—or watch others "play" at clubs or private parties. Vanilla people have heterosexual sex with one person at a time, no kink. The subtext? Vanilla people are afraid of exploring, pushing, testing the limits. The players, heavy and casual, think we'd love it their way, if only we weren't too wimpy to give whipping a try.

In fact, the vanilla person has probably fantasized about bondage or spanking, about making love to more than one person at a time, or about having anal sex. "Forced sex," often including bondage, and sex with more than one person at a time are two of the top five fantasies reported by both men and women in several research studies. Nancy Friday's 1992 book on contemporary female fantasies, *Woman on Top*, reported female participants have far more sadomasochistic fantasies than women surveyed for her books twenty years ago.

How could you not have bondage-inspired fantasies, for instance, when bondage is featured in films like *Basic Instinct, Tie Me Up, Tie Me Down*, and the Madonna clunker, *Body of Evidence* (sold in video stores with an accompanying "passion pack," including handcuffs and a candle for dripping hot wax onto the body of the bound one you love)? How could you not have a stray S/M thought if you read magazines, watch television, go to the movies, or walk through the districts in every major city favored by artists and gays, from St. Louis's Central West End to San Francisco's Castro District to Washington, D.C.'s Dupont Circle?

Twenty years ago, oral sex was considered kinky—and people seldom admitted doing it, though surely they must have. Today, cunnilingus and fellatio are acceptable forms of sexual behavior, acknowledged by the majority. Will light bondage perhaps be viewed as just another sex trick in the skilled lover's bag twenty years from now? Possibly. Sex has changed in America and throughout the world and continues to change, but probably not the way you think it has.

Ask the average American how sex has changed in the past decade and he or she will say, "People are having less sex—or fewer partners—because of fear of AIDS."

Wrong.

Whether undertaken by magazines, universities, or such national giants of headcounting as the Alan Guttmacher Institute, the behavioral surveys *do not show much change at all in the number of partners or the frequency of sexual encounters we have now as compared with ten years ago.* The *Cosmopolitan* reader has an average of four partners per year now, down from five partners a year in 1980—a more significant decline than that shown by most polls and studies. The typical survey respondent reporting less sex is an aging baby boomer whose drive for children and security is stronger than his or her craving for sexual variety. People give lip service to disease fears but, with the exception of homosexual men, have so far failed to change significantly their sexual behavior in terms of partners or numbers of encounters in the face of a growing AIDS epidemic. *Only 17 percent of heterosexuals who have multiple partners even use condoms regularly.*

"How often?" has not significantly changed. "How?" is the new hot question. Sex in America has gotten kinkier. The practice of some forms of kink is more or less sanctioned by some experts who view it as a way of reducing exposure to disease. S/M rarely involves penetration or the exchange of bodily fluids. And a little kink can keep a monogamous partner from straying back out into the disease pool, can't it?

"Many experts predicted the demise of American sex in the wake of the panic generated by AIDS," say Samuel S. Janus, Ph.D., and Cynthia L. Janus, M.D., authors of *The Janus Report* (1992), the first broadscale scientific national sex survey since the Kinsey report. "We found instead a continuous and increasing variety of [sexual deviance]."

The evidence is everywhere. The sadomasochistic images that dominate MTV now appear regularly in our fashion magazines. Society women dress in bondage outfits designed by Gianni Versace. A mainstream pinup wears a leather bikini, hands suggestively raised over her head. Phil and Oprah and Sally and Geraldo have introduced us to practitioners of every imaginable sexual perversion. Your grandmother can define *transvestite*. *Time* magazine has reported on the "growing phenomenon" of sex toy shops in suburban shopping malls, where handcuffs, whips, and ankle and wrist restraints are sold alongside the honey dust, flavored condoms, body paints, and disposable panties that titillated us a dozen or more years ago.

The face of kinkiness is far more diverse, and private, than a public collage of such media types as Madonna and the publisher of the *S & M News*, who turns up on daytime talk shows regularly with one of his devoted slaves in chain. Junior League wives attend sex toy parties and purchase fur-lined handcuffs. Solid Republican husbands dress in women's silk panties beneath their pinstriped suits. The typical practitioner of kinky sex is more like Chuck Jones, Marla Maples's publicist who was arrested for stealing her shoes, than the urban transvestite hooker. Before being exposed by the national media as a foot fetishist, Jones led his secret sex life behind the facade of a successful entrepreneur, husband, and father. The difference between him and your neighbor? Donald Trump caught Jones on film with a camera he'd hidden in Marla's closet.

Irrefutable numbers are hard to come by in a nation that eschews funding sex surveys. Who knows exactly how many people practice kink now—or did ten or twenty years ago? Researchers at the Kinsey Institute in Bloomington, Indiana, estimated that approximately 50 percent of Americans have tried bondage at least once, 40 percent have experimented with S/M games at least once, and that 5 to 10 percent engage in sadomasochism for sexual pleasure on a regular basis. In the most recent *Redbook* magazine reader sex survey, 46 percent of the respondents said they practiced anal sex at least occasionally, and 50 percent of them reported enjoying the experience. Almost 5 percent of married Americans told a Guttmacher pollster they have had sex with another partner while the spouse was present. And, again, the interview subjects are middle class and above, with the highest concentrations found in the upper middle classes. One survey of men who subscribe to a magazine for transvestites reported the majority were above average in intelligence and career advancement and financial attainment, and more than 75 percent were married and were parents.

Before 1980, intercourse was the sexual activity most men requested from prostitutes. Now, according to a spokesperson for PONY (Prostitutes of New York), it is fellatio, closely followed by some form of S/M, typically spanking with the hand, a belt, or a cane. (He pays her to spank him.) A Southern dominatrix told me she'd given up "turning tricks" for "whipping bottoms," because "smart women are doms now, the dumber ones are hookers. It takes a lot of brains and creativity to be a dom. Any woman can spread her legs."

Sex certainly *has* changed in America. What has driven so many people to the sexual limits?

The social acceptability of kink, especially among the avant-garde. Once everyone with money had at least one gay friend. Yet middle-class gays were afraid to tell their friends about their sexual orientation. Now the rich may have a transvestite friend, too. No one knows whether there has been an actual increase in hardcore S/M activity— heavy whipping, cutting and branding of flesh, prolonged discipline sessions in which masters torture and humiliate slaves for hours. Social observers and sex researchers agree that light forms of bondage and S/M, as an occasional game, are practiced by more people now, in part because the prevalence of such imagery makes the behavior acceptable to us in our bedrooms. In *The New Joy of Sex*, Dr. Alex Comfort treats "loving" S/M as just another sexual variation. Even Dr. Ruth, a self-described "square," has a benevolent view of spanking and light bondage and once dismissed one of her reader's serious concerns about them.

"As long as nobody gets hurt," she said, "what is the harm in indulging your partner's occasional request for something a little kinky?"

Fear of disease or boredom or intimacy. Some experts believe disease fears may play at least a small role in the increase in kinky behavior, particularly among gay men, bisexuals, and the kind of sexual adventurers who attended orgies in the Seventies or early Eighties. They often claim S/M games make monogamy more interesting. Possibly, in this advanced stage of the sexual revolution, the boldest players are looking for new taboos to break. Nothing but kinky sex is left in a world where mothers have sex with their daughters' boyfriends and go public with the details on *The Jenny Jones Show*. For the sexually avant-garde, the Vault, a Manhattan S/M club modeled after a dungeon, is the Nineties version of the public sexual decadence that once drew the same crowd to Plato's Retreat, a club where all manner of sex acts took place between consenting adults with the price of admission. Instead of participating in orgies, the Vault's clientele safely watch nonpenetrative activities between masters and mistresses and their slaves, rough sex play as a spectator sport.

At Paddles, in Manhattan, I recently stood at the bar with wineglass in hand and watched for over an hour as a "master" immobilized his slave within an intricate web of silky ropes, blindfolded and gagged her, then whipped her breasts, buttocks, back, and thighs. Sweat trickled down her face, between her breasts, down her belly, and dropped from her hard nipples. Her hips moved, and her pelvis rocked against the ropes as if she were rocking against her lover's body.

The sounds of whips and paddles smacking against flesh, the muffled groans, moans, and gasps from participants, the sights of erect penises and hard nipples straining against cloth, welts forming, and sweat pouring off contorted bodies are the spectacle here. House rules forbid exchange of bodily fluids, the drawing of blood, or exposure of genitals. By contrast, many swingers, who still Do It in public, now hold safe-sex parties in which "sex" may be masturbating a partner, hands and genitals covered in latex. Tame by comparison?

Some experts, however, believe something other than

fear of contracting a disease is more likely to motivate a couple into experimenting with bondage and discipline: Fear of intimacy. Fear of the loss of control. Fear of the consequences of genuine sexual equality. Fear of impotence. Is it a surprise that "kink" should be the new sex now that baby boomers are aging and men, especially, need more to arouse them sexually? Should we be shocked that S/M, with its set of rigid rules for role-playing, would surface now when people of all ages are grappling, often unsuccessfully, with redefining male and female roles?

These fears, the experts tell us, are more prevalent in our rapidly changing society than they were twenty years ago. They make the ritualized emotional safety of fetishism or sadomasochistic sex appealing. Contrary to what many believe, most forms of kinky behavior, especially S/M or fetish play, are not practiced by people who are wildly passionate and out of control. The further one ventures into kinky territory, the more rules and rituals one must learn. The game is power exchange. The issue is control. The "scenes" are planned and executed according to plan, with less spontaneity than the derided vanilla couple might exhibit on Saturday night in the missionary position.

The sexual repression that underlies our Puritanical culture. Researchers who specialize in the treatment of sexual paraphilias are a growing breed, one that includes Robert Kolodony and Mark Schwartz, the heirs apparent at the Masters and Johnson Institute. Perversion, the experts believe, often results from a rigid, religiously repressed background. The sons of Southern Baptist preachers may be more likely to be foot fetishists than the sons of East Coast liberals. All of America's sons and daughters have come of age under the long, lingering shadow of the Puritans, which makes us less likely to indulge joyously in sex than people from many other countries—though the Japanese, British, and German people share some of our hangups, if not our heritage.

Freud saw sadomasochism as an eruption of man's darkest, most primitive nature. He said sexual deviants were "poor devils who have to pay a high price for their limited pleasure." In America today, S/M seems more like a game. A man can walk into a brightly lit sex toys shop, put down his credit card, and have the nipple clamps and leather restraints wrapped in pink tissue paper for presentation to his beloved, along with a bunch of roses and a bottle of champagne. Is the sex play he will have with his lover a mere form of sport? Something more sinister?

That seems to depend upon whether or not this game is his only means of achieving arousal and orgasm—whether or not it represents the single narrow path he has for finding arousal and release. In this book, you will meet people who regard kink as a part of their private erotic repertoire and pull out the silk ties or leather restraints once or twice a month. You will meet others who hang around the fringes of The Scene, the clubs and social groups, and a small number who are totally immersed in this Scene, to the point of selecting their partners, finding their friends, and often choosing their employment among a group of people who *live,* not merely practice, S/M.

I have arranged the book in an order of ascending kinkiness, beginning with behaviors common to many of us, such as anal sex, light spanking, and bondage, progressing through heavier forms of kink, such as the master-slave relationship and the sort of masochism that sends its practitioners to the hospital, even the grave. I chose to end with body piercing, a practice which to me, and I suspect to most readers, seems to have little or nothing to do with sex—with intercourse and orgasms—but has achieved widespread acceptance among the young.

Many people were open with me in describing what they do and why they do it. Often, I was invited to witness private scenes, including domination sessions in dungeons. I have been inside sex clubs and private parties, the kinds of places to which other curious vanilla people might secretly want to go. I have met people who are doing things we may fantasize or fear doing ourselves. Outside their sexual realm, these people look, for the most part, like you and me. Only the full-time Scene members and the extravagantly pierced are identifiable in public—because they choose to flaunt their lifestyle.

The typical participants in kinky sex could be that attractive, quiet professional couple in the condo across the hall. Was that the shadow of a nipple ring you spied beneath her clingy blouse in the elevator you shared with her today?

Part 1
Almost Every
Sexually
Adventurous Person
Has Tried . . .

Chapter 1

What's the One Thing He Says She Won't Do That He Really Wants to Do? Heterosexual Anal Sex

Wendy is holding a butt plug in the palm of her hand. About two inches in length and less in diameter, the plug is designed with a wide flat base, presumably so it won't get lost inside the lower intestine. I look at it and remember the urban myth that swept the country several years ago. Surely you heard the story about _____ (fill in the blank with the name of a local, national, or international celebrity suspected of being secretly gay) who was taken to the hospital after a gerbil inserted into his anus for fun ran amok. This is the societal message we send about people who have anal sex: They are foolish and lust-crazed enough to introduce live rodents into their bodies, via their assholes.

"I don't get the point of this," Wendy says to the sales-clerk, jiggling the plug in her hand. She is wearing a sleek navy gabardine coatdress with gold buttons that comple-

3

ment her heavy gold earrings and watchband. Her chin-length blond hair is turned gracefully under. Wendy looks more *Working Woman* magazine than Frederick's of Hollywood. "It isn't big enough to get you off," she observes.

"Some people use them to prepare for anal sex," the saleswoman explains. She is in her early twenties, very pretty with long, curly brown hair, and tiny, probably a size two. Her diminutiveness is emphasized by the strapless black rubber dress she wears. The dress is ugly and expensive. Two hundred ninety-nine dollars for something that wouldn't look good on your front tire? "The plug opens them up a little bit and gets them used to the feeling of something inside, so penetration won't be as difficult," she adds helpfully, walking toward us on four-inch-spiked heel shoes, in the vulnerable, tentative gait such shoes impose upon the wearer. "You might enjoy a bigger one more. They come in different sizes."

While Wendy examines butt plugs and anal vibrators, I look around Dressing for Pleasure, an upscale "erotique," a clothing and sex toys boutique. DFP is more spacious than shops I've visited in New York, Philadelphia, or Washington, D.C. The product line is more diverse, the selection of books and videos quite large. The merchandise, however, which ranges from bras with holes cut out for nipples to custom-made whips, still evokes a suppressed giggle, with "tacky" the basic descriptive adjective I would choose. No matter how you display a bondage mask or a pair of crotchless panties, they will never have class. Nor are they, in this setting, threatening. Like the raw sexuality of Elvis in his prime translated into a head and torso lamp base in shades of pink, gold, and turquoise, kink has become domesticated, rendered powerless to reduce much response beyond an embarrassed chuckle.

Constance, the owner of the shop, and her partner and submissive, John, run more than a retail business. DFP is almost a community center for the upwardly mobile and kinky in northern New Jersey, land of luxurious bedroom communities, expanding industrial parks, and vast shopping malls. Their customers talk about Constance in effusive terms, and underlying the praise of her is respect. They speak of her as though she had been the firm but fair headmistress of their boarding school.

The week before Wendy's and my visit, I scheduled an appointment with Constance for a private tour of the shop, then promptly forgot about it. The message she eventually left on my answering machine was stern. In a British accent, she said, ''I am so disappointed in you. I was expecting you and you did not arrive. You must certainly have an explanation for this.'' It isn't nice to ignore dominant women—my first lesson communicated by a woman so powerful she can make you hang your head or square your shoulders through phone-voice contact alone.

I glance around, surreptitiously smirking at the edible panties, not wanting her to see me, though she couldn't possibly know who I am.

I am examining the condom selection when Wendy walks over, wrapped purchase in hand. She has bought an anal vibrator, a device that looks like the nozzle of an old-fashioned douche bag attached to a battery compartment. The pursuit of kink is not often a path marked by beautiful adornments. The gadgets, the clothing, the disciplinary accessories—all lack a certain grace and charm, the kind possessed by lace, silk, satin, and scented oils and creams, those classic accoutrements of seduction. On the other hand, good leather does have an enticing erotic smell.

"Our salesgirl is a submissive," she whispers excitedly in my ear. "If you look really closely at her back, you can see some fading marks. Notice on your way out." She picks up a package of anal condoms, but then puts them back down.

"I wish I needed these," she says wistfully.

Wendy can't remember if her first experience with anal sex was inspired by a story in *Penthouse Forum* or *Penthouse Variations,* but it was definitely one or the other. Almost ten years ago, when she was in her late twenties, she was living in a large L-shaped studio, a fourth-floor walk-up, in the East Village section of Manhattan with her boyfriend, Alan. She was a part-time waitress at the Lion's Head Pub, a Greenwich Village restaurant. She considered herself an actress, an opinion occasionally buttressed by a minor part on a daytime soap. Alan, two years younger, dark, bearded, and intense, worked for a trade publication by day and wrote his novel at night. They came together at a point in their lives when each needed a partner for mutually sustaining illusions as much as for sharing the rent and the bed.

"He cribbed his sex scenes from those sex magazines," Wendy recalls. "We never admitted he did. I don't know if he ever finished that novel, or any novel. We broke up after two years; I haven't seen anything by him in a bookstore, but I don't buy a lot of books. I could have missed him."

"Those sex magazines," *Forum* and *Variations,* inspired Wendy's fantasies. While Alan worked at the noisy old electric Royal typewriter his parents had given him as a high school graduation gift, Wendy sometimes masturbated, a magazine in the other hand, in the bed, covered by an Indian-print spread, tucked back into the alcove. If she made enough noise, Alan would turn off the machine and join her in bed. He would ask her what she was thinking about when she masturbated; what had turned her on.

"I said it was him, but he knew it wasn't. One night he handed me the magazine and told me to read from something that aroused me. I opened it to a story about anal sex. My heart was beating faster as I started reading. It was a first-person piece, by a wife who gave her husband the gift of anal sex for his birthday. She had prepared by occasionally inserting an anal plug to get used to the feeling—you know, like the girl in the sex boutique described, but I didn't want to let on that I knew. My face was sweaty when I finished reading, and he had a huge erection.

" 'You want me to fuck you in the ass, don't you?' he said. Not, *I* want to, but *you* want it. Of course, I knew he wanted it, too. He'd brought it up a few times, and once, had tried to sort of slip his penis in my asshole, but it isn't that easily done. I was scared. I knew this was going to hurt like hell, but, yes, I did want him to fuck my ass. From fear and excitement, my heart was beating wildly.

"I insisted we take it slowly and use lots of lube. He started by using one finger, then two, working them very slowly and gently into my asshole. I made him put on a condom and more lube. We did it the first time with me lying on my back, legs up and over my shoulders.

"I knew it was going to hurt, which it did at first. But,

God, it felt good, so good. I couldn't believe how much I liked it. Your asshole is incredibly sensitive. And you can feel everything, every tiny movement of a cock or finger inside you.

"I know the joke about buttfucking. It's something a woman does twice—once to find out what it's like and the second time to see if it was really that bad. And I know some women believe this is something only passive women do to please their men.

"Buttfucking is seen as the ultimate male sexual fantasy. We, as a culture, don't understand how much women can like taking it up the ass."

Alan liked it, too. On their last night in the apartment together, he said he considered "the gift" of her "anal virginity" the best thing she'd ever given him. He credited "that magazine" with encouraging her to explore this aspect of her sexuality.

"He may have been right," she says. "I think I would have discovered anal sex eventually anyway, but the young wife's story did turn me on to the idea that night."

How kinky is anal sex?

"The anal taboo is so strong in this country, most bookstores won't carry my book [*Anal Pleasure and Health*]" Dr. Jack Morin says. "That hasn't changed in the twelve years since the book was first published." He laughs when he says, "This has been good for my book." He's right: There is no other book on anal sex, which is astonishing when you consider how many sex books are on the market. "There's no competition. I can't think of any other area of sex which isn't covered by several books."

Even though surveys show an increase in heterosexual anal sex (and a decrease in homosexual anal sex, attributed to AIDS fears), Dr. Morin explains that "the taboo remains strong. This is a very secret sex practice. People don't talk about it. The association of the anus with feces, with dirtiness and nastiness, goes way back. Beliefs learned that early are entrenched.

"The good side of a taboo is what I call 'the naughtiness factor.' Some people like feeling they're violating a prohibition. This makes sex more exciting for them. The bad side of a taboo, of course, is that people who break the taboo feel bad about what they're doing, about themselves for doing it—and inhibited about getting information."

Is Wendy so rare a woman in her desire for anal intercourse?

Anal Pleasure and Health grew out of Dr. Morin's workshops, where participants learned how to enjoy anal stimulation, including intercourse, without pain or injury. In the beginning, the participants were largely gay men. Then heterosexual women discovered his classes. Their questions and concerns, he says, were very similar to those of the men.

"Some women had to work through their feelings about what enjoying anal sex said about them. They would ask, 'What kind of woman does this?' or 'How sleazy is this?' while gay men worried more about issues of power and submission. Did receiving anal sex make them too submissive?"

Most men will eventually ask for anal sex from some woman; and many, perhaps most, women will say no.

However, thirty years ago, many, perhaps most, women were saying no to fellatio and cunnilingus, then considered "kinky" because they weren't practiced by the average American. The symbol of sexual licentiousness was the wholesome *Playboy* centerfold, her delicate tuft of pubic hair covering inner lips, which apparently few men imagined penetrating with their tongues. Anal sex is as kinky today as oral sex was then.

Studies show that at least 30 percent of American heterosexual couples have tried anal sex—and some practice it regularly. This form of intercourse provides the possibility of an easier transmission for the AIDS virus, if damage is done to the rectal tissue—which can easily occur without liberal use of a lubricant such as KY jelly. Yet, for straight monogamous couples, anal sex is the way to be kinky—perhaps, because it is the cultural taboo most easily broken. Not surprisingly, many men and women who have been in the forefront of the sexual revolution are more afraid of anal play than the young married couple next door.

The legendary former porn star/cult figure Annie Sprinkle, who has done just about everything and confessed it all in print or on camera, once responded to my question of whether she did or didn't take it up the ass: "No way! No one is fucking me up the ass!" That was the only time in the ten years I've known Annie that I can recall seeing her draw herself up in the posture of a Sunday-school teacher.

Another woman, a friend, not well known, answered the same question in the classic way: "I tried it once. It hurt. When he pulled his penis out, there were bits of fecal matter clinging to it. Gross! The next day I hurt more, especially when I had a bowel movement. But he wanted to do it again. No! No! No! Why do men want this anyway? I don't understand it.''

I do understand. Men aren't the sex who were sent out to play in ruffled rompers and admonished, "Don't get dirty!," so they aren't as put off by the possibility of an unclean moment as we are. Aesthetics aside, they are the products of millions of years of social conditioning to be the sexual aggressors. And the issue in sex is erotic power, dominance and submission, the same issue, whether we're talking about a couple in the missionary position or the mistress with her slave tied to the rack. The impulse to dominate the female must be programmed somewhere like a tiny microchip implanted in the male brain—into the majority of the male brains, at least. (Many men are more submissive than I ever could be.) Plunging into a hot, tight corridor that yields each opening reluctantly must feel like entering a snug virgin every time. Could that sense of newness fail to arouse the average man? Can he be blamed for wanting to feel his penis being grasped so tightly? No and no; and, of course, there's more.

There is what he wants her to be, not always, not even the majority of the time, but sometimes: *submissive*.

A woman is never as submissive as when she offers a man her ass to plumb. She fears pain or discomfort or a streak left on the sheets less than the total surrender accompanying that act. She must trust him in order to let go of herself completely. She must also trust herself to regain the control she's temporarily relinquished when the sex is over. The ability to trust could lead a woman to say yes to anal sex. But will she *want* it the way she wants intercourse? Only rarely do I enjoy being submissive or saying yes to anal sex, though when I do, I enjoy it enormously.

I've never failed to have an intense orgasm from anal sex, though it still isn't something I do often or have done with many men. I don't *want* it that often. I have to be open to the experience. He has to be a special man. I know nothing will move me in the same way this does, but I hold off, saying no many times for every yes.

The ass is a gift. When a woman kneels with her ass in the air, head well down, she feels erotic dread grow in the pit of her stomach and spread through her loins. She can want for this and fear it. In my anticipation of the entry thrust, my heart beats faster, the walls of my vagina swell. It is all up to him. How will he take me?

The sex advice books say that a man should push gently, entering only glans deep, and move slowly, taking the friction on the pulling out of the stroke not the pushing in of it. According to Dr. Alex Comfort, author of *The Joy of Sex*, one does not "joyously" thrust into the anus. This is how careful people would behave when they were experimenting with a new form of sex.

"Hot anal sex with a man is a milestone in the relationship," one woman explained. "Doing it proves something to both of you. When I think about anal sex, I'm always turned on. It's a potent fantasy element. In actuality, I seldom want to do it. That does seem strange, not wanting to repeat a great experience. Maybe deep down, I'm afraid of doing damage to my body or my psyche if I allow this to happen very often."

Some women do, of course, want more. Wendy does.

* * *

"After Alan, I was the one who suggested anal sex in relationships," Wendy says. "The next man told me he wasn't particularly interested in doing it, but he would to please me, or if I was on my period. My periods go on for several days, so he was glad to fuck my ass, because he was glad to still be fucking. He was the least interested in my butt of all the men I've ever known. I mean, he didn't particularly like to look at my ass or fondle it. I think he was afraid that male interest in anal sex indicated homosexual tendencies. He never said this, but I think that's what he thought."

Five years ago, Wendy traded acting and the East Village for a job in retail management and an apartment in a comfortable New Jersey suburb approximately forty-five minutes from Manhattan. She started dating Doug, a lawyer she met when he came into her store to buy gifts for his mother and sister on Christmas Eve. The following Christmas Eve, they were married. Now she lives in an even more comfortable Jersey suburb, in a spacious two-story house with a swimming pool. Their baby girl is almost a year old. The nanny speaks halting English. Wendy works part-time selling clothing and jewelry in an exclusive boutique. An enthusiastic homemaker, she subscribes to *Redbook* magazine and belongs to the Junior League.

"I still read *Forum* and sometimes *Variations,* and they get me hot, hotter than they do Doug. I can be excited by everything, including the lesbian and S/M stuff, though these are things I have no interest in trying. He knows I've been to Dressing for Pleasure. I buy things he likes, leather bras and G-strings, body oils and honey dust. He likes me to make a big production out of dressing for sex. I won't show him the anal vibrator. That will stay in the bottom of my drawer, something for me to use when he isn't here.

"We very rarely have anal sex. He loves my ass, looking at it and touching it. I know I can get him interested in sex just by putting on a pair of shorts that are so short my cheeks show. He just doesn't feel comfortable doing it to me that way. He says it makes him feel like a rapist, even with my consent. The first time we tried, he lost his erection before he could get inside me. I feel like the only woman in America who wants anal sex from a man who doesn't want to give it to her.

"I wouldn't break up my marriage over something like this. It isn't that important. Sometimes I fantasize running into Alan accidentally and checking into a hotel room where he has a real go at my ass. Fantasy, pure fantasy."

She sighs theatrically, pauses, then adds: "Call me in a few years to see if I'm involved in a discreet but hot affair with a man who likes anal sex as much as I do. *That* I can see happening."

Chapter 2

Bondage 101, Tie and Tease

"A rosy pink corset enhances my tiny waist and full hips. The little white stays stand out like valentines. I wear adorable clothes. . . . She leads me to a tree in the backyard, where I am bound and suspended. Her husband silently takes pictures. I am the captive slave girl, prized for my beauty. I am the chaste virgin who must be taken by force. My pussy quivers. My ribs and muscles stretch from the earth to the sky, between heaven and hell."

Veronica Vera,
writing about her initiation into bondage

WASHINGTON, D.C.

Veronica testified before the Meese Commission on pornography in defense of bondage. Dark-haired and beautiful, she somewhat resembles the cult bondage pin-up queen of the Fifties, Betty Page, who was called before a previous porn inquiry, the Kefauver Commission. Ironically, and perhaps tellingly, underground S/M groups flourish in D.C., home base of the inquisitors. The exclusive Black Rose, a social group, reputedly counts almost half its membership from among the various ranks of government.

Michael says he finally understood why women become aroused by bondage when he read Veronica's story, printed in a sex magazine he purchased used for a dollar at a Times Square shop.

"Women like bondage," Michael assures me. "They like being tied up, because it takes the responsibility away from them, permits them to indulge their true submissive natures. I love women. I am a true romantic, the guy who always brings a single red rose," he says, tapping with his index finger the long-stemmed red rosebud surrounded by baby's breath and sheathed in plastic, which makes me think of a condom.

The flower is lying beside my tape recorder on the table between us at Kramer's Books and Afterwords Café in Washington, D.C. Has he brought me the rose as a visual aide to the interview? Or does he think this, our second meeting, will end in his showing me "up close and personal" how he practices his favorite sex game, "tie and tease"?

A light coating of sweat lays across his brow. This is the eighth day of above-95-degree temperatures in D.C., and he has broken a sweat walking the half block from the Metro stop. He smiles. At our first meeting, we established his personal and sexual history, excluding bondage. His mother gave birth to him when she was sixteen and died in an automobile accident when he was three. His grandmother and two aunts raised him. He's never known his father. Could he enjoy tying up women because, as an adult, he's acting out against his female-dominated childhood? They never tied him up, he points out. He doesn't remember playing cowboys and Indians, though surely he "must have; in those days the Saturday-morning shows included a lot of half-hour cowboy dramas, 'The Lone Ranger,' 'Sky King,' all that."

I signal the waitress to place our order for iced cappuccinos. He gives me a significant look—his eyes moving slowly from the rose to my wrists and finally to my eyes.

"In your dreams," I tell him.

"Fantasies," he corrects me. "In my fantasies. You know the movie women love—and I'm sure you love it, I can tell you are the type—is *Tie Me Up, Tie Me Down*, which—you've read enough psychology to know this—is the ultimate female rape fantasy. She's kidnapped by a man who ties her to the bed and makes love to her like no man ever has. When she is accidentally freed, she ties herself back up again. Get it?"

Who didn't get it? You didn't need a reviewer to tell you this movie was *Sleeping Beauty* meets the "Rape Fantasy."

"Tell me about the first time you tied a woman up," I say, flipping on the recorder.

Bondage is erotic restraint, the sensual experience of safe captivity, and the beginning in any discussion of S/M—though some sadists find the tying of ropes too tedious, and some masochists can endure pain, but not restraint. Depictions of bound women are found in the ancient pornogra-

phy of Japan and China. In fact, the bondage tradition
thrives in modern Japan. One can see how some men find
the sight of a compliant, helplessly bound female arousing—but what does the woman, or man, who desires the
restraint get from the experience?

The bonds encase and embrace you rough and close.
They change the way you feel the world; and in a sustained
bondage encounter, they seem to become more confining
over time, though they have not been physically tightened.
Even comfortable, gentle bondage places stress on the
body. The classic bondage pose, arms above head, looks
hot in photos, but cannot be sustained in real life for long.
A spread-eagle-flat-on-the-bed position can lead to muscle
cramping. Bondage isn't as easy as it looks or sounds.

Though they may be nothing more than flimsy silk
scarves, the bonds take you to the place where you played
as a child, where the Indian tied the cowboy to the chair, to
the place where you sat in the darkened theater holding
your breath while the heroine or the hero was tied by the
bad guys to a bigger chair, to that place of safe captivity
where whatever happens isn't in your hands. Bondage is
the starting place. The one who is bound relinquishes control and *accepts.*

For many couples, bondage is the stopping place, too,
because they never take their "play" any further than a
simple game of "tie and tease," in which control is relinquished to the partner who then becomes responsible for
providing the pleasure. I have tied a few partners to bedposts with their ties or the sashes to my silk robes and fel-
lated them to orgasm; on those occasions, I felt like a
person who has planned the surprise party, not a dominant.

Once I secured my partner's wrists and ankles together, then covered his eyes with another scarf. I put on a feathered mask from Mardi Gras and licked his body from nipples to groin, the feathers trailing in the wake of my tongue. He could have worked himself free, but why would he have wanted to do that? I have likewise been tied and teased to multiple orgasms, sometimes by men who pulled their tongues away just before an orgasm could begin, and then made me wait, probably only seconds, before slowly lowering their faces back to my body. What we practiced together was the ancient technique of strengthening the orgasmic response by extending the arousal process, a game almost every sexually adventurous person has tried at least once. Yet it was an erotic power exchange, however symbolic.

A female friend says, "I had an affair with a man who loved to handcuff me to the bed. I let him because he performed cunnilingus forever as long as he had me cuffed. One night he left the bedroom door open while he went to the bathroom. His roommate walked past and saw me. I was so embarrassed, I broke up with him."

And from another friend, "I tried bondage in college. We were drunk, and the guy dropped the key to the handcuffs down the heating grate. When my roommate, who was my cousin, came in, there we were. We had to call campus security. I've played with bondage since, but no handcuffs. Only fabric, something you can cut with a pair of scissors."

Like others who engage in this comfortable form of restraint some call "love bondage," neither these two friends nor I have any interest in participating in heavy bondage, extremely uncomfortable forms of being trussed, sometimes accompanied by spanking, whipping, or other forms of "discipline."

Michael is forty, twice-divorced from wives who ceased to excite him after they failed to lose the weight gained with pregnancy. He is ever in search of a love to match his signature rosebuds—*perfect.* He earns approximately $75,000 a year as "a highly skilled technician." To protect his privacy, he has asked that I limit his job description to this one ambiguous phrase. A physical description of him will be no less useful in locating him among the thousands of men in his age group who live in the Washington metropolitan area: medium height and build. A reasonable crop of brown hair, graying at the edges, blue eyes, neatly trimmed beard flecked with red and gray. He is wearing Top-Siders without socks, faded and frayed denim shorts, and a black short-sleeved T-shirt with the sleeves rolled up.

I met Michael through an ad placed in a bondage publication. "Researching a book, looking for interview subjects, anonymity guaranteed." He and fourteen others, including eight women, responded.

"I'm not into serious bondage," he explained over the phone. "Not a B&D-er. No Japanese rope tricks. I can take it or leave it. This is something I do for women. Women really get off on bondage. Have you ever read a romance novel? They like you to overcome their resistance. I'm an erotic game player. Bondage is the game."

According to the respected professional journal *Archives of Sexual Behavior,* more women than men, when asked to rank their sadomasochistic interests, preferred spanking, oral sex, masturbation, erotic lingerie, and bondage. More men than women preferred master-slave relationships, humiliation, anal sex, and transvestism. The sexes were equally inclined toward rubber and leather.

B&D—bondage and discipline—is what people in The Scene call Michael's game. A B&D-er, according to their definition, is one who incorporates aspects of bondage and discipline into erotic play. If you've ever held your partner's wrists together over his or her head during lovemaking, or had your own wrists held in this way, you've indulged in a little B&D. The dominant is the person placing the restraint; the submissive is the one restrained. Finding oneself bound, and thus unable to resist or control pleasure, can relieve the responsibility for sex, and the guilt. For some people, being bound is enough to give them spontaneous orgasm. And, for others, orgasm is beside the point. Aficionados of tie and tease don't take it to those outer limits.

"The first time I tied a woman up," Michael says, "it began with holding her arms over her head. This woman was very aggressive, the type who's humping and bumping out there in the world. I don't know why I held her arms together, but when I did, she got really hot. Which made me get hotter."

As he talks, I remember a former Puerto Rican lover who was fond of holding my wrists together, arms over my head, as he whispered Spanish words of love into my ear and rubbed the head of his penis across my clitoris. I shiver at the memory. This man was hot, and I was definitely not turned off by his sexual dominance.

"We did it this way several times," Michael continues. "Then I asked her if I could use silk scarves to tie her wrists to the bed, and she said okay. She acted like she was going along with it to please me, but that was not true. She wanted this. I watched her responses carefully; she responded more when I was holding her down in some way than when I wasn't."

I glance at Michael's rose. A thorn has pressed a tiny hole in the plastic cover. The bloom is no longer hermetically sealed.

"Bondage evolved slowly for me from that point," he says, following my eye to the rose, then touching the end of the thorn briefly with his index finger. "With the next woman, I never got past holding her arms, because she didn't like it. Then I got involved with a real hot little number who wanted to try things. She asked me to spank her. I'm not into doing that, so I said I would tie her up. We were at her place. She opened the drawer in the chest beside her bed. This gal had police-issue handcuffs, leather wrist and ankle restraints, several lengths of silk drapery cord, a red satin blindfold, and a ball gag. The ball looked like one of those hard rubber things you throw out for the dog to fetch. It turned me off. I talked her into letting me tie a scarf around her mouth instead.

"She had a lot of stuff, but basically she wanted to be spread-eagled and blindfolded while I sucked and fucked the hell out of her. Only this one scenario. She thought it was varied because she never knew whether my mouth or my dick was going to end up inside her."

Could he speculate on what drove this "hot little number," a comely cosmetics company executive, to pursue

22

the spread-eagled and blindfolded state at night? No. "She never talked about being abused. One of her parents was a church deacon or something like that, no ugly stuff in her background."

Did he get tired of her limited erotic scenario?

"No, no. I lost interest in her for a lot of reasons. The magic wasn't there. You get to know a woman and you find she isn't who you thought she was. It doesn't matter if the woman is into bondage or not. That isn't the issue. It wasn't like 'I'm tired of this because she wants to fuck the same old way every night.' I might have been able to take her further if that's where my head was, but it wasn't.

"After her, I got involved with women who were either not interested in bondage or kept getting progressively into it. The bondage definitely added to the experience with these women. As we moved into tighter bondage, their responses heightened.

"I was taught breast bondage by one woman. You wrap the base of the breasts in rope and circle the rope around the body and over the shoulders to create like an open bra effect. Then you wrap her waist in rope. Her breasts look big; and her waist looks small. I can see why this woman got off on having it done. She never looked better than she did in breast bondage. More feminine."

Who were these women?

"A teacher. A nurse. Businesswomen. The one who taught me breast bondage has her own communications company, but not here in the D.C. area. She can communicate all right. In fact, the women who were most into bondage could tell me exactly how they liked having it done.

You always hear that women can't tell you what they want in bed. Kinky women can.

"But, you know, I believe," he says, pausing in what I'm sure he means to be a pregnant way, "all women are kinky. Some of them just need a little encouragement to let their hair down."

I ask him if he could put me in touch with some of these women. He says he will contact them and get back to me if they are interested in being interviewed. Meanwhile, he has brought me something, a copy of a letter from the breast-bound beauty detailing a fantasy she wanted to make real with him.

In the letter she told him to tie one end of the rope around her waist and then tie it in a knot. She explained how to cross the rope over her chest and make loops around each breast. By pulling the rope tighter, she said, he could make her breasts swell and stand out in front of her, creating an aesthetically pleasing arrangement. Finally, she instructed him on how to pull the rope between her labia and tie the ends behind her back. She would be, she said, wrapped like a present for him.

She dotted each I with a tiny, precise circle. And she did not say what she wanted done with this "present," which she told him in such explicit detail how to wrap.

"What about your wives?" I ask. "Did you practice bondage with them?"

"Oh, no. I didn't discover bondage until after the second divorce. Do you think that would have kept the marriages alive?"

When we get up to leave, he wants me to take the rose because he will feel "silly" carrying it back home. I need to talk with him one more time and I think accepting his bud, laden with his symbolism, will taint the future conversation. I demur. We compromise and leave it for the waitress.

Most of Michael's encounters have been with women who used mild restraint, perhaps, as he speculates, to free them from their own sex guilt or from the responsibility of making the sex work. If a woman's hands are free, she can be expected to take her own orgasm into those very hands, can't she? She can use her hand to masturbate herself or to guide his hand or mouth toward the places where she wants and needs stimulation. An unbound woman is an equal partner in sex. She has no one to blame but herself if the encounter ends without her reaching orgasm. However, if her hands are tied, he must "give" her the orgasm she wants.

The Januses say in *The Janus Report*, "For some individuals, being tied up is exciting enough to give them spontaneous orgasms. For others, it relieves their guilt about voluntarily performing a sexual act (which they were taught as children was 'bad' and 'dirty'), even with their spouse."

Ginni, one of Michael's lovers who seems to find the restraint of bondage what she needs to free her from sexual responsibility, did agree to talk to me.

Afraid of being overheard in a public place, Ginni comes to my apartment. A slender redhead in her late twenties, she appears to be taller than Michael, whom she hasn't seen "sexually" for over a year, though they remain casual friends and occasionally have lunch together. She is a high school teacher.

"Michael tapped into my essence through bondage," she explains. I wonder how it is that someone's "essence" could be freed through bondage. Isn't that a paradox? "I had never shared my bondage fantasies with anyone. He asked me one night after we'd made love if I would tell him my fantasies and I refused, because I was ashamed of them.

" 'If I guess, will you tell me?' he persisted. He guessed and I opened up to him. Rather than being disgusted by my fantasies, he was excited by them. That was such a relief, because I expected rejection. Once a man told me he couldn't get an erection with me because I was disappointing with my clothes off. He said I was too thin"—she put her hands up to her breasts, covering them, as if she still felt the sting of his rejection—"I had too many moles on my body, and my pubic hair needed to be trimmed. I'll never forget how bad that felt. I was expecting something similar to happen when I told Michael about my desire to be bound, but he accepted it, and me, completely.

"When I was a little girl, I played this game of 'tying up' with another little girl. We tied each other to chairs mostly. One day we were in the bathroom. She told me to take off all my clothes, and she tied me with towels to the shower rod. I can still remember how excited I felt, my heart pounding in my ears. My mother knocked on the door, asked what we were doing, and told us to come out. I've always wondered if she knew what was going on.

"My friend untied me, and I dressed quickly, but my heart didn't settle down for a long time after we were in my room playing with our dolls.

"I told Michael this, and the next time we saw each other, he suggested we shower together before lovemaking. In the shower, he tied me to the rod with the belt from his terry-cloth robe. Then he turned the spray on my vagina and left me in there alone for several minutes. I was so excited by the time he came back, I had an orgasm as soon as he started soaping up my body and fondling me.

"This was the most loving, liberating experience for me. I know it sounds crazy, but I feel more free when I am tied up. It's okay then for me to be who I really am."

When Ginni began the interview, she spoke in a high, nervous voice. Now she is more relaxed, and her voice has dropped down an octave, settling into the comfortable tones she must use when teaching. I ask her if she has practiced bondage with anyone else since Michael set her free.

"No, not yet. But I know I will. My orgasms are stronger when I'm bound in some way. Michael has taught me there is nothing wrong with sharing and acting out these fantasies. When I am comfortable with a new man in my life, I will tell him what I really want."

What happened between her and Michael?

"He's not ready for a committed relationship and I am. It had nothing to do with bondage. Michael just can't let go of the idea that around the next corner may lurk the most wonderful, perfect woman in the world. He's always looking ahead for her to appear in his life.

"Michael is a romantic idealist."

With rope.

Ginni has mailed me a copy of a book called *Learning the Ropes: A Basic Guide to Safe and Fun S/M Lovemaking,* by Race Bannon. I open it and a sheet of flowery paper accompanying the gift flutters to the floor: ''Every beginner should read this!'' I flip to the section on bondage technique, which includes the following tips:

Never leave someone in bondage unattended.
Never tie anything around the neck.
Be careful not to tie too tightly anywhere the flow of blood might be restricted. Be especially careful at the wrists and crotch.
When tying around the chest area, ask the person to inhale deeply and hold the breath before you secure the bondage. This way you know they have enough room to breathe comfortably while in bondage.
Do not cover the mouth or nostrils.

They seem like fairly obvious points to me. If you're putting a rope around someone's throat, doesn't that escalate the game from bondage to something more violent? I like, however, his section on turning ordinary household items into S/M tools. This is stuff you don't get from Heloise. Bannon suggests beginners start with rope, preferably braided nylon rope, number 8 (1/4 inch), 50 to 100 feet in length. Why this particular rope? It's readily available in hardware stores, smooth on the skin, and easily cut.

I put down the book and suddenly have a flashback. I was having drinks with a colleague who reached down into his briefcase to pull out a book proposal for my perusal. Coiled at the bottom of the leather case was a piece of rope, braided, nylon, smooth, and shiny. I had wondered what the rope was doing in his briefcase at the time, but for some inexplicable reason, I, who have few qualms about asking intimate questions, didn't ask him.

Now I think I know what he might have been doing with that rope. Maybe I also know why I didn't ask.

Chapter 3

The Spanking Game

St. Louis County

Meredith is holding a rolled-up copy of *Stand Corrected,* a magazine "dedicated to the romance of discipline." An astonishing array of magazines, newsletters, and books devoted to the practice of erotic spanking is available in this country. Occasionally Meredith punctuates her conversation by thwacking a tabletop or her arm, wrist, or opposite hand with the slender, low-gloss tube. "Sixty-four pages. One hundred percent spanking." Contents include: Lesbian super-hero spanking, EuroSpank, exclusive spanking photos from Great Britain, hundreds of personal ads, a new episode of "Shadow Lane," which is "quite possibly the most tasteful enema story ever written," and more. The blonde on the cover, butt exposed, has clearly just been spanked. She is smiling over her shoulder at her reddened cheeks. You will not find this magazine at your neighborhood newsstand.

"He met his new wife through the personals," Meredith says. " 'DWF, looking for divorced or single WM adept at administering playful spankings, preferably by hand. If the need for sterner discipline arises, he will know how to use a belt, paddle, or hairbrush. No whips. I am a forty-year-old girl and naughty, naughty, naughty. Daddy, oh, Daddy, where are you?'

"I know it by heart. He showed me the ad and told me he was going to answer it. We were having drinks at TGI-Friday's and going over the divorce settlement agreement before we signed it.

"Steve's like that. He talks." She thwacks the cocktail table between us, jiggling the wine in her half-full glass. Fortunately, I am holding my full one. "Oh, does he talk. He's a sensitive man. Just ask him."

In less politically correct times than our own, spanking, the administering of blows exclusively to the buttocks, was widely regarded as a form of lighthearted sex play between partners—typically the dominant male partner and the woman who must occasionally be tamed into submission. Movie heroes sometimes gave their heroines a swat or two. Tracy spanked Hepburn. Cary Grant turned more than one woman over his knee. On "I Love Lucy," Ricky (Desi Arnaz) once took Lucy over his lap and soundly spanked her, to the delight of the audience. The *Kama Sutra* offers detailed directions on administering the four kinds of blows to produce the eight kinds of sounds.

Today, spanking of female buttocks in a romantic comedy—something starring Julia Roberts and a middle-aged man, perhaps—would be very politically incorrect. Yet men, as well as women, get their buttocks reddened in the name of love.

Years before Steve, Meredith's first time was a slap during intercourse. She had been stunned by the sound and the sensation. A sharp, quick stinging slap had echoed in her ears as her pulse raced. She had felt confused, cheapened, and violated as much by her arousal as by the corporal liberty he'd taken with her. What had made him think he could? Why had her body betrayed her? Unable to deal with the welter of conflicting emotions awakened by this one glancing blow, she never saw the man again.

A year later another man spanked her, more than once, during intercourse. She was on top, and the rhythmic smacks drove her deep into a pulsating orgasm. The irony was not lost on her.

"I was disciplined in the female superior position," she says. "Maybe he felt he had to do that because I was on top."

Afterward, she cried. The man was solicitous. He didn't know why he'd spanked her, he said. It just happened. Then he'd felt her grow hotter and wetter, so he had continued spanking. She cried harder. Finally, she fell asleep in his arms, intensely aware of the heat in her buttocks and shamed by that afterglow. The spanking episode was not repeated in their brief relationship, which ended more or less by mutual consent when they stopped calling each other, no explanations asked or given. She was never able to admit to him she'd *enjoyed* what he'd done to her.

"But I thought about it sometimes when we were making love or when I was masturbating alone. I was aroused by the memory of the spanking, and I played the scene over and over again in my mind. After my orgasm, I was flooded with feelings of guilt and shame. What was wrong with me? Where did this come from? I don't remember being spanked as a child. My father didn't hit my mother. They didn't have loud fights. Why was I reacting like this to being hit? My own sexual response was repugnant to me. I wanted to bury it so deeply that no other man would know; I thought I had succeeded until I met Steve two years later.''

Meredith was thirty-three when she met Steve, then forty, at the Unitarian Church, which they had both recently joined. His divorce, after nearly ten years of marriage, had been final for six months and he was ready to "rejoin the world," as he explained to her. She'd relocated to the St. Louis area from Chicago to take a corporate job at the same salary as the one she'd had in Chicago, with a far better chance for advancement. The cost of living was less in St. Louis, so she was living more comfortably than she had since leaving her parents' home. Church, she thought, was a good place for meeting new people, though not necessarily datable men. She wanted to expand her new life, open up her private spaces, and fill them with good people.

"I was delighted to meet Steve the first Sunday," she says. "He was the kind of man your mother has in mind when she says, 'You should go to church; maybe you'll meet a nice man.' We talked in the parking lot for an hour after every other car had pulled out.''

They were a match on many levels. She was very nearly his professional equal. Both wanted marriage and children.

They were comparable in looks: he, nearly bald but blessed with large expressive green eyes and a trim athletic build that made him seem taller than his five foot nine; she, at five-three, was a blue-eyed brunette with a curvaceous body that offset ordinary features and coloring. They shared an interest in tennis, racquetball, classical music, theater, Italian food, and foreign films.

He asked her out the first time by calling on a Tuesday for a Friday dinner and symphony date. He took her to Anthony's, a four-star restaurant in downtown St. Louis. There was no pressure on her to become sexual. The next day he sent a bouquet of flowers and a note thanking her for the lovely evening. They immediately fell into a pattern of regular weekend dates, and by the time they'd known each other a month, an anniversary marked by his sending thirty-one roses to her office, they were seeing each other nearly every night.

"Our first sexual experience together was by the book," she says. "Third date, my place. He gave me the first orgasm via cunnilingus. I sucked him briefly to return the favor. We had intercourse, first in the missionary style, then with me on top. I thought the sex was very good. He was a skilled lover, particularly at the oral part. Looking back, I can say he seemed a little too controlled sexually, never really letting go until right before the point of orgasm. But a lot of men hold themselves in check pretty well to make the experience last longer.

"Once, and this happened sometime in the first month, he got very angry when I tickled him in bed. He grabbed my hands and yelled, 'Don't do that!' I felt like he'd slapped me, but the moment passed quickly as we resumed lovemaking.

"The spanking started after we'd been together three months—and after I had accepted his proposal of marriage. It started like this: Steve had taken to entering me before I was lubricated. It hurt, but I didn't stop him. It felt like rape. Maybe I wanted to play at rape, and somehow he knew that. One night he sort of rolled over on top of me and started fucking and I said, 'Ouch!'

"He didn't say anything or pull out of me. He took his hand and began slapping at the side of my ass. I raised my hips. He sort of scooped his hand under me and spanked me that way. It made funny noises, like sucking slaps. I started getting wet, very wet, and moaning. He kept it up until I came. We didn't talk about it. Afterward, while he was holding me, he was sort of stroking the places where he'd hit me and we were talking about the mundane sorts of things we always talked about after sex—what we were going to do that weekend, or what kind of frozen yogurt was in the fridge.

"The next morning I felt nauseated, thinking about what had happened. I said I was coming down with the flu and called in sick at work. After he left, I threw off the blankets, ran into the bathroom and inspected my ass in the full-length mirror. I had some redness, no bruising. He called me half a dozen times during the day to check on me. That night, he brought all my favorite deli items and flowers and a box of molasses lollipops from Bissengers'—for which he'd had to drive fifteen minutes out of his way.

"I was going to talk to him about the way we'd had sex, but the words got stuck inside me and never came out. It was a few weeks before he spanked me again. We'd been having a lighthearted disagreement about a movie we were watching on the VCR. He turned me over his knee, pulled down my sweat pants and panties and blistered my ass. I wanted to scream, but I didn't. I worked very hard to control myself. Little grunt sounds were all I made. Tears were running down my face, and I was gasping for breath by the time he finished.

"He groped for his zipper, freeing his penis, then lifted me up and sat me down on him. We both came almost immediately. He held me for a few minutes, and then he said, 'Let me up, baby. I'm going to get some ice for your butt.'

"What happened after that was as strange as the spanking. He laid me across his lap and ran ice cubes over my ass while we finished watching the movie. The ice felt so good, melting into my hot skin. A little rivulet of water ran down the crack of my ass into my cunt. I felt like a child, a pet, a bad girl, a good girl. Yet I've never felt more womanly in my life."

Among the twenty-seven people I interviewed who indulge in spanking, only one man said it made him feel "more like a real man" to spank his wife from time to time. The others saw no connection between what they do and S/M—though the Kinsey Institute labels spanking a "paraphilia called sadism." The institute, under the able direction of June Reinisch, Ph.D., serves as a national clearinghouse for sex research information. In categorizing spanking as a paraphilia, they are disseminating information based on the prevailing opinion of sex therapists, educators, and counselors, not making a behavioral judgment.

In *The Kinsey Institute's New Report on Sex* (1990), Reinisch answered a man who'd written to say he believed "most women in their deep subconscious mind *want* to be spanked," by saying, "the vast majority of women do *not* want to be spanked and do *not* associate being spanked with sexual pleasure."

Those who do are, by the institute's definition, "masochists."

"I don't like pain," one man who likes to be spanked told me. "I am not a masochist. I like the intense sensations that accompany spanking, the feelings of powerlessness, of being controlled by an authority figure. But once the spanking is over, I want the status quo resumed. You don't hear spanking enthusiasts call what they do a 'lifestyle,' like so many of the S/M crowd."

Many spankers are careful to distance themselves from S/M devotees. In their book about The Scene, *Different Loving,* Gloria and William Brame note "many spankers, whether givers or receivers, vehemently insist they have nothing in common with sadomasochists." The Brames point out that the spankers even think bondage is a little kinky.

Some spankers and spankees I interviewed expressed wonder that anyone would get excited about being tied to the bedposts during sex. In general, spanking devotees, or "purists," are happy within the confines of their particular self-imposed sexual limits. They have preferences for position, whether over the knee or over a chair, table, or bench, and rules about how many blows they will receive, how hard the blows may be, and with what instrument other than the hand may be used. As long as the limits are observed, they accept their own erotic drives as being, according to one participant, "within the normal boundaries of sex play."

Yet some, like Meredith, feel very uncomfortable about the erotic feelings the act of spanking arouses in them.

Why didn't Meredith back away from this man as she had the other two men who'd spanked her?

"Now I knew it was me. The men were responding to something in me. Could I tell Steve I didn't like the spankings when my body clearly told him I did? He was so logical and rational about everything. I knew we would end up having this intelligent discussion about eroticized violence, in which we would both agree the bottom line was that we were consenting adults. I didn't want to have that conversation.

"Maybe I didn't want to hear the rest of what Steve might have told me, either. I have the suspicion I wouldn't have liked to know his deepest fantasies."

The wedding, a year exactly after their first date, delighted her parents, who had accepted Steve as a son almost as quickly as Meredith had taken him into her bed. Their two-week honeymoon in Greece was an odyssey of sexual and emotional intimacy. The last good time, or so she remembers it now. No spanking.

"I thought marriage would take away that part of us I didn't feel comfortable with," she says. "And for almost six months, there was no spanking. The sex wasn't very satisfactory, either. We had a lot of things going on—my promotion, his problems at work after he didn't get the promotion he thought he was going to get. He went through a crisis period. Then the fog seemed to lift.

"We spent a weekend in the Ozarks at Tan-Tar-A resort. Good sex, sunshine, water. He opened up to me about the situation at work. Apparently his boss had made it pretty clear to him that he wasn't going any further there. He had hit his own personal ceiling. I felt so close to him, touched that he would share his vulnerability with me.

"The day after we came home, he brought me a beautifully wrapped gift. A teddy bear. He said he had decided it was time we started a family. I went ballistic on him. *He* had decided? What about me? Pregnancy wasn't part of my plan for a few more years at that point. He said I was kidding myself, didn't I realize how old I was, how my chances to conceive were shrinking all the time. We didn't speak for two days.

"Then he spanked me again, hard. I wouldn't give him the satisfaction of crying out. When we had sex, we were slamming into each other, tearing at each other, like animals mating. He said it was the best sex he'd ever had. I couldn't argue with him."

The teddy bear sat on top of the oak wardrobe in their bedroom, and their sex life became more centered on spanking. They made love once a week, or less, and always the lovemaking was preceded by some form of spanking, if only a light slap or two. This went on for six months. Meredith acknowledges that it might have gone on indefinitely if she hadn't inadvertently overheard a remark at his company Christmas party.

"Do you suppose he's going to take her home and spank

her tonight?'' Steve's secretary had whispered to Alice, his friend and coworker, loudly enough for her to hear.

"I turned around and looked at them. I knew I was blushing, and when they saw me staring hard at them, they blushed, too. In a way, it wasn't a shock. I knew how much Steve loved to dish the details of other people's lives. Steve gossips and tells personal details, just like women do. He knew how Alice liked to do it with her husband. Why had I thought he wasn't telling as much as he was hearing?

"Yet I was still hit hard by the realization that these women, and God knows who else, knew Steve spanked me. It was too much.''

That night, Meredith and Steve had a fight ending in smashed crockery and packed bags, not spanking and intercourse. Steve apologized for telling the details of their sex life and admitted he should have known better—because he knew how "funny" she was about her "mildly kinky tendencies.'' Even his apology sounded like a putdown in her ears.

"Everything came together for me that night,'' she says. "I saw our marriage for what it was. Steve, in his pseudo-therapeutic way, had always been putting me down. He had this way of withdrawing, observing, and sitting in judgment. The talking to others was part of the behavior. He had assumed superiority, and I let him. The spanking was all part of that, of my need to be humbled and his need to humble.''

Steve is drinking a Michelob Lite from a frosted glass. On the table between us is an envelope full of pictures, featuring Steve and his third wife, Donna. She looks a lot like his second wife, Meredith—average features, curvaceous body, blue eyes. Her hair is bleached blond and worn in a big style, layers of hair puffed up and out.

There are also some pictures of her daughters, Jessica and Samantha, ages five and seven. In one typical studio family portrait, he stands behind Donna, who is seated on a velvet love seat, the girls on either side. He is leaning in toward the family, his hand resting on his wife's shoulder. Everyone smiles. And there are pictures of Donna wearing a white ruffled corset with garters attached to white stockings, wearing nothing else, her back to the camera, smiling over her shoulder at her reddened ass cheeks, a smaller version of the chastised maiden on the *Stand Corrected* cover that Meredith had used to swat her own bursts of anger, like flies that had shot from her mouth.

"Meredith is a very angry woman," Steve says. "I feel sorry for her. She needs help. I believe she may be a sociopath."

A sociopath?

"Someone who has no conscience or feeling about how they use other people for their own means. Meredith used me for her sexual purposes, then she turned me into a villain when I gave her what she needed."

"I thought it was a friendly divorce," I counter evenly. Water is condensing on the sides of my wineglass. I ask the waitress for ice. California jug wine can't be iced down too much. "Meredith said it was a friendly divorce."

"Oh, of course, it was," he says, waving his hand in the air. His wedding ring has three fat diamonds lined up across the top of the band. I can't help but notice his fingers look fat, too. "Friendly. I didn't mean to imply otherwise. I

41

was trying to help you understand Meredith and what happened between us.''

He leans back in his chair, smiles expansively, and agrees first to tell me the story of his life.

Steve's mother was forty-one when she gave birth to him in Chicago, two months after his father, a police officer, was killed in the line of duty. There was insurance, a paid-up mortgage on their modest Hyde Park house, a pension, and, later, a small inheritance from her mother. They weren't rich, but they certainly weren't poor. Steve's mother didn't have to go to work, so she didn't.

''She nearly suffocated me. You think I mean that figuratively, but I mean it literally. I really believe my mother wanted to kill me when I was an infant, because she hated me for being alive while my father was dead. She had huge breasts and she nursed me until I was three years old. In therapy, I regressed to the point where I could remember her trying to suffocate me between her breasts. She finally stopped nursing me because I wasn't getting enough to eat. I was a skinny little kid.''

After nursing, he remembers masturbation.

''I don't know how young I was when I started masturbating, but I wasn't in school yet. I thought I discovered it.'' He laughs. His eyes ignite as he talks. ''In my mind, I was center stage, not center bed. The world was watching and applauding. When I came—and don't let anybody tell you little boys don't come, they do—I could actually hear the clapping.''

But no spanking.

''It didn't happen. I wasn't spanked. I didn't see spanking. My first wife wanted to be spanked. I didn't understand that's what she wanted for a long time. She would provoke me by drinking too much in public, or tease me about my hair falling out in front of our friends, or taunt me by flirting with other men or telling me how attracted she was to someone at the office. Then she would say, 'I know you're mad at me. Don't you just want to take off that belt and whack me?'

"Believe it or not, I didn't catch on until she had had an affair. I was broken up. I was crying and begging her to tell me why. She lifted her skirt and showed me her butt and said, 'He did this to me.' I said, 'Is that what you want? Is it?' She started crying, and I took off my belt. I laid into her pretty hard, especially in view of what she'd already sustained. She loved it. Afterward, she told me she wouldn't ever cheat on me again. We kept the belt on the bedpost and called it 'her' belt. I never wore it again, but I used it a lot. She said she creamed her pants every time I took it off the post. One day I caught her sniffing it. She said it smelled like sweat and sex."

Why didn't the marriage last?

"She left me for someone else, probably someone who would give it to her harder than I would." He finishes his beer, signals for another one. "We remained friends, really friends, like I don't think Meredith and I will. After the first affair, the barriers went down between us. She told me her fantasies, how she couldn't ever come without fantasizing about being spanked or whipped. Those elements were always in the fantasy. Without them, she was unable to reach orgasm. She attended my second wedding. Did Meredith tell you that?

"And I told her my fantasies, some I've never told another woman. I have this recurring fantasy of making love to a young virgin. She has been waiting for me in a beautiful castle in the middle of the desert since she was born. When I come to her, she is thrilled and scared at the same time. I initiate her into the joys of sex. It's a beautiful, gentle fantasy, no spanking or roughness."

He pauses, giving me a chance to comment on his fantasy. I don't. We look at each other awhile. I suddenly remember a story told to me by another man who spanks. He was first aroused by spanking, he said, as a boy in grade school in the South when he witnessed a girl being swatted with a paddle by the teacher. ("I was glad it wasn't me. At the same time, I was getting an erection watching her take the paddle. He really swatted her good. I guess you're going to say I never outgrew my adolescent sexuality.")

"How many men can say their ex-wives came to their second wedding?" Steve asks proudly, breaking the silence between us.

"Okay," I say. "Have I got this straight? You tried to keep your first marriage together by fulfilling her fantasies, meeting her sexual needs. You saw the same needs in Meredith. Were you looking for a woman who wanted to be spanked?"

"No. Not consciously, at least."

"But, you were by the time you got around to number three."

"She told you," he says. Anger flares briefly in his eyes. "Meredith told you about the ad. Okay. Yes, by number three, I was looking for what I knew I could handle. Is there anything wrong with that?"

* * *

Donna would not agree to see me alone. Her condition for being interviewed was that her husband be present. He is on his third beer when she joins us, I on my second glass of ice. Her hair is even bigger than it was in the pictures. I cannot imagine this hair getting mussed during sex—or spanking.

"We don't do it every time we have sex, the spanking, and we don't have sex every time we do a spanking," she says. "I know what you really want to talk about, and it isn't how many nights we do it in the missionary position.

"For me, spanking and sexual intercourse don't necessarily go together. I want to be spanked almost every day, but most of the spankings are light ones. It makes me feel sexy all day if David spanks me gently in the morning before he goes to work. We pretend I am the naughty wife when he gives me these soft spanks. On Saturday mornings, we almost always have sex after this." She pauses and takes a deep pull on her frozen margarita through the straw, leaving traces of red lipstick on the plastic. "When we have more time, he spanks me in a slow, sensual scene. I pretend I am a slut who cannot be true to any man except this one who has the courage to dominate me. The slaps get progressively harder. He stops periodically to massage my buttocks or finger my genitals. I get very hot. He tells me I am a slut because I am getting so wet. I like these sessions always to end in sex, but sometimes he makes me wait until later because he doesn't have time or isn't in the mood.

"Other times we pretend I have been a very naughty child and must be punished by Daddy.

"The punishments are hardest. They happen maybe one or two times a month, with a hairbrush, a leather paddle, or a very thin cane."

I think about a recent segment of *Real Sex* on HBO, which featured a couple, their bondage equipment, whips, and canes. The very thin cane, they agreed, caused the most intense, painful sensations and had to be used sparingly.

"I am always over his lap with the other spankings, but for punishments, he puts me over the sofa arm or ties me over the kitchen table, my wrists and ankles fastened to the legs. He starts by using his hand to warm me up. We read somewhere that bruising is minimalized if you start with light slaps to bring the blood to the surface. After a hard session, I don't mind seeing the marks for a few days, but I don't want them to last longer than that, so we are careful.

"He makes me count the strokes. I am not supposed to count one if it isn't hard enough. If I cheat and count it anyway, he makes the next one twice as hard. David can be a stern disciplinarian when he knows I need him to be. Sometimes during a punishment, he gives me a little bit more than I think I can take. If he didn't, then I would be in control of my punishment, and that wouldn't be what I want.

"Once, we tried something we'd read in a book that had turned me on so much I couldn't stop thinking about it. A man had made his partner kneel on the bed, her ass in the air, and take one hundred strokes with a thin cane in that part of her buttocks where the ass meets the upper thighs—take it without moving. We knew this was too much for me to bear, so we adapted the idea.

"We agreed that David would give me twenty-five strokes on the buttocks, not just in that one place alone, and that he would start over if I moved. After the eighth stroke, I thought I couldn't stand anymore. I jerked away.

"His voice was calm and very patient. He told me he was going to start over as he had promised and, if I moved again, he would make the strokes very hard. My legs were trembling, and it was difficult to keep still."

David reaches across the table and takes her hand in his. His eyes are misted over with love or lust for her. Her own eyes briefly fill with tears.

"You were testing me, weren't you?" he asks her gently. "Tell her why you did that."

"I needed to know he would follow through. When we are playing Daddy punishing naughty girl, I need to know he is going to be a strong Daddy. If I can whine and get him to ease up, I feel cheated." She took another deep swallow of her drink. "That was the hardest punishment he's ever given me. I didn't move, except for the involuntary trembling in my legs, and I counted each stroke, from one again to twenty-five. Around twelve or thirteen, I could actually feel something kick in inside my brain, and the pain turned into something that was part pain, part pleasure.

"Afterward, he made me stay bound to the table for thirty minutes while he watched the national news. I kept pressing my genitals into the wood and reliving those strokes. When he came back into the room, he asked me what I was doing. I was ashamed to tell him. I wouldn't ask him to let me come then, because it felt wrong."

David took her hand to his lips.

* * *

Donna was spanked as a child, by her mother, who was the family disciplinarian, frequently administering punishments, physical and verbal, to Donna and her two brothers.

"My father was the classic emotionally absent father," she says. "Mother handled everything, except earning the money and painting ceilings and cleaning out the gutters, which were his jobs. I remember being spanked a lot by her, but she never used the strap on me like she did on my brothers.

"My most vivid memory is of the last time she ever spanked me. I was thirteen. She turned me over her knee. I don't remember what I'd done to earn her wrath, but she was very angry. I had learned how to take a spanking pretty well by then, but she was relentless that day. Finally, I yelled, 'Stop!' and pulled away from her. She pulled me back across her knee and started pounding on me again. When she finally finished, I ran upstairs to my room and threw myself across the bed. My bottom was on fire. I was panting and crying. When I'd cried myself out, I was still panting. I didn't understand then exactly what was happening to me, but I do now.

"I was sexually aroused, *highly* sexually aroused. I wonder if Mother understood that, if she stopped spanking me because of it. Or maybe she was telling the truth when she said I'd hurt her hand so bad, she knew it was time to give up on spanking her children."

In high school, Donna played spanking games with another girl.

"We had this elaborate scenario worked out to make us feel okay about what we were doing. We pretended we wanted to be actresses. She loved playing Katharine Hepburn being spanked by Spencer Tracy, the spunky woman drawn lovingly across her exasperated man's knee. I played Spencer.

"When it was her turn to spank me, I was Kate in *The Taming of the Shrew*. I told her she wasn't spanking hard, even when she was, because I wanted it harder.

"My boyfriends in high school and college didn't spank me. I didn't know how to suggest it. My first husband didn't spank me. We had a very boring, unsatisfactory sex life together. After I was divorced, I answered an ad in *The Riverfront Times* from a 'strict, demanding man seeking compliant young novice.' He was too much into heavy corporal punishment for me, but I did discover spanking publications through him. I had no idea before I met him that you could actually find someone who was just what you wanted by placing an ad."

Steve calls me a week after our interview as "an informational follow-up" for my benefit. He wants to be sure I understand that a couple should establish their own guidelines before the hand, or the flyswatter, touches flesh. How hard? How long? Will you use a hand or an implement, a brush, paddle, spatula from the kitchen drawer? Will the spanking be a form of foreplay, or will it be an erotic act outside the context of sexual intercourse? Do I understand that, for some people, intercourse after a hard spanking from "Mommy" or "Daddy" can seem like a violation of the incest taboo?

He sounds like a therapist as he assures me that spanking "need not change the power dynamics in a relationship. Your readers should know that."

I thank him for his concern. I do not tell him that the therapists to whom I have been speaking doubt spanking, or another form of S/M, can exist separately within a relationship, or at least not for long. Can one partner always play the dominant and another the submissive without affecting the power dynamics? Not likely, they say.

If one partner is sometimes Mommy or Daddy with whom sex is forbidden, can the couple have an egalitarian relationship outside the bedroom? Even less likely.

"Have a nice day," Steve says. The ubiquitous sign-off suits him.

Part 2
Pushing the Limits

Chapter 4

S/M as Foreplay

SOUTHERN CALIFORNIA

"My personal belief is that whatever consenting adults do together without causing permanent injury is okay," Anthony says.

We are sitting on one of the many balconies of this, one of his many homes, watching the sun sink slowly into the Pacific Ocean. The big red ball appears to sit on the lap of the sea before burning its way through and disappearing. We sit quietly until nothing is left of the sun but a pink and purple sheen on the surface of the water. Waves crash rhythmically on the rocks several feet below us. Sunset is an event in Southern California, an event that, like all others, is set to the music of the surf.

"I don't put my value system on anybody else, and I don't want them to put theirs on me," Anthony says, refilling our delicate crystal champagne flutes into which calla lilies have been etched. "Having said that, I'll tell you I'm not into S/M on any heavy level. I don't believe in drawing blood. To me, S/M is a game to liven up things that were starting to get dull.

"First, you need a relationship. You can't start with the S/M. And you don't need it at the start of the relationship, when things are hot enough on their own. It's later, when you begin to slow down. As you get older, especially as you've been involved with one person longer, you find yourself slowing down. You need more to get excited, to keep your sexual interest up. That's where S/M comes into play.

"I also believe this is something you're more likely to get into if you have money. I've lived extensively in Europe and more recently in both Manhattan and L.A. The people I know who play around with S/M on any level have money. It's not a poor person's game."

Anthony is an entrepreneur who starts up companies and sells them when they become successful. An amateur photographer, world traveler, and gourmet cook, he is, at forty-nine, fit and trim, stylish and handsome—the kind of man avidly sought by single women of all ages. He knows he is.

"I can have my pick of women," he says confidently. "I'm not kidding myself about why, either. Money. Women find money very sexy."

He spreads a minimal amount of low-fat goat's milk cheese on a very thin cracker and offers it to me. I open my mouth, take in half the cracker, and bite down. My tongue touches his fingers before he withdraws the hand. It is a sensual moment. I suspect such moments are rare with Anthony.

"I know what women want from me," he says, and the

glint in his eyes is cool, controlled. I recognize the same chill in his eyes that I've seen in the eyes of other S/M aficionados. "I know what I want from them. Young and beautiful isn't enough anymore. After I fuck her once or twice, she had better be willing to get into some light play with belts, tit clamps, what have you, if she wants me to fuck her again."

Over time, Anthony has upped the sexual ante. When he became sexually active at age sixteen, the stakes for a woman were risky, but simple: If you love me, you'll let me fuck you. Later, the sexual challenge might have been: If you love me, you'll let me come in your mouth or fuck you in the ass.

Now, Anthony says, if you want me, you have to keep my sexual attention through a little game of S/M.

The majority of S/M participants are, like Anthony, dabblers in this form of erotic "play." The people for whom S/M is a lifestyle choice seldom have *sex* as the rest of us know sex: the mutual pursuit of orgasm through oral and manual genital manipulation and/or intercourse. These people are into The Scene, in capital letters. Anthony and his compatriots stage "scenes," little S/M tableaux, which culminate in intercourse and orgasm for both parties.

S/M as foreplay may actually involve less pain than a heavy spanking, but it registers higher on the kink scale than anal sex or "tie and tease" bondage or spanking. The limits of what is acceptable have been expanded beyond a single practice, the geography of the body upon which the game is played taken beyond the confines of the wrists, ankles, and buttocks. The component of humiliation, either verbal or physical or both, becomes more pronounced. The question of control, which might have been submerged in the one-note play of spanking, bondage, or anal sex, is clearly an issue here.

The goal is to intensify the sex, not replace it with something else. Control is the intensifying force. S/M activities involve consensual power exchanges in sexually charged settings. To the outsider, it is often difficult to determine who is really wielding the power, the top who dishes out the pain, or the bottom whose limits determine how far the top will go. Often, it is even more difficult to feel the sexual charge in a scene that looks silly, not erotic.

At a private play party in the Midwest, held in a home, not a club, I watched a woman discipline a man. Her outfit, a leather creation that looked like a thigh-high teddy, accentuated the twenty extra pounds she carried around the middle. She hobbled on five-inch heels, size ten. The hair on his unshaven legs was matted beneath his glossy black pantyhose, making his flesh appear mottled. His own red teddy was stained in circles under the arms from sweat. She led him around the room on a leash and periodically asked one of the guests to spank him with a large wooden paddle or flick a thin whip across his nipples.

When they were both sufficiently aroused by the process, they sneaked into the bathroom to have sex. A man who had watched the scene with me commented: "They would have had a hotter time if they could have waited until they got home. You know they just did this so we'd think they couldn't wait."

* * *

"Do you know the definition of S/M?" Anthony asks me.

He is grilling shrimp, which Conchita, the Hispanic woman who tends this house, has washed, deveined, skewered, and marinated for him. The sky is purple and blue, shot through with ribbons of pale pink. The waves and the champagne have a cumulative numbing effect.

"Power playing," he says, flipping the skewers of shrimp. Conchita appears with bowls of salsa and rice, which she puts on the table set for two. "Nothing more than that. Sexual power playing. That Marquis de Sade stuff is over the top. Only a pervert would want to whip someone until she bleeds."

"Or *he*," I interject. "Until *he* bleeds."

"Oh, sure. She or *he*. We must be politically correct here, mustn't we?"

There are more submissives of both sexes than dominants, more men who wish to be disciplined than those who fervently desire to wield the rod—a fact dominant men like Anthony either don't believe or find too wincingly uncomfortable to acknowledge. Why is this so? Men are more likely to be driven by S/M desires; women more likely to go along for the sake of pleasing their men.

Paraphilias are almost exclusively male, according to Fred Berlin, M.D., an associate in the department of psychiatry at Johns Hopkins University who specializes in the treatment of paraphilias. "There are almost no female compulsive voyeurs, exhibitionists, sadists," he says. "Masochism is the exception. However, there are still more male masochists than female."

V. K. McCarty, the longtime editor of *Penthouse Varia-*

tions, a publication dedicated to non-vanilla sex practices, speculates that "men as well as women have sex guilt, which is alleviated by being 'punished' for being sexual. Also, men are still more likely to be burdened with heavy responsibilities in high-anxiety jobs. They find release from their tensions in being tied down and disciplined."

For whatever reasons, submissives outnumber dominants by as much as ten to one. Perhaps that is why so many people "switch"—alternate playing the dominant or submissive role in S/M play.

If you both want to be disciplined, you have to play fair and take turns, don't you?

"A woman I turned on to S/M told me she liked doing a scene because it was like riding the Screaming Eagle roller coaster at Six Flags over MidAmerica," Anthony says. Bits of rice fall off his fork poised to enter his mouth. They land on his white cotton shorts. He brushes them off irritably. "She said she liked it when someone created a roller-coaster ride for her," he continues. "A ride that scared her a little bit, even though she knew it was perfectly safe."

"How did she know it was perfectly safe?"

"Because I was running it. I was in charge of her ride. She knew I was in control of the situation and she trusted me. If I was in control, she knew she didn't need to be. She didn't have to worry. That's what women tell me they like about S/M. They just sit back and enjoy the ride. At the end, they're gasping for breath and loving it. They want to go around again, maybe not that night, maybe they're too sore to go around again that night, but again, soon."

"Tell me about a scene."

He puts down his fork, pushes his plate an inch or so toward the center of the table, and, magically, Conchita appears. He stands, excuses himself to change his "soiled" clothing, and goes inside. She clears the table, then returns with coffee and bowls of mixed berries. A few minutes later, he comes back on the balcony, dressed this time in soft white slacks and a turquoise silk short-sleeved shirt.

"My favorite scene," he says after he's sipped his coffee flavored with chocolate mint and nodded his satisfaction, "goes like this: I like a woman with long arms and legs, the better to play pony girl with me. I dress her in nipple clamps, a leather choker, wristbands, and thigh-high high-heeled boots, the heels four to five inches in height. Nothing else. I attach a leash to her collar and make her prance like a pony around the room for me until she's worked up a sweat.

"If she doesn't get her knees up high enough for my satisfaction, I flick her backside with a riding crop. When I know she's excited enough to take a little more pain, I flick it across her clamped titties. That really makes a woman jump like a skittish Thoroughbred.

"It's very exciting to me to watch a sweating, panting woman perform like a prize horse in a contest ring.

"When my dick feels like it's ready to burst, I put her across a piece of furniture and fuck her. Or maybe I'll just make her bend over and I'll fuck her across the room, if she's exactly the right height for that. Believe me, I've never had a hard time getting inside a pussy after this game. The women are always wet and ready for me.

"They tell me it's as exciting for them as it is for me.

When I treat them like animals, I free the sexual animal inside them.''

He picks up his coffee again. His hands are small, curiously effeminate for a man his size, nearly six feet tall and broad-shouldered, but I admire his manicure.

''Come inside and look at the game room,'' he says, standing up abruptly. ''You can't write about this without seeing the scene of the plays now, can you?''

The house is over fourteen thousand square feet, light and plant filled, decorated with occasional huge pieces of furniture or sculpture, and has lots of empty space. Photos of family members and friends fill the walls leading up staircases and down hallways. He has many pictures of his mother.

Anthony loves his mother. If you're looking for a peg on which to hang him, by the scruff of the neck or by the scrotum, it isn't the Bad Mother one. He loves his mother, but not in a slavishly devoted way. She didn't tell him sex was bad. She didn't wallop him with a belt or play with his little penis when he was small—or if she did, he doesn't remember or bear a grudge, and frankly, the possibility of that is too slim for me to consider. Dad was a kind man who keeled over from a major coronary on the eve of his fortieth birthday.

''My parents were Republicans,'' Anthony says, grinning evilly at me. ''Do you think that explains it?

''I have some books,'' he says, indicating a small collection of paperback erotica lined up neatly in a corner of a bookshelf, their spines largely hidden from casual view by a wood carving of a bear. I see a copy of Anne Rice's *Exit to Eden.* "No how-to books. I've never needed a sex manual, and I don't think I need one in this area, either. It's common sense. I've had horses. I know what a whip can do if you let your arm go with the swing.

"There's a limit to what any normal woman should be expected to handle in a sex game."

S/M dabblers seldom talk of "limits," the level of a submissive's tolerance for pain; and Anthony isn't using the word in that sense. The motto "Safe, sane, and consensual," by which Scene members swear they live, hardly needs to be spoken by someone like Anthony.

"Common sense," he says, "Sex is all between the ears anyway."

He opens a large entertainment cabinet, a six-foot expanse of rich teakwood, housing a twenty-seven-inch television, a VCR, a library of tapes, and an assortment of riding crops, whips, high-heeled black boots in several sizes, and enough leather collars, wrist cuffs, and leashes to turn the neighborhood women into a twenty or more horse team.

"Feel the quality of the leather," he says, handing me a collar. "Like butter. I buy this stuff from a guy in L.A. who handles custom orders. That stuff you buy in those shops is junk. I wouldn't put a woman of mine into a leather miniskirt from Kmart. Why would I dress her in something from the Erotic Bazaar or whatever? In the closet, there's a whole wardrobe of costumes, from the French maid's outfit to some elegant backless gowns."

I put down the collar and scan the titles of the tapes. *Story of O. Paula's Punishment. The Leather Mistress. Slave Girls. Spanked Students.* And more.

"Would you like to see something?" he asks. When I demur, he says, "Sure, you've seen this stuff. But I've got something here you haven't seen. My own private collection."

He points to a shelf on which the tapes are labeled simply by women's names. *Christy. Lisa. Lyndie.* More than two dozen names, including *Tiffany,* numbers one and two.

"Two different women named Tiffany," he explains. "What can I say? This is California."

We watch a few minutes of each tape. In addition to the pony girl scene, he and his partners have played, among others, the games of naughty maid and chastising master, Daddy and girl, spoiled rich bitch and the man who tames her. There is almost always a whip, which he handles judiciously, leaving nothing more severe than a slightly reddened streak across very white flesh. He is proud of this skill.

"Let me show you the stills," he says, pulling down a large and heavy leather-bound scrapbook from a top shelf of the entertainment cabinet. "I'm good for an amateur photographer. Some of these are professional quality, don't you think?"

He's right. They are, particularly the ones at the end of the book, taken by a camera on tripod, of him and a lovely, lissome blonde having intercourse, doggy style. They glisten and gleam with real sweat and lust, like the pictures in Madonna's book, *Sex,* should have done, but didn't.

Anthony's interest in photography led him to S/M.

"In my twenties, I just wanted to get laid. By the time I

was thirty, I had more money and less trouble getting laid. I liked to photograph my lovers, at first in tasteful lingerie shots. When I got tired of those, I sought out unusual collections of pornography for ideas on how to pose my women.

"In a few years' time, I'd moved up to S/M scenes, but I didn't really play the games. I just put women into the clothing, the poses. That was highly arousing in itself to me. I enjoy being in control of women, of their bodies and their emotions. It was inevitable that I would want to act out a scene, but I wasn't the one who escalated the action the first time around. That was a woman.

"When I had her in the classic submissive's pose, ankles bound, wrists bound behind her back, ass in the air, she begged me to hit her with the crop.

" 'I've always wanted to find a man who was man enough to do this to me,' she said. My first whipping was a revelation, about myself and about women. I wanted to do it, they wanted to have it done."

Anthony is quick to concede that not all women want "to have it done." "Maybe half, maybe two-thirds" of the women he's dated accepted that his lust died after several straight sex encounters and chose to move on, their parting gifts and the memories of all those exquisite meals tucked inside mental scrapbooks. They didn't feel sufficiently challenged by his flagging erection to put on a collar and prance for his steadfast approval.

"With so many women out there," he says, shrugging his shoulders, "I should regret the ones who don't want to play? I read somewhere that the ratio is something like twenty available women for every one straight man in New

York City. Run out of playmates here? New York is an option."

He promises "to put me together" with some of the women in his collection. Proudly, he boasts, "some of them have gone on to other S/M relationships, where they are the dominants. I helped them find their true selves."

Vicki, who learned S/M from Anthony, has been in a monogamous relationship with a man named Ted for five years. She appears to be in her early forties, though she refuses to disclose her age; Ted is several years younger. A redhead with fair skin given to crinkles at the stress points, with green eyes and a soft, pillowy bosom on an otherwise taut body, she is attractive. He, however, is gorgeous, a blue-eyed blond Nordic god with the kind of muscled body women dream of running their hands over. This is the kind of pairing that leads to the inevitable question: Why did he choose her—not that there's anything wrong with her, but why her when he could have anyone? You ask this even before you learn he sometimes likes to pretend he's her slave.

"That's only pretend," she says. "People in porn novels live S/M. Real people don't. It isn't a twenty-four-hour-a-day dynamic. I would have no respect for Ted if he was capable of being a full-time slave. He isn't. Occasionally, he likes to be dominated. No woman ever did it to him before me. That's my secret power over him. I found his submissive side, and he told me it was like finally being completely known and completely accepted by another person. He was in heaven."

The episode she describes is oddly reminiscent of a

scene in *Guest of a Sinner,* a novel by James Wilcox, which I've recently read. Wilcox, a literary author, and one of my favorites, introduces an element of S/M into the relationship between his main characters, Wanda and Eric, who are sharing an apartment for financial reasons. Wanda, the plain one, has suffered the pangs of unrequited lust for the more comely Eric for more than two-thirds of the book when, in exasperation, she yanks him from a bath and takes a hairbrush to his bottom. And, then:

> Resting his elbows on the sink, he submitted to the brush. At first the strokes were somewhat symbolic. But later, as she became more certain of the power welling up inside her, all the anger and frustration, her hand left red marks on his cheeks as he sprawled across her lap on the narrow bed in her own quiet sanctuary.

Mere pages later, Eric, the previously unattainable man, marries Wanda. The brush is replaced by a Ping-Pong paddle, and her uncle, the self-flagellator who never leaves home without his whip, comes to visit. I've read Wilcox's previous five novels, about gentle, quirky, and neurotic characters. No S/M until now. Has Wilcox tapped into the national pulse and found its beat emanating lower than the heart, in the region of reddened buttocks?

"It happened the first time quite by accident," Vicki says, pulling me back into the present. "Ted was on top, fucking me, and I wasn't comfortable. I was also irritable because he was fucking me in, like, this lethargic way. I tried shifting him, but he was out there in his own space. Without thinking about it—and I hadn't thought about S/M after the little thing with Anthony—I slapped him hard on the side of his ass. His erection immediately got harder. I had his attention. I slapped him again. He was moving with me, lifting his weight off me, pushing harder inside me. I kept slapping him, and he fucked me like he never had before.

"We didn't talk about what had happened, not until it happened several more times. I was afraid to analyze the situation for fear that speaking the words would destroy this new passion. He was embarrassed. One morning, when we were edging each other out for mirror space in the bathroom, I asked him quite casually if he'd like me to try a brush or another implement, and he said he would. That opened the door."

The door they opened led to their own erotic backroom, where a plastic spatula improves the sex in a way no Victoria's Secret confection could. Vicki, who played the submissive in Anthony's posh little theater, is always the dominant partner, though she and Ted never use the words *dominant* or *submissive*. They live a few blocks from the beach in a tiny cottage painted dusty rose trimmed in white, surrounded by bougainvillea, palm trees, hibiscus, and a profusion of other plants and flowers too numerous to catalog.

"We have the white picket fence," she says, laughing merrily. "The American Dream. Maybe more women would see their dreams come true if they understood that some men want to be overpowered."

Ted finds discussing his sex life more difficult than Vicki does, but he complies because "this is something she has

asked me to do for her." His comment reminds me of a
similar remark made by a male submissive in Maryland,
who also agreed to talk to please his dominant lover. In
their case, the couple described their relationship in completely different terms, she claiming her disciplining of
him was a "spiritual power exchange that energizes both,"
he saying, "I just get off on getting whacked."

Ted lights a cigarette at the beginning of the conversation. We are sitting on green iron and wicker chairs on the
redwood deck he has built on the back of the cottage. The
deck and the small planted yard below are enclosed with a
high redwood fence.

"I don't know what makes me feel more uncomfortable,
lighting this," he says, waving the cigarette, "or telling
you how I feel when Vicki manhandles me. I'm trying to
quit. Smoking in California is about the most politically incorrect thing you can do.

"I might as well start at the beginning. I thought I was
gay as a kid because I liked to read my sisters' romance
novels. My dad left right after I was born, and my mom
raised me and my two older sisters by herself. They took
care of me a lot while she worked, and romance novels
were part of our mostly girl household.

"Whenever the heroine got turned over the hero's knee,
I got an erection. I was identifying with her. My first girlfriend used to bite my nipples really hard, and that excited
me more than anything else she did. Sometimes they were
sore for a few days after the weekend. I felt like they were
my private badge of manhood, proof of my virility, which
only I knew existed.

"Girls were always after me. I could have had any one

of them in high school and college. There's no point in being modest about my looks—or bragging about them, either. It's genetics. I was born this way. The crazy part is how people respond to beauty, not the beauty itself. Beauty is far too highly rewarded in our society. People should be able to admire it without being caught in the trap, but they can't. Over the years, the women I've stayed with the longest have been those who weren't so taken with my physical charms. Nobody, until Vicki, tapped into my secret fantasy life.

"She knows how to be rough with me in the way I crave. Love bites. Slaps. Spankings. We don't have any S/M paraphernalia. Those sex toy shops are turnoffs to me. We use things you find around the house."

He declines to say what those ordinary household items are, much less how they are used, but he does concede the spatula is a "favorite—and you can surely figure out how she uses it." I guess as a spanking implement on the buttocks, but I can also imagine her spreading open his legs and spanking his inner thighs with it. I don't want to picture Vicki doing anything more creative to beautiful Ted. I've heard some "creative" means of torture I wouldn't want to imagine applied to him.

One woman, for example, told me she made her slave/husband stand naked in the center of the room at a holiday party while she attached two strings of miniature Christmas tree lights to him with long, thin needles holding the strings to his flesh. The bloody procedure took nearly an hour. When she was finished, she turned off the other lights and plugged him in.

Vicki joins us with a tray supporting a pot of herbal tea,

three cups, and a plate of morning glory muffins, which she has made. They contain dried fruit and seeds and are delicious.

"Ted won't tell me any details," I complain.

"Oh, give her one little story, just one," she wheedles, cupping his chin with her hands and feeding him a bite of muffin.

Here is the story:

Ted pretends he is a Chippendale's dancer who doesn't know his lover, Vicki, is in the audience. She has told him to quit the job or lose her. At the end of his act, he walks backstage to find her waiting. She grabs his crotch and chastises him for having an erection. While the other dancers watch, she takes off her belt and beats the shit out of him. When he is reduced to a whimpering, blistered hunk on the floor at her feet, she spreads her legs and makes him eat her, again as the other men watch. She is, of course, not wearing panties.

"In real life," he says, "she doesn't beat the shit out of me. But I dance for her. She punishes me. I eat her out. She lets me jerk myself off at the same time. We talk through the story as we're acting it out."

Anthony calls several days later to ask what I thought of Vicki and Ted.

"She's great, isn't she?" he asks. Not waiting for an answer, he adds, "He's a real weenie. Every now and then she comes over here to play with me. She says she has to have a real man occasionally, one who knows how to dish it out. Otherwise, she says she's happy with him. Different strokes, huh?"

Susan Crain Bakos

I wonder if Ted knows. And, if he does, does the knowing increase his humiliation, and therefore his joy, in being with Vicki? And does Vicki consider Anthony "a real man"?

70

Chapter 5

Advanced Bondage

San Francisco

"You will call me at two o'clock tomorrow afternoon," Cleo Dubois says over the phone. "I will give you directions and you will come here for an interview lasting until four. You will call me at nine in the morning to confirm this."

Cleo is a dom, one of several on my list to see in San Francisco. I found her name in *The Black Book,* a national resource guide for products, publications, and services aimed at consumers who can't find what they want or need in the Yellow Pages or the aisles of B. Dalton. A rumor spread among the San Francisco S/M community has it that a scion of one of the city's most revered families found his dom of choice through this book.

Cleo's listing reads: "Real S/M and skillful bondage in a private dungeon—sensitive sadistic focus—advanced S/M techniques for experienced masochists, and consultations for novices. All genders and sexual persuasions welcome.''

Both aficionados and practitioners of the art admit bondage is done better in California than on the East Coast. The symmetry of the bonds nears perfection here in the Golden State. The bindings on ankles and wrists, for example, will be aligned so that to the naked eye they appear to be identical, each equidistant from fingertips or shinbone or whatever else you care to use as a measure.

''Bondage is more aesthetically pleasing in California,'' says a man who has spent approximately $25,000 on being tied up this year, not counting airfare and hotels.

As I am scribbling Cleo's terms in my datebook, she repeats them as if speaking to a child. Men pay to be treated this way—receiving instruction from haughty, controlling women who seem to have no other phone voice inflection than condescending. I shove the book into my bag, next to a videotape of an S/M wedding, in which the groom pierced the clitoral hood of his bride/slave on the makeshift altar where they exchanged vows. The wedding took place in the Sonoma Valley, in a home with a breathtaking view of the wine country, with forty guests, all members of the ''S/M family,'' in attendance.

In a cab heading toward a dungeon in the Castro district, I wonder: What excuse did the bride and groom give their families, the biological kind, for excluding them from the wedding?

I tell the driver I am writing a book on kinky sex. He gives me the company card with his cab number listed and says, ''Call me. I can take you to a lesbian hangout where they have sex in the bar, sometimes with gay boys, I kid you not. Is that a confusion?''

As per instructions, I hit the bell at Kaye Buckley's three times. (''I know it's a friend if I hear three rings.'') She buzzes me into a Victorian house that has neither been desecrated by owners who lower ceilings and slap fake wood on walls, nor lovingly preserved by the ministrations only cash flow can provide. Like an old lady with good genes, this house has aged gracefully, wrinkling into herself with dignity. The stairwells are filled with light from the huge windows. A five-foot-tall, reasonably healthy umbrella plant grows in a pot on the second landing. I walk up the steps toward Kaye's voice. The lights go out when the door opens on her domain.

She is a dominatrix, a mistress paid by her clients, largely upscale married men, to bind and sometimes sexually torture them. Today she is not dressed for work. A small woman in her mid-forties, Kaye has hair dyed in two shades, very black with a clump of blond in the front. She wears glasses and no makeup, tight ankle-length black pants, black ballet slippers, and a loose black tunic. In a black linen suit and sling-back high-heeled pumps, and carrying a Coach bag, the ubiquitous accessory for women who work at more or less regular jobs, I feel overdressed.

We shake hands, and she leads me down a hallway lined with S/M photos in black and white. Some are of her dressed for work. She looks surprisingly different and very good in them, her body lean and trim, *aggressive,* the kind of exercised body other women admire on a woman. She looks a little sexy. We start at the back, in the last of her three rooms, the leather dungeon. Serious bondage takes place in this dark room, where the ceiling and walls are painted black. The windows are covered completely in black velvet. A vampire could live here. In fact, the one piece of furniture, aside from the straight-backed chair where she seats me, is a long box that looks like a sarcophagus with a padded leather lid. Implements of torture hang from the black Peg-Boards on two walls. On another wall hangs something that looks like a frame filled with interconnecting mattress springs. You don't need much imagination to guess clients are tied into—or onto?—this piece.

"Would you like a cup of tea before we get started?" she asks. "I have chamomile, mint, and apple."

I examine the room while she prepares the mint tea. The languid, discordant twangs of Eastern music pour out of her portable boom box. The art includes a statue of Pan and a photo of a nude man kneeling, head encased in leather hood, arms held behind him by leather wrist restraints fastened together. Only the shapely leg of a dom wearing high-heeled boots is visible. Her foot is resting on his head.

"You like the photo?" Kaye asks me from the door.

I admit the pose has a certain sense of humor, which elevates this photo from the typical work of S/M porn. The man, his average middle-aged flabby ass exposed to the world; the woman, in power, her identity a secret. Bondage that exposes the ass or genitals is considered humiliating or embarrassing bondage. The position of her foot underscores the obvious in an amusing way. I would consider it a symbol of raw female power if I did not know the man beneath the foot paid her to place it there.

"My particular specialty is bondage, both rope and leather," Kaye says, handing me the tea.

Many doms have specialties. They may cater to a variety of needs but consider themselves most proficient in one area—bondage or fetishism or caning or whipping, for example. I met a woman in Houston so skilled with the cane that she is often summoned, by first-class flight, to other cities where doms have clients willing to pay all expenses plus $250 an hour for the very best cane hand. Twice a year she travels to England to buy new canes.

"That's why I'm here," I reply. "I know that some men pay for a session that involves only heavy bondage. I don't understand why."

The point of "tie and tease" bondage is to intensify the restrained partner's orgasm by prolonging the excitation phase, or exerting some control over when he can climax. You tease him close to ejaculation with your mouth or hands or pussy, or probably all three, then pull away near the ejaculation point. If you mount him after having pulled away two or three times, you can ride him to a thundering orgasm—his, and several of your own of equal magnitude. But you will want his hands free before you come so he can hold your hips, fondle your breasts, pull you down to his chest at the end. You will want his hands free because you crave his touch and the feel of his arms around you. The bonds, easily slipped, are more symbolic than real, in case he really cannot wait.

Heavy bondage, however, places the bound one in a position he or she couldn't possibly escape without help. This sense of powerlessness, real not pretend, is what the devotee most craves. He may be chained to a wooden apparatus reminiscent of Colonial stocks, or fitted into leather garments that can be laced tightly together, binding the body in contorted positions, or tied with ropes into an intricate webbing. However he is bound, he is completely dependent on the dom to bring him safely through the experience. Nothing is up to him anymore. Men, and it is overwhelmingly men who are bound this way, often say they are only truly free when completely trussed.

Sensory deprivation is typically part of a heavy bondage scenario. The submissive wears a gag, earplugs, blindfold, or hood. Some doms favor inflatable hoods with breathing tubes, which immobilize the head. His body may be forced into a contorted position, even suspended. During suspension bondage, the submissive is hoisted off the ground with winches. The best dungeons are equipped with safety devices capable of releasing the bound victim quickly into the arms of his dom, who has been trained in CPR, if he faints.

Where is the pleasure in a web of rope so tight and intense it may take the dom hours to spin around captive flesh? What does a man get from this experience when she will not touch his genitals, unless she perhaps lashes them gently with a suede flogger? Why would he pay to be wrapped up tighter than a fly in a spider's web, then possibly turned upside down, only to be released from his bonds without being allowed sexual release?

Heavy-bondage devotees, for whom bondage is the chief source of erotic pleasure, say they welcome the restraints that remove all responsibility from them. They are tired of being in control of their lives and the lives of oth-

ers—wives, children, employees, clients, or patients—
whose futures they hold in their hands. In the captive position, the bound go deep within themselves, to a place they
describe as an altered state, where senses are heightened—
and nothing is required of them, not even sexual response.
He doesn't have to get an erection or give a woman an orgasm. He is free to do nothing. Some men have told me that
they know this freedom in no other place.

"Lean against it and see what it feels like," Kaye says. She
has noticed me eyeing the inner-spring device on the wall
as I walk back to my chair.

I lean against it, raising my arms above my head for effect. It gives with my weight. The feeling is neither pleas-
ant nor unpleasant, but it is vaguely sexual. Perhaps raising
my arms and opening my body elicited this brief erotic tingle. Or perhaps it is the sense that I have placed my body
where naked men have placed theirs in submission to a
woman.

"I lived in Japan, worked in the sex clubs as both a dominant and submissive, and was married to a Japanese
man," Kaye says, sitting on the coffin-like thing, sipping
her tea. "Rope bondage is part of the Japanese tradition.
That's where I learned how to do this."

"What are you sitting on?" I ask.

"Do you like it?" Smiling gently, she seems pleased I
ask. "I made it myself. This dungeon is all my design. I'm
not a very good carpenter, but I built everything myself,
with a little help from friends. I call this my bondage table
sarcophagus."

"I was going to say it looks like a sarcophagus."

"Every dungeon has a bondage table, something on which to lash the submissive down. See the hooks along the edges? You fasten the lacings through the hooks." She stands and opens the lid. "I use the inside for sensory deprivation."

"You mean you put people inside?"

"Sometimes." She walks to the rear wall and opens the doors of a large cabinet, built in three sections, which nearly covers the entire space, perhaps ten or twelve feet in length. "Some of my clients want some pain in addition to bondage. Would you like to see?"

She throws open the doors on whips, paddles, belts, floggers, collars, and cuffs. There must be thousands of dollars invested in this equipment. I put down my teacup, walk over to the collection, and stroke something that looks like a feather duster.

"You went immediately to the feathers," she says, nodding as if she has expected this and I, like a good student, have fulfilled her expectations. "That would be something I'd use in sensual play. For someone wanting a more sadistic approach, it would be maddening." She takes a suede flogger down and hands it to me. "Or something like this, this is sensual." I run my fingers through the strips of soft leather. They feel innocent in my hands. "I would use this in sensual play."

"Would you use this on someone who has come to you purely for the experience of bondage?"

"Maybe. Probably not. For this person, the bondage alone is the experience."

We walk back to our positions, sit, and pick up teacups.

"Who are your clients?" I ask. "I don't mean names or identifying descriptions," I add hastily.

She nods, but first she tells me about herself.

Kaye had her first orgasm at twenty-nine and shortly thereafter became involved sexually with a couple while she was married to a Japanese man and living in his country. The threesome was a "triad" who formed a "committed relationship." The male was dominant; Kaye and his partner were submissive, her first experience in S/M, the encounter with the "pain dynamic" that changed her life. Japanese-style rope bondage was part of what they did together, and under the man's tutelage, she became proficient at this method of wrapping the body in layers of rope and the accompanying tying of complicated knots to hold the flesh in place.

"Some people have a need to surrender," she says, "to lose control through submission. I believe submission takes power. It is a letting go, which takes power. For some, this power is only realized through bondage."

She is capable of sitting quietly, without balancing the teacup in its saucer or picking at a piece of dead skin on her finger or stroking the implements that surround her. Her hands in her lap, she sits on the sarcophagus and speaks in a voice so still it seems to appear in the middle of the room, with no projection from her. Not even her eyes dart from side to side. I admire her ability to be this still.

"It is very hard for me to talk about being a child or about the decade in my life I spent as a submissive. I also worked as a submissive, and later as a dominant, in the sex clubs of Tokyo. I have marks from those years." I wince, but she waves her hands at my discomfort. "Some of us are proud of our scars.

"As a kid, I was topped by people who didn't know what they were doing; I had no support. I saw my father four times in my life. My mother had a complete breakdown when I was six months old and she spent the next six months in a mental institution. The people in charge of me didn't know what they were doing. My two marriages were both traditional and restrictive. I wasn't topped by someone who knew what he was doing until I found S/M.

"When I found this form of eroticism, it spoke to me. I couldn't be in a relationship with someone who didn't understand and practice some kind of erotic power play."

She is in a relationship now, with a submissive man who is "exploring his feminine side." Her clients are mostly heterosexual men, typically married, though she does on occasion see couples and, more infrequently, a woman alone. The men are corporate executives, entrepreneurs, lawyers, doctors, brokers, and bankers. She will talk to them about their fantasies, but she won't let them dictate how a scene will be run. Like many people in The Scene, she gives credence to the belief that AIDS fears have sparked more interest in "creative" means of sex play. Does she really think her clients would turn to sex if they weren't afraid of AIDS?

"If someone comes to me and says, 'I want to be led down the hall on a leash and forced to sniff panties,' I tell him, 'You have to see someone else.' I won't be topped from the bottom, which means I won't let my submissive control the scene. He has to trust me. What I do is a professional service. I do not sell a commercial product."

Some people, she says, "like to put on leather restraints, the glitzy trappings, and have sex wearing leather. There is nothing wrong with having sex wearing leather wristbands. That is a fine thing to do, but that isn't what I do with my clients.

"I consider myself an S/M sex educator. And, I can't take a client unless I feel ethically good about what we are going to do. There is a strong spiritual element in this, particularly in bondage."

In bondage, she says, one can find one's senses heightened by the feeling of "primal helplessness."

"The first thing I do with a submissive is put a collar on him. That establishes the roles, who is in charge and who is—well, who is the submissive."

Spirituality is the theme running through much of what the San Francisco S/M community says in defining itself. Kaye Buckley derides the New York City scene as being "commercial," while describing herself as a "professional." Another dom, who considers herself a "therapist," told me, "If you do it right, S/M is spiritually empowering. On the East Coast, they just beat the shit out of each other. When I bring a whip down across flesh, I am bringing a soul closer to ecstasy."

Standing in the Japanese room, Kaye's other dungeon, I feel smothered in the spiritual S/M blanket, as if I were in the airless quarters of a monk who flagellated himself, and his fellow monks, on a daily basis. This room doubles as her bedroom; the bed is a wood-framed mat, over which hangs the hoisting apparatus. I can't imagine what it must feel like to go to sleep each night under that thing. Do the images of trussed men march through her dreams like so many sheep? In this room, the taped music on the boom box is Kodo, which is composed largely of monotonous drumbeats. (Kodo drummers are skinny guys dressed in loincloths who look like sumo wrestlers after several years on Ultra Slimfast.) A gong sits on a shelf. There is another Pan figure, a goddess of unidentifiable lineage, some incense in a holder, and a feather mask, all atop a small black lacquer cabinet. The room is spare, austere. Does Kaye have snapshots of nieces or nephews, paperback romances or mysteries, candy bars, and lace bras? If she does, they are out of sight.

"You notice the leather dungeon has a different feel than this room," she says. "Theater is a very important aspect of S/M."

"Do you suspend clients in that?" I ask, looking over my head at the hoist.

"Sometimes. Not too many clients want this experience. It is very different from the leather bondage I perform on the table. I did have someone in here this week. He comes once a month, and this is what he wants." She hands me a book of photos. "This is the sort of thing I can do."

I turn the pages. Some men, mostly women, all Asian—Japanese, I presume—bound by row upon row of rope. In one photograph, I count fifteen rows of rope around the wrists of one small woman. Her breasts are little pointed cones peaking from small hills of rope.

"Well," I say, handing her the book.

"Yes," she says. "It is impressive. It took me almost four hours to bind and hoist my client this week." We both look up at the empty apparatus. "That's an unusually long and complicated session. Two hours is more typical.''

"How long did he stay up there?" I ask.

"Only a few minutes." She pauses, waiting for a response, but I have none. "It's a spiritual thing," she says.

"Would he like to talk about it?" I ask.

"I doubt it."

In the cab I take away from Kaye's place, the driver tells me his transmission is "weirding out." He blames himself.

"I didn't plan my life," he says. "I drifted through. I never took charge of my own destiny."

Briefly, I consider telling him he can be glad of one thing: He doesn't have to pay a dom to relieve him at the controls. Instead, I tell him I'm researching a book on sex.

"You came to the right town," he says. "There used to be a lot of sex here."

I found Don through the maze of connections that exist within every profession and also within every underground community. The real six degrees of separation: Every journalist is only six phone calls away from the right source. A prominent professional, Don sits on a coveted arts board, is known by the headwaiters at the best restaurants on both sides of the bay, and has a beautiful yacht docked in Sausalito. Around fifty, he is married and the father of two. Why would he want to talk about his experience with bondage? He says he trusts me. I suspect that, while fearing discovery, he simultaneously yearns for the yanking open of the closet door that would end his double life. He takes small risks that could, but probably won't, lead to exposure.

"I have not established a relationship with one dom,"

he says, "but I have seen at least once all the top women who specialize in bondage in this country and in some European cities. I travel a lot in my work. Money allows me to be discriminating. If I'm in Brussels on business, I can afford the side trip to Hamburg to see Karen Hensall. Maybe I'm afraid to see one woman on a regular basis."

"Afraid of what?" I ask.

We are sitting on the deck of a Sausalito restaurant overlooking the bay. We can see his yacht. Across the bay, the lights of San Francisco are beginning to glitter in the dusk. Behind us, the rich hills of Marin County climb into the purple sky. Don has a home in those hills and an apartment in San Francisco. What could he possibly fear?

"Becoming too dependent on one woman," he says. "If I have a relationship with a dom, she will exert more control over me than she can in a single session. I've seen Kaye Buckley twice in the past few years. She is very good at what she does, one of the best. But if I saw her once a week or even once a month, she might have more influence in my life. She really understands me."

He smooths back a lock of blond hair that the sea breeze has swept down on his forehead. His hands are strong. I can imagine them caressing my breasts, parting my thighs. When Kaye Buckley takes hands like these and places them behind broad backs, does she ever wonder what they would feel like on her own body?

Don's hair is highlighted, but skillfully so. I can see him sitting patiently under one of those little caps in an exclusive salon where they can hide him in a curtained room, waiting for the color to take hold. His hands are manicured. The tan linen slacks still hold a crease at day's end. Noticing the attention I am paying to the physical details, he smiles at me. His eyes are too blue to be real. Contacts.

"I try to keep in shape," he says, "for a variety of reasons, one of them being I don't want to look like a ridiculous flabby slob when I'm being hoisted up in suspension bondage." We both laugh. I can see him suspended from a hoist, his stomach not betraying him. "Vain," he admits. "They say men are more vain than women. I am proof it's true." He pauses. "I wonder if the women are laughing silently at the absurdity of their captives. I've heard Cleo Dubois laughs when she has a man hoisted up. I can't imagine anything more humiliating than being laughed at."

"Where did you hear that?" I ask him, but I've heard it, too, heard furthermore from *her,* that derisive laughter is part of the service she provides. Is there an infinite yearning for humiliation within these men?

"From a dom in New York City." He puts his hands around the double cappuccino in front of him, as if he were warming himself on a chilly night, and says, "I consider myself a submissive. It's a secret I can't share with my wife."

Imagine being unable to share your deepest sexual desire with your partner because you are too shy to vocalize your needs. Then imagine believing your desire is too shameful, too vile for the ears of your beloved, and you will know how Don lives his life. He thinks he is "sick." Doms have told him he isn't, but he doesn't believe them. ("Why should I put stock in their opinions? They make their living off sick bastards like me.")

Therapy is an option he hasn't seriously considered, maybe because he doesn't believe in change, maybe because he doesn't want to let go of that which ultimately brings him pleasure. He is having his needs met. In therapy, he might be expected to sacrifice fulfillment of those needs in the hopes of learning some other path to pleasure. This is the path he's mapped out, however tortuous and indirect it may appear from the outside.

"I don't believe in therapy," he says, his voice low, confiding. "My wife and I had marital counseling several years back when we were going through a rough patch. I went to please her, so she would understand I was serious about making her happy within our marriage. I said what the counselor wanted to hear, and we were pronounced a cured couple and sent on our way. Therapy is all B.S. You learn the language and speak it back to them and they're happy with you.

"Our problems at the time had nothing to do with sex," he assures me, spreading his hands wide and placing them flat on the table. I wonder if this is an example of powerful body language, the sort of gesture he might make at a board meeting. "She thought I was too involved in my work and not enough involved in our marriage and the rearing of our children. She has no complaints about the sex. We have it twice a week in a reasonable variety of positions. I perform cunnilingus on her." He smiles. "She is satisfied. The one thing that makes my sexual behavior more tolerable to me is knowing I am able to please her by using the bondage fantasies to keep me excited during sex."

I would like to put my hand on top of one of his and stroke the underside of his wrist with my thumb. I know

Don's secret and find him an attractive man. Does his submissiveness trigger a response in me?

"Have you ever tied a man up?" he asks.

"No," I reply, because I think Don would not consider my play with silk sashes "tying up."

Don recalls seeing old magazines featuring cult bondage pinup queen Betty Page when he was a high school freshman. He was aroused by the photos of her in various stages of undress, though rarely nude, bound most often by rope. While Betty was widely photographed by many different photographers as a calendar model and centerfold, the bondage photos were taken by Irving Klaw, who must have been obsessed with sexual bondage. Betty quickly became his most famous model, and their collaboration is often credited with establishing bondage as erotica in this country.

Don identified with Betty. He felt himself in her position, helpless and subdued, held in a state of suspended sexual animation. Unlike other men, he did not put himself into the role of the captor, the unseen person who had tied the ropes around her. He didn't think there was anything strange about this until he was in the senior-class play. Who thinks their adolescent fantasies are so much unlike those of others?

"I can't remember what the play was, but I had a fairly minor role. I spent most of my brief time onstage tied to a chair. I had a half-dozen lines. Whether I was the victim or a captured criminal, I can't tell you.

"All I remember is getting a tremendous erection each time I was tied into that chair. I was praying no one would notice, but, of course, they did. A couple of the guys kidded me unmercifully. They assumed I had the hots for the star of the play, a little blonde who was prancing back and forth in front of me while I was tied up, her pointy breasts pushing out her sweater. I took her to the senior prom because I wanted to be sure the guys who ribbed me about my hard-on continued to blame the condition on her. I've never been back for a high school class reunion. My old classmates probably think success went to my head. But I don't want to be reminded of the senior-class play.''

That incident forced Don to examine his sexual responses, which he concluded were ''abnormal.'' He didn't like what he saw in the psychic mirror, and, to combat his negative self-image, he became skilled at pleasing his partners, particularly through oral sex.

''Where does something like this come from?'' he asks. ''I can't believe I developed this fixation because I saw those old photos of Betty. How many men and boys masturbated to Betty Page without turning into bondage freaks?

''I can't recall anything in my childhood, in the way my parents treated me, which would cause me to be this way. Sex wasn't a topic in our family. My parents are descended from Calvinists, strict and upright people who don't have much truck with pleasure. I can't recall seeing much affection, and no signs of overt sexuality, between my parents. Nor was there anything even vaguely abusive in their treatment of each other or me. I have read about people burying memories of childhood abuse, but I don't think I have.''

Perplexed and embarrassed about the evolution of his desire, he has never told anyone else that he can't sustain an erection or ejaculate without fantasizing about an intense bondage situation. When he has tried to hold other fantasies or focus on his partner, his erection has wilted. Nothing makes him hard again except the bondage fantasies.

"As long as I can fantasize, I'm fine," he says, laughing self-consciously. "If my wife ever becomes a mind reader, I'm in trouble. On those few occasions when I've tried to have sex without fantasizing about bondage, I haven't been able to perform."

Don keeps his fantasies fueled by visiting a dom once a month or less often. He pays for an intense bondage experience only, no whipping, electric prodding of the genitals, or "play piercing" (the inserting of rings onto nipples or scrotum, which will be removed after the session), practices he considers "really over the line." When he can see a dom who specializes in Japanese rope bondage, he does, because it is "much more satisfying" than being laced with leather straps onto a table. The experience lasts anywhere from an hour to three and a half, costing from two hundred dollars to one thousand dollars for the session.

He also practices solitary bondage at least once a month, sometimes more often, and only when traveling.

"A dom in Amsterdam taught me how to tie myself to the bed with a system of ropes attached to a combination lock. Before I do this, I set an automatic timer on the lamp next to the bed. I have about ten minutes after I tie myself up before the timer goes off. After it does, I can't see the combination lock until the lamp comes back on again, usually three hours later.

"This is an intense experience for me. Before the light goes off, I think about all the things that could go wrong while I'm unable to see the lock to free myself. What if there's a fire? Another emergency? What if my wife calls in the middle of the night? If I am traveling with business companions, what if they call or come to the door? In my worst scenario, they become alarmed when they can't raise me and call hotel security who lets them into the room. There I am, naked as a jaybird, tied to the bed, my peter standing at attention. It would be the end of me, wouldn't it?"

When the lights come back on, Don frees himself. He coils the ropes and hides them with the lock and timer in the false bottom of his suitcase. But he does not masturbate.

"I never masturbate following a bondage experience," he says. "That would change the dynamics for me, somehow. I just don't do it that way."

Several weeks after meeting Don, I see a bondage photo layout in *The Spectator,* California's weekly sex newsmagazine, which makes me think of him. The photos are of a bound woman, a brunette who, although she looks nothing like Don, has a quality of vulnerability that evokes his memory. Later I show the photo layout to a woman, a submissive who also likes to be bound. I ask why this arouses her. She speaks of love, the love the submissive believes is pouring from the dominant who binds. Her flowery words answer no questions for me, explain nothing to the uninitiated who doesn't understand the need, the desire to be tightly bound.

It's about "love," she insists. What has this got to do with love?

Chapter 6

Master/Mistress and Slave Relationships

PHILADELPHIA

"People don't understand that being free means living your true nature. For some people, their true nature requires them to be a total slave to another person. This is their freedom. It is an idea too complex for the average person's small mind to comprehend. Know what I mean?"

Having pontificated on sexual slavery mere blocks from the site of the Liberty Bell, Alan leans back in the uncomfortable chair, which rocks slightly on the uneven floor at Copabanana's on South Street. He reaches out to take Alicia's hand. Alan is a tall, lean black man in his late thirties with a shaved head that shines under the bright overhead light. She is his very white blond wife, also in her late thirties. At first glance, they seem like a sexy couple. His shining blackness with her contrasting paleness brings to mind all the clichés about ebony and ivory love. You look at them and think *hot forbidden sex* because of their skin tones. They could be a Calvin Klein ad shot in black and white. You imagine them on pristine white cotton sheets, their limbs passionately intertwined.

He is a midlevel executive in a firm headquartered somewhere in the Northeast, but not Philadelphia. We have picked this city as a meeting place because they do not live here. Alicia, who is also his slave, returns his squeeze of her hand and looks into his eyes lovingly.

The moment makes me uncomfortable. I am reminded of a similar loving gaze directed from a slave to her mistress, Ava Taurel, a prominent Swedish dom now practicing in New York City. The slave stood quietly in the room awaiting orders of a secretarial nature, while I interviewed her mistress, who had forgotten to dismiss her. When Ava noticed her presence and sent her away, the slave pouted. Ava complained to me, ''She wants me to humiliate her all the time. It's so boring.''

How awful to be boring one's adored master or mistress. More to the point, how can one who always submits not become a bore? In your fantasies you may want someone who lives to please you, but not in real life.

''We have an S/M marriage,'' Alicia told me on the phone before we met. ''Because we are both highly visible professionals and are also an interracial couple, we have to be very careful about who knows. We have a few friends in the S/M community, but we aren't joiners. You won't see us participating in support or social groups. Professionally, this could hurt me more than Alan.''

Alicia, whose lineage can be traced to the American Revolution, is a licensed marital and sex therapist. Would you be entirely comfortable with your therapist if you knew in her private life she sometimes kneels naked on all fours for an hour or more while her husband rests his wine-glass or his ashtray on her back as he reads the daily papers and watches the television news?

"When I am with him, I cannot discern the difference be-tween pain and pleasure. I am body, nothing more."

Another wife/slave said this as she was describing her relationship with her husband/master. The phrase "I am body, nothing more" conjures visions of hot, wild genital-writhing sex, leaving the sheets sticky wet—animal lust, animal sex. Later in the interview she said they had "gone beyond penetrative sex."

How can you be a "body, nothing more," yet forgo the primal satisfaction of "penetrative sex"?

People who have taken S/M beyond foreplay seem to have desexualized pleasure and sexualized pain. They have redefined "sex," eliminating, or greatly reducing, genital contact. Intercourse is, for most heterosexuals, the ulti-mate—though by no means the only—sexual expression, because the act fulfills emotional as well as physical needs for connection. I want penetration as much as my man wants to be inside me. Couples deep into S/M seem to have that need met by connecting whip or paddle or clamp to flesh. In some way, the implement of torture becomes a psychological extension of the one who wields it. More than one submissive has described the whip in phallic terms.

A thirty-five-year-old submissive male, an East Coast dentist, described his initiation into sadomasochism with his dominant lover as a "gradual process of learning to need the pain as much as the pleasure. She started by whipping me a little each day. I learned to take it. Then I realized I had learned to need it. The pain and pleasure are inseparable to me. One can't exist without the other.'' Later in the conversation, he added, ''Her use of the whip is masculine, my craving for it feminine.''

An S/M relationship is two people plus their implements. The accoutrements of pain are more significant to them than the vanilla couple's sex toys, videos, or favorite lingerie. Often, a submissive speaks warmly of his or her special whip, belt, paddle, or hairbrush. Alicia, like the majority of submissives I interviewed, says these relationships are ''more intense'' than others.

''This encompasses our lives,'' she says. ''We would not exist without it now.''

The typical couple who play S/M games as a form of foreplay do not describe themselves as being ''in an S/M relationship.'' The dabblers insist the roles they assume during sex play are shed when the game is done. She or he may become submissive sexually without affecting the egalitarian nature of their relationship. Whether or not they can move into and out of those roles easily probably depends on how often and how hard they play—and on whether or not they switch roles. At the level of master or mistress and slave, the roles have become their primary reality. The master or mistress may claim to respect the slave and consider him or her an ''equal,'' but this is not ''equality'' as the rest of us define the word.

One gay man who is a slave to another man told me: ''He owns my property and my money. He tells me what I can and cannot do. This is a total commitment we have to each other. We aren't role-playing. He owns me, which is a tremendous responsibility for him.''

"I don't believe Alicia is a slave just because she's a woman," Alan says. He wipes the grease from his fingers on a napkin and looks at the basket of fries. "I never should have ordered these," he says. "My best friend, Roger, is as highly evolved as I am. He is a fine person. I think someday Roger will admit he is a truly submissive man.

"Maybe that won't happen until he meets the right woman who can be his mistress in all senses of the word." He smiles smugly. "I'll bet you're surprised to hear me saying this, aren't you? I'll bet you thought I thought only women could be slaves."

Sexual slave. The phrase makes you think of women in historical romances, their beaded bodices yanked from heaving breasts by masterful men who satisfy these proud beauties beyond imagining—and against their will. In our fantasies, a slave submits her body, not her mind. Her submission eventually brings the master to his knees.

In reality, more men than women live as willing slaves. Yet male sexual submissiveness remains our culture's secret. Almost twenty years ago, journalist Nancy Friday disclosed that two-thirds of the men she interviewed for *Men in Love* reported fantasies of being dominated sexually by women. Numerous other research studies have shown men's desire to lose sexual control, at least on occasion. We cling to the image of the dominant male—and assume S/M will always be *The Story of O,* or the story of Alicia, a modern working woman privately subjugated to her man.

S/M social clubs and dating services offer free admission to women but charge men, because there are ten men, often more, for every one woman. Nine out of ten of these men are submissives. There may be hundreds of men for every woman willing to train them, according to Nancy Ava Miller, founder of People Exchanging Power (PEP), which has chapters in several cities nationwide, including Baltimore, Philadelphia, Atlanta, Phoenix, Dallas, Houston, and Honolulu. Several years ago she ran this ad in the *Albuquerque Journal:* "Attractive, domineering, sincere female seeks submissive, obedient, smart, sane, reliable man." From the 170 responses, she eventually chose her husband and slave, Barry. His penis was pierced during their wedding ceremony.

In a master or mistress and slave relationship, the power dynamics go beyond sex. In fact, they may often replace sex. Cleo Dubois describes sadomasochistic activities as "erotic power play, not sex." Miller claims that she and her husband/slave "rarely" have intercourse. The same is true of Alicia and Alan.

"I am a healer, a teacher," Alan says. "I am very spiritual. I consider myself an evolved person, and I am here to help others evolve."

He picks a French fry from the basket in front of him. A vegetarian, he has found nothing on the menu suitable for his consumption, except the fries. When I had suggested the Spanish fries—a mix of onions, jalapeño peppers, and potatoes—he frowned. Alan doesn't eat spicy food. He doesn't drink alcohol, except for the occasional glass of wine. Alicia, after consulting him, has ordered a cheese-burger and a margarita. She has not given up meat, though they do not cook or serve it at home. He is in a benevolent mood.

"You're on holiday," he tells her. "It won't hurt you."

"Do you consider yourself Alicia's spiritual leader?" I ask him.

"You might put it that way," he says. "In your mind, that's how it would be phrased. I don't see spiritual leadership as some form of authoritarianism, but I can see you do. Know what I mean?"

He uses this phrase repeatedly throughout our interview. "Know what I mean?" seems to be his way of emphasizing his points. I can imagine him checking to be sure all the appliances are turned off at least twice before leaving for the office every morning. I do not think he compulsively repeats "Know what I mean?" because he deems me any more stupid than the next person. His use of the phrase annoys me, anyway. He is like a dripping faucet I want to shut off.

My eyes wander away from his as he speaks. I glance at Alicia's reddened wrists, exposed when the cuffs of her long-sleeved white blouse ride up as she handles her burger. She has recently worn restraints. He follows my gaze, and then meets my eyes. His smile is sardonic.

"You think it is all about sex, don't you?"

Erotic sadomasochism is a consensual exchange of control between two people that can be practiced in many forms and on differing levels of intensity. Named after the famed Marquis de Sade, the French erotica writer known for inflicting cruelty upon women, the sadist causes pain and humiliation. The masochist, named after Austrian novelist Leopold von Sacher-Masoch, receives the pain and humiliation. Both achieve some level of sexual gratification through the process.

Why does Alan seem disdainful of the presumption that what they are doing is "about sex"?

An S/M relationship may begin with "sex"—two people aroused and sated by acting out scenarios of dominance and submission. Costumes such as uniforms are frequently involved. Bondage, spanking, verbal and physical humiliation, sensory deprivation, whipping—all of these and more may be elements of their lovemaking. For some of these couples, people like Nancy Miller and Barry, Alan and Alicia, the punishments, or power exchanges, become more elaborate with time. The games last longer and are less likely to end in sexual release. "Playing" has become an end in itself.

Hardcore S/M people believe what they do is more interesting than having "sex," by which they mean intercourse and orgasm.

"There are so many wonderful things you can do with household items," Nancy says, "that are so much more interesting than having intercourse."

Her favored household items include candles for dripping hot wax on Barry's nipples and genitals, a feather duster, a paint stirrer for spanking, plastic wrap for mummifying him, clothespins to "decorate" his penis, and an oral thermometer for sticking into his urethra. That's only a partial list.

A growing number of heavy S/M devotees believe the

practice of inflicting pain brings themselves and their partners onto a higher spiritual plane than the rest of us occupy. They speak of S/M with reverence, almost as if it were some kind of religion. I have identified these spiritualists as one of three groups of serious sadomasochists. The other two include punishers, those who use S/M as the stage for acting out humiliation and punishment as a catharsis, and the romanticists, people, most often women, who must be romantically involved with their partners before they can participate.

A lesbian mistress, a Chicago executive, told me: "I take responsibility for the whole being of my lover, who is my slave. Her mind and her spirituality are my concern as much as her body. Through pain, I take her to spiritual levels she could never achieve otherwise."

A master said of his relationship with his slave, "I know how to use her pain, to use the endorphins that kick in at a certain level of pain, to bring her to a state of euphoria, which is both physical and spiritual. The closeness of our union could never be reached any other way. Simply stated, we have a deeper, closer, more spiritual relationship than a couple who does not practice S/M." (It is worth noting that both partners have trust funds, no jobs or need for them, and thus have the time to devote to disciplinary sessions that can last up to six hours.)

Alan and Alicia also subscribe to the belief that S/M can be used as a path to spiritual enlightenment and marital unity. They resemble religious zealots who will only have intercourse when it suits a higher purpose: procreation. One seeks religious euphoria through whipping, the other through prayer. They are both rigidly moralistic, living their lives on a very narrow path.

"It took me many years to recognize and accept my own submissiveness," Alicia says.

She tugs nervously at an end of her long blond hair, so dry and overprocessed it looks as though it might break off in her hand. Except for her hair, Alicia is pretty in a conventional way. Thin, well-groomed, dressed in jeans and a crisp white blouse, her basic Keds spotlessly white, she looks like the typical thirtysomething suburban mother. Toss a sweater casually around her shoulders, put her in a Toyota, park her in front of a soccer field, and someone's child would surely wander her way, thinking he had found home.

"My mother was submissive in the worst way," Alicia continues, dropping the piece of hair, which falls limply to her shoulder. Alan reaches over and tucks the hair back, behind her collar, as if he has suddenly noticed its sad condition. "She deferred to my father in every way. He got the choice cuts of meat, the last piece of cake. Nobody could read the newspaper before he was finished with it. Every night of their life together, she went to bed when he decided it was time to go to bed, not before him or after. Sometimes he pushed her around. No, I don't think they were into S/M at all. They would have been better off if they had been."

"Do you understand why that is?" Alan interjects.

"No," I admit. "I really don't."

"There is a difference between abuse and dominance," he says. "Her father was abusive. I am dominant. I want to

102

bring Alicia to a greater pleasure than she could know any other way. An abusive man doesn't want his woman to have any pleasure at all. Her mother was subservient. Alicia is submissive. There is a difference between subservient and submissive. Know what I mean?''

"He's right," Alicia says, nodding her head vigorously. "Alan respects me. He respects my limits. My father had no respect for my mother."

She finishes her drink, and Alan asks the waiter to bring her another. Again, she gives him the look, the submissive's look of love. In her eyes, there is no question, no challenge, no hint of independence or promise of individuality, no sure glint that says, "I love you, but you cannot cross my lines." How does Alan sustain interest in someone who gives him no resistance?

"When I first got interested in S/M, I wondered if it was an expression of my desire to be abused as my mother was," Alicia continues. "I've worked my way through that."

Alicia's first S/M experience was with a dominant woman, her roommate after college. This woman liked to tie Alicia down to the kitchen table and put clothespins on her nipples and labia. ("She would kiss and stroke me as she pinned me. Then she would perform cunnilingus as she slowly removed the pins one by one.") After that relationship ended, Alicia actively sought out dominant men.

"I perform cunnilingus on Alicia," Alan says. "Are you surprised to hear that? Sometimes I think she needs to feel her body is worshiped, too. Know what I mean?"

I know I would like to stop his clock. Alan is bringing out the latent dom in me.

"I knew I wasn't gay," she explains. "The attraction for me in that relationship was the S/M, not the lesbian aspect. She taught me a lot, mainly how to look for what I wanted. I never knew there were bars where S/M people hung out, or social clubs. She took me on the train to New York City to those places. After we split, I would do those things in New York City alone when I visited for a weekend, because it was far enough away I wasn't worried about being seen by a patient or associate.

"Sometimes I got into situations that were heavier than I wanted. I remember one man who was into tit torture. He kept the clamps and weights on me for too long. I was in agony. I was crying, and I called out the safeword to stop him, but he wouldn't stop. My breasts hurt for two weeks afterward." Her eyes fill with tears. "That was a scary time in my life. I knew what I needed. Finding him was hard."

She met Alan at a Christmas party in the common room of the apartment complex where she lived. He was another woman's escort, but he unobtrusively gave Alicia his card and told her to call him. She did.

"We recognized each other immediately," she says. "I knew he was a dominant male; he saw my submissiveness, though I wasn't dressed at all that way."

"I have the power of looking into someone's eyes and really seeing them," he adds. "When we looked at each other that night, it was like we knew everything we needed to know. She took her eyes away first, and I could tell she was shaken. She saw my power. It was inevitable we would be together. Know what I mean?"

* * *

Their relationship escalated to the status of master/slave much faster than the period of nine-and-a-half weeks made famous in the popular S/M novel of that name. The first time Alan made love to her, on their first date, he slapped her thighs, pummeled her clitoris with a vigorous thumb massage, and thrust violently in and out of her during intercourse. She was sore the next day—and a little confused about whether she wanted to see him again or not. Maybe she'd had nothing more than rough sex. And did she want that again?

"Then he called me and told me to touch myself in all the places that hurt," she says. "I did. He kept talking me through the touching exercise until I was very hot. 'Do you want to come?' he asked. I said I did. He ordered me not to let myself reach orgasm. 'Touch yourself until you are on the verge of orgasm, then stop,' he said. I did.

"I was covered in sweat, gasping for air, I wanted to come so bad, but I did what he told me to do. That's when I understood he was my dominant. If he had that much power over me when he wasn't in the room with me—well, I had to be impressed.

"Before he hung up, he asked, 'Do you understand why I was so rough with you last night?' I did. He wanted me to feel the sore spots the next day and, in them, feel him and his power over me. He wanted to mark me."

One month after their first date, she was wearing his rings through her nipples and labia.

"The piercings were painful," she says, "but I was never so happy in my life. I swooned into his arms when it was over. I was in ecstasy pain."

* * *

For Alicia, ecstasy is achieved through pain and humiliation. ("It is necessary for him to humble me, necessary for me, not him.") Humiliation, verbal and physical, is a strong component of S/M, particularly on the master/slave level. Submissives may be required to crawl across the room while wearing a collar or stand naked with genitals prominently exposed in front of company. One male slave told me his mistress was fond of "playing dog" with him in the backyard of their suburban home. Dressed in leather jockstrap and collar, he, on all fours, chases after the ball she throws, picks it up with his mouth, and deposits it at her feet. Another male slave said his mistress enjoyed walking him on collar and leash through their Greenwich Village neighborhood, where, to be honest, such behavior is unlikely to garner them more than mildly curious glances. If they were to move to a small town in Maine, now *that* could be a humiliating experience.

Some masters and mistresses escalate the risks of discovery by neighbors, strangers, even the police, as the relationship progresses. Fearful of the effect such behavior could have on her practice, which brings in three-fourths of their family income, Alan and Alicia are more cautious. When he wishes to humiliate her in public, he takes her to an S/M club in New York City, ties her to the whipping post, and hands the whip to a stranger. If she cries too loudly, he makes her stay fastened to the post for an hour following the whipping.

Most of the time, however, he humiliates her verbally in the privacy of their own home.

* * *

"How can you speak of love and spiritual evolution when you call her 'slut' and 'whore'?" I ask him. "When you verbally castigate her for offenses such as trembling while she's pretending to be your table holding your wineglass?"

"That doesn't sound loving to you," he says, "because you don't understand anyone else's way of loving."

"When he calls me a 'slut,' " she says, "he is reminding me that I am redeemed by every stroke of the lash. By whipping me, with a real whip or his tongue, he takes away my imperfections."

What does "redeem" mean in this context? How does she equate whipping with the taking away of her imperfections? To the uninitiated, this is nonsense speak. But I have repeatedly heard such phrases from submissives in describing how they believe suffering pain and humiliation inflicted by their dominants brings them closer to a state of spiritual perfection. Inevitably, they say their dominants act in a way that we would see as cruel out of "love."

"Most people don't see the beauty in *The Story of O*," he adds. "They see her losing herself, giving up her personality and her will, to her master. They think this is cruel. People don't see the beautiful part, how the master has really helped her replace that personality with something much better in taking over her will.

"I have tremendous willpower and discipline. I gave up seafood, which I love, because I wanted to purify myself, to make myself a better person. You don't see that by surrendering her will to me, Alicia has put herself in the hands of someone who is evolved."

"Besides," Alicia says, "he doesn't give me anything I can't handle. People not into S/M think we are mutilating our bodies, but we aren't. That isn't true.''

I think about her pierced nipples and labia. Isn't that mutilation? Aren't the rings cold inside her flesh in the winter? Sometimes my earlobes feel frozen from wearing earrings.

We leave Copabanana together and walk up South Street. Alan is critical of the trash on the street, the crossdressers, the Japanese tourists, and the kids from the burbs dressed in leather. As an interracial couple, they get little attention here in this ''anything goes'' part of town, and what they do get seems to be positive. I notice two young white women casting covetous glances at him. Why wouldn't they? He's tall and slender and moves with elegance and grace. As a couple they are striking.

Even knowing what I know about them, I look at these two and want to believe their sex life is as hot as an X-rated video. His big, glistening penis parts the pale lips of her vagina, covered in the finest grade of almost white pubic hair. His full lips close softly on her pink nipple, and he sucks while she moans in ecstasy. I want them to be a fantasy of interlocking parts, gleaming black and juicy pink. I want them to be my fantasy. They aren't. More important, I don't want a black man, a descendant of slaves, to be a slave master. He is. No wonder I am easily annoyed by him.

''Boys shouldn't wear lipstick,'' he says. And later, ''Did you see that girl? She had blue hair in the front. Does she think she is attractive to men?'' He grimaces at the man wearing a sandwich board advertising Condom Nation, the condom store.

"Freaks," he says.

I ask him if the wonderful smell of cheesesteaks laced with onions coming from Jim's Steaks doesn't drive him wild. He grimaces again as he patiently explains to me why he gave up meat. We part at the corner of South and 6th with his promise that I will be allowed to interview Alicia alone. I want to know how her submissive lifestyle affects her ability to counsel others. Can she help other women to grow, to get out of bad relationships, to ask for their sexual pleasure? She says she can, but how? Weeks later, after much rescheduling, she admits he's changed his mind.

Several weeks later, Alan sends me a letter describing his childhood in the South, his stint in the Army in West Germany where he discovered S/M with a willing prostitute, and the various jobs he's held in his life. His mother was a "healer," he writes, given to putting her hand on his head when he was sick in lieu of aspirin or antibiotic. He hated his mother because she was never there for him—literally never there. Most mornings he woke alone, fed himself if he could find food, dressed himself, and walked to a neighbor's, where he waited for the school bus. His father was truly never there, having disappeared shortly after impregnating his mother.

"I didn't go to my mother's funeral," Alan writes, "so that tells you pretty much everything."

With no siblings, aunts, uncles, or grandparents, Alan was alone in the world until he married Alicia. Now she is almost alone except for Alan, because he has limited the amount of time she can spend with her family. "They don't understand what she sees in me," he writes. "I think they are racists."

The quintessential question those who do not practice hardcore S/M have of those who do is: *Why are you people doing this stuff?*

After meeting Alicia and Alan, I was troubled by the question. Why does she submit? Why does he dominate? How can they call this love? I felt badly about Alicia. Don, who pays to be tightly bound, is in control of his submission. Alicia seems far less in control of hers, though I may be wrong about that. She does earn a lot more money than Alan does. Is money her hidden power asset? Will she become even more submissive? I imagined her someday sleeping in a box built inside their mattress and box spring while he slept on top of the bed—like another slave and master I'd met.

Before I began researching this book, I was a guest on *The Richard Bey Show* when the subject was S/M and fetishistic behaviors. As a journalist who reports on sex, I was placed in the middle, between a foot fetishist, a master and his slave, a mistress and her slave—and a cop who thought they should all be arrested. The mistress sometimes put her slave inside a box built into the inner springs of a bed while she made love on the top of the mattress with someone else. I had been selected for this panel to be the neutral voice, the objective journalist who would say: We may not understand, condone, or accept what these people do, but we must respect their right to do it. Sitting between a master in leather, suede flogger tucked into his belt, and a cop in a conservative suit, white shirt, and tie, I said my lines.

Predictably, some audience members denounced the "sinners" and "sickos" while others blamed "dysfunctional families" for creating S/M-ers. Then, one nonjudgmental but truly mystified person stood and said, "I'm not criticizing any of you. I just don't get it. Why do you do these things?"

They had no explanation that made any more sense to *us* than Alan and Alicia's explanation of why she finds fulfillment and personal freedom in being his sexual slave. No matter how many times someone patiently says to me, "I am free because I no longer have to make any choices for myself," I will never understand how they can regard that as freedom. Yes, I realize they mean free in the sense of "without responsibility"—for their lives and their pleasure. To me, freedom is taking that responsibility and making those choices.

George, a noted East Coast S/M master who has been active in The Scene for nearly thirty years, took on my education as a pet project. He suggested I read *The Q. Letters: True Stories of Sadomasochism* by "Sir" John Q. This book, he promised, would help me understand the why—understand with my gut, not just my head.

Sir John, a very wealthy man, insists his slaves were intelligent, strong "equals"—and a few pages later reminds us that a good slave must consider her master "superior." He types his slaves in five categories, from the classic masochist, who loves pain for the sake of pain, through the challenger, who rebels against her master to test her own limits and his ability to dominate her. The experiences he details with the women he has mastered range from simple whipping and bondage to an encounter with a woman named Margot, who wanted more pain than even he was willing to administer.

During one four-day ordeal before he set her free rather than continue to meet her needs, Sir John whipped Margot for twenty hours, pierced her clitoris and nipples, branded his initials into the flesh of her inner thighs, applied electrical shocks to her genitals—and more. She wanted all this and more.

Sir John quotes from the diaries, letters, and conversations of slaves who adored him for his whip hand. Everyone seemed to write thank-you letters, except Margot, whom he presumes is dead at the hands of a man more willing to push her limits than he was. Apparently, Sir John's slaves got what they wanted from him, except for Margot, of course, who couldn't get enough.

I did not find the answer to the question of why. In fact, I came away with more questions—mainly, What does all this have to do with sex?

But I realize that some people would not understand why I can enjoy anal sex or "tie and tease." And some people don't really get the appeal of oral sex.

"You come at this with no basis for understanding, being hopelessly mired in your genitalism," a lesbian mistress told me, and she may be right. I do love intercourse. Maybe it is not possible for someone who loves intercourse to grasp fully the lure and power of S/M.

"You get it or you don't," a member of an S/M social club told me. "It's as simple as that. If you get it, it's part of you, like faith in God."

Chapter 7

Homosexual S/M: Lesbians Do It Harder

"S/M has changed in the gay leather community because of AIDS fears," explains Gary, a member of what he calls the "new" leather scene.

At thirty-two, Gary looks like a typical big-city Guppie—a gay Yuppie—hair cut in a "fade," long on top and close on the sides, manicured nails, astute gray eyes made for sincere eye contact, casual clothing from the Gap. He carries an expensive tan leather shoulder bag containing his Filofax, health club ID, and the other necessities of life. In my black jeans, black cowboy boots, black silk shirt, and long, dangling silver earrings, I look more leather than he does.

Police raids and legal actions taken against S/M social groups and the clubs and bars, particularly gay bars, where they congregate in various parts of the country have made many lifestylers—gay, straight, and bisexual—paranoid about talking to journalists. Gary consented to introduce me to his community only if I promised not to name their hometown. He was there, he says, when a Pittsburgh party was raided in a private home. Newspaper coverage listed names.

Gary says, "We fear something happening here like what happened in England, where a man is serving time for consensual S/M. The judge acknowledged he was a safe player, but ruled he had to be sentenced to a four-year prison term because he set a bad example for people who might not be able to play safely. Can you imagine that? Some of us drove to Chicago and marched on the British consulate in protest. Anyone into S/M has to be nervous, but especially gays. The leather community is blamed for starting AIDS in this country.

"We were hit first and hardest by the epidemic. We have lost a lot of people. And the leather community has been in the forefront of the battle against AIDS. The Scene has changed. Safe, sane, and consensual are more than by-words. They are bylaws. Drawing blood, having un-protected anal sex—these are things you just don't do anymore when you play. Anal fistfucking isn't happening as much as it once did.

"If you want to see the hard action, you'll have to go to a lesbian play party. They do it harder."

The gay leather scene peaked in the late Seventies and early Eighties, its heyday marked by the brief success of the camp disco group The Village People, men in the uni-forms of cop, cowboy, construction worker, Indian, and leather man singing about the qualities of "macho." Uniforms play a vital role in S/M scenes for straights as well as gays. Dozens of people have described "scenes" in which the dominant partner was dressed as a cop, soldier, doctor or nurse, or construction worker wearing hard hat and tool belt. The leather community, however, established leather, from cap down to biker boots, as an S/M uniform of its own.

"The leather bar scene is tame in comparison to how it was when masters used to tie up their slaves to posts while they drank," Gary admits. "You saw bloody stripes across backs in those days."

Now the San Francisco leather dykes are the acknowledged toughest players.

Gary takes me to the one gay bar with a leather room in this city. The main bar area is filled with men, mostly under thirty-five, mostly trim and clean-cut, dressed in suits or slacks and sport jackets or pressed jeans and immaculate white T-shirts. There are some couples who, like heterosexual couples, occasionally touch, a hand laid on an arm to make a conversational point, a finger run lightly down a cheek, a chin caressed. The bulk of the patrons are singles, making eye contact, exchanging smiles, and approaching each other with the mixture of wariness and hope familiar to anyone who has been single past age thirty.

Neighbors have complained about this bar, and occasionally the police have raided it. The owner considers the harassment "generalized gay bashing." According to Gary and some of the other patrons, the source of the problem is the backroom, the leather room to which only men dressed in full leather regalia are admitted. I am allowed to enter as a guest after each one of the fifteen backroom patrons has been asked if he objects to my being there. One no would have kept me out.

You can almost smell the testosterone rising above the scent of leather. The room is small, stark, and simple, done in smoky glass and wood stained black. Men posture like horses pawing the ground. Brightly colored bandannas in back pockets signal predilections. Turquoise worn on the left signals "cock and ball torturer"; on the right, "cock and ball torturee." Burgundy indicates "two-handed fister" if worn on the left and "two-handed fist fuckee" if worn on the right.

"There are twenty, twenty-five colors," Gary says, "depending on which city you're in, more in San Francisco, or so I've heard."

Among this group of fifteen men, there is one turquoise bandanna worn on the left, but no matching signal from a submissive in sight. In fact, there are few bandannas. Two of them are black, worn in left-hand pockets, which indicates that the bearers are S/M masters.

"Who is entitled to wear the black?" I ask one of the men, Tony, who appears to be in his late forties, wearing a leather vest under a leather jacket, chaps, and boots decorated with chains and spurs.

"Someone who has the experience and skill to accommodate any man's need for S/M on his own level," he says. "Being a master does not mean being a brute."

Tony has tanned, weathered skin reminiscent of hide, which makes one assume he has worked outdoors at some rugged occupation for most of his life. Wrong. He's a certified public accountant with a lifetime membership at a tanning salon. His colleagues at the office and the people he sees regularly at the salon don't know he is part of the leather scene, though, he says, most know he is gay.

He is looking for a slave, having recently set free the man he "owned" for seven years. The relationship ended over another man, a master for whom his slave secretly yearned. A proud man, Tony wouldn't tolerate his slave having lust in his heart for another man.

"If you own someone, he isn't supposed to think about another master," Tony says. "I blame myself for what happened. If I had been paying closer attention to his needs at the time, he wouldn't have been looking around."

I buy Tony a drink, and he tells me the story of his sexual life.

"I knew I was homosexual when I was eleven or twelve, the age where the girls begin getting breasts," he says. "I didn't care about their breasts. I didn't like girls at all, but I did like other boys.

"I knew I was S/M when I was five years old. Oh, I didn't have the language for it, but I knew what I was. I liked to inflict pain. I beat up on other kids, and I liked the sound my fists made on their flesh. I liked seeing welts and bruises form on them.

"My dad used to beat us kids, six of us, with his belt when we were really bad. The others couldn't stand to watch anyone take a licking. But I liked to watch. I would hide behind the door and peek through the crack or the keyhole if he shut the door. I liked to hear the screams from the one who was being beat."

"How did you feel when it was your turn to get the belt?" I ask.

"I took it," he says, shrugging. "I didn't like it, but I respected it."

Tony put the parts together, his sadism and his desire for men, in the military. A commissioned officer, he had an affair with a noncommissioned officer—an affair that ended when Tony beat the other man so brutally he had to be hospitalized.

"I took him to the hospital and said I'd found him like that. He told the same story. They were suspicious, but they thought he'd been the victim of a gay bashing. I don't think they suspected me of doing it, maybe of being his boyfriend, but not hurting him. I learned something from that experience. When I got out of the service, I started hanging out with the leather crowd, where I learned how to inflict pain without doing serious injury.

"In order to learn, I had to experience the whip myself. You will hear people tell you that you can't be a good dominant unless you've felt what the submissive feels. It's true. I had my limits pushed by a few masters, and it taught me a lot."

Gary comes up behind me and touches my shoulder.

"The guy who just came in has some heavy objections to you being in here," he says, gesturing toward a slender young blond with a yellow bandanna—for "pisser"—in his left-hand pocket. "We'll have to go."

"Call me at home," Tony says, handing me a business card, which has his home number in addition to his office number. "Be glad to talk some more."

Gary has arranged for Jay and Jim, a couple from his social group who have been together for five years, to tell me about their relationship. I am waiting for them in my room at the Holiday Inn. Five minutes before their scheduled arrival, the phone rings. Gary says, "They wimped out. They're both doctors. The possibility of having their cover blown leaves them limp."

Gary and I arrange to meet several hours later at a shopping mall. From there, he will take me to a lesbian bar with a backroom for S/M, where, he says, "You'll have a better chance of finding a communicative couple."

Meanwhile, I make some phone calls on my own. Jan, in another Midwestern city, smaller than this one, belongs to a lesbian S/M support group, Briar Rose.

"You can come here if you can't get anyone to talk there," she says. "There are only fourteen of us, a small group, but we're friendly to outsiders."

I take apart a club sandwich ordered from room service and nibble quietly on the layers as Jan tells me about her life. She is five-foot-three and weighs one hundred ninety pounds; her lover is six feet and weighs "well over two hundred. We're big girls. That's why we like to do it in swings."

Swings, which hang on big hooks from ceilings, are popular with sadomasochists. They have canvas or leather bucket seats, like the versions made for babies. Some have holes through which to put your legs. Jan puts her partner's legs through the holes and fastens her wrists to the ropes suspending the seat.

"She likes me to fuck her hard with a twelve-inch battery-operated dildo while she's in the swing," Jan says. "After a good whipping, of course.

"S/M sex is much more interesting than vanilla sex,"

she continues. "We put so much energy into it."

Then she tells me about the scene she created for her lover, who is also a "pre-op transsexual, which means she dresses in men's clothing all the time, but has a woman's body." For their anniversary, Jan gave her a replica of a Civil War uniform, took her, dressed in the uniform, to dinner at the historical society restaurant, then brought her home to the "playroom" for the special treat of the evening. Jan popped a videocassette of *Glory,* about a regiment of black Civil War soldiers, into the VCR, and, with the movie playing in the background, stripped off her partner's uniform, fastened her to the ceiling hook, and "lovingly" whipped her.

When she is finished with the story, I ask if the uniform was North or South. There is an uncomfortable pause. "North, of course," she says. "What do you think we are—racist bigots or something?"

At the lesbian bar, which is brighter than the gay bar we visited, Gary introduces me to Beanie and The Crew, who have been living together for three years. Both are in their late twenties. Beanie is tall, nearly six feet, and very thin. Her red hair is cropped so close it forms tiny curls the width of a slight little finger all over her head. She wears heavy eye makeup—green eyeliner, lighter green eyeshadow, a thick layer of mascara, and pink lipstick. The Crew, who was a member of a champion rowing team in college, has even less hair, pale blond fuzz not much longer than Beanie's eyelashes. She is of medium height and build, with muscular arms, a legacy from her rowing days. They are dressed in identical red ribbed muscle shirts and frayed, faded jeans. A fashion cop would throw the book of citations at them.

"You want to know how we do it?" The Crew asks, smirking for the benefit of the women at the bar, who are listening.

"I'd like to know how you met first," I reply.

Beanie, the self-proclaimed "romantic half of the couple" and the submissive, relishes telling the story. They met at a meeting of Lesbian Sex and Love Addicts Anonymous. Beanie went because she "needed help to get out of the pattern of being slavishly devoted" to a woman who was cheating on her. The Crew was there because she'd been told it was a great place to pick up women.

"Our eyes met, and we knew it was going to be love," Beanie says. The Crew is rolling her eyes fondly as Beanie speaks. She reminds me of a very young man in love and embarrassed by his feelings. "We went out for a drink together after the meeting. She gave me the courage to go straight back to my place and tell my lover I no longer needed the humiliation of her neglecting me. The next day I moved into The Crew's loft. We've been together ever since."

"Isn't that a great story?" Gary asks. "It moves me every time I hear it."

Both Beanie and The Crew claim to be victims of childhood sexual abuse. Beanie was raped, she says, periodically by her mother, beginning at age six.

"She would come into my room dressed in a cop's uniform," Beanie says, "and rape me. First she would take off my pajamas and touch me all over my body. I can close my eyes and feel her fingernails raking across my little girl's pussy and pushing open my crack. She raped me with her hands. It hurt. I would cry and she'd comfort me for a while. If I cried too much, she got mad and spanked me.''

The Crew puts an arm tenderly across Beanie's shoulders as she describes her childhood ordeal in a dispassionate voice. They look at each other meaningfully. I sense they are sharing what they might describe, given their familiarity with recovery terminology, as a "healing moment.''

"It was my father who did me,'' The Crew says in a stagy offhand way, her arm still in place around her lover. "He started when I was six or seven. I stopped him when I was maybe ten or twelve. I kicked him and broke his wrist. I was aiming for his balls, but he put his hand in front of them, so I got his wrist. He never came in my room again.'' She laughs. "Ha, ha. I didn't mean the double entendre. Came and came. Well, he didn't with me anymore after I broke his wrist.''

Jan, from Briar Rose, told me earlier in our phone conversation that she thought a lot of S/M people, "heteros and homos,'' come from backgrounds of abuse—physical, psychological, and sexual. I remember her comment as this couple talk about their childhoods.

"It's too simplistic to say we do what we do because we were abused as kids,'' The Crew says, slicing neatly into my thoughts. "I think there is more to it than that. I knew I was S/M when I was two or three, years before my father stuck me with his prick.''

"I was little, too, when I knew,'' Beanie says. "I always knew I was. If you are, you know who you are. You know right away. You know who is. Even if nobody in your family or circle of friends is doing it so you can't possibly know what S/M is all about, you still know you are.

"I remember seeing things on television, maybe even cartoons. They were images of domination and submission. I stood in front of the TV transfixed because I knew what they were. I don't know if anybody else did or not, but I did."

Nodding her head in agreement, The Crew tightens her grip on Beanie, who looks up adoringly at her.

"I lived in New York City—in the East Village and the Williamsburg section of Brooklyn—for two years before I came here," Beanie says. "I couldn't get a date. There's a lot of hostility to S/M among lesbians who are committed feminists in the big cities. I was in with that crowd. I guess I missed finding the people who were doing what I was doing."

"Well, aren't you glad you did?" Gary teases, punching her arm lightly below the place where The Crew's hand is embedded in it. "You wouldn't have met The Crew if you hadn't left the Apple."

An older woman sitting at the end of the bar, who somewhat resembles Margaret Thatcher, buys us a round of drinks. Then she joins us.

"I couldn't help overhearing you talking about New York feminists," she says. "Can I put my two cents' worth in?"

"You're buying, you're talking," The Crew says.

For the next half hour, they complain about lesbian feminists who are opposed to S/M, whom they label "Andrea Dworkin-ites," after the militant antiporn crusader.

"S/M has helped me get rid of my passive-aggressive behaviors," the bestower of two cents says. "I communicate better. In a relationship, you're going to cause pain anyway. Why not agree on how much pain and what kind, right up front? If you can't trust another dyke to respect your limits, who can you trust?"

"What we're doing is unleashing our sexual energy in its purest, rawest power," The Crew says, and Beanie nods enthusiastically, standing so close that her chin bangs against The Crew's chest.

The women agree that other lesbians "confuse" lesbian S/M with "prick violence and pornography." Again, they blame Dworkin and her sisters for all the confusion. They don't seem to know that Dworkin, who has never been identified on TV talk shows as a lesbian, has written lesbian erotica under her own name, erotica heavily laced with S/M scenes. Not wanting to prolong an ideological discussion, I don't tell them.

"You still want to know how we do it, don't you?" The Crew asks.

The two of us are sitting in the backroom, the S/M room, of the bar. Beanie has gone to work. She is a waitress at a truck stop outside the city. Beanie plans to mark time as a waitress until her parents are both dead, when she will inherit their several-million-dollar estate. The Crew has been drawing unemployment for three months since her employer eliminated several middle-management jobs. She doesn't have to get up in the morning, and she wants to play.

"Watch me do a gay boy," she says quietly.

She approaches two beautifully androgynous and unnaturally blond young men sitting in a tiny wooden booth along the wall. Within minutes, she brings one of them back to the bar, where she orders him to take off his belt and hand it to her. He complies. Then she tells him to pull down his pants, bend over and clasp his ankles, and present his ass to her. Again, he complies. She hits him with the belt, reasonably hard, ten times. He grunts, but never sobs or cries out. His erection is solid, bobbing and throbbing in time with her swats.

Jan told me she sometimes "plays with gay boys." They like, she says, "to be spanked, nothing heavy, by lesbian dominants. If you see a gay boy in the backroom of a lesbian bar, that's what he wants."

I glance at Gary, whose face is red. I wonder if his presence is so casually accepted in this bar because he is, or has been, one of the "gay boys" who likes to play.

"Tell me what you and Beanie do," I say to The Crew after the "gay boy" has pulled up his pants and returned to his hard wooden booth.

"Suspense getting to you?" She laughs. "Okay, I'm the top, but you probably know that. We don't like the terms 'dominant' and 'submissive.' We use 'bottom' and 'top.' I top Beanie. She was never topped before me. She just took abuse.

"I like to tie her up in the big bay window in our upstairs bedroom. We live in a big old house—an architectural delight, the realtor calls it—which Beanie bought with one of her trust funds. I put a big hook in the wood above the window seat and took out the seat, so I can hang her, with her feet on a stool, of course. She couldn't very well hang by her wrists for long, could she?

"We have sheers in the window, but if you're really looking, you can tell she's hanging there." She pauses to take a theatrical swallow of her beer. "When she's worked up a good sweat, I whip her with a braided leather whip we had specially made by a whip master on the West Coast, a bitch goddess with huge tits and a shaved head. Her picture is on her brochure.

"We play games, too, like anybody else. Daddy/Boy is our favorite game. She dresses like a boy in a little navy romper suit with anchors sewn on the front; and I dress like Daddy with a strap-on dildo. She can take more punishment this way than any other time."

The Crew goes on to describe at length the copiousness of both their vaginal secretions and the quality of their erections—in their nipples.

Before I leave this city, Gary takes me to a private play party, where thirty heterosexuals, homosexuals, and bisexuals—members of a social group—are gathered in a typical suburban sprawling ranch house. Jill and Dick, the married couple who are hosting the party, have sent the children, ages three and ten, to Grandma's for the night. They proudly show me their "den," a twenty-by-thirty-foot room painted black and fitted with wall chains and shackles, a bondage rack, two whipping posts in the middle of the room, a spanking saddle, a hanging swing, and a cupboard filled with paraphernalia ranging from whips to candles for dripping hot wax.

They are both in their mid-thirties. Dick is dressed as an

errant cowboy in black leather chaps, black hat, black boots—and something resembling a triangle of stretchy red bandanna covering his scrotum and penis, which swells solidly beneath the cloth. She plays cowgirl in boots, gunbelt, hat, and G-string, all in white. I think tasseled pasties would be a nice comic touch, but her wide brown nipples are bare. They have almost identical short blond blown-dry hairstyles and reasonably trim and tanned bodies, with no tan lines.

"People will tease me all night for this white outfit," she says.

"How do you keep the children out of the dungeon when they're home?" I ask.

"We keep it locked," he says. She offers me a tray piled high with crab puffs. I take one. "They know this room is off-limits."

I have never known a child who wasn't up to the challenge of unlocking a room in his or her own house, but I don't know their children.

Their guests range in age from a young woman who doesn't yet look twenty-one to the group's founding father, a robust sixty-year-old man who has been in The Scene almost forty years, or as he puts it, "before there was a Scene." Most are in their mid-thirties to late forties and dressed largely in black leather, rubber, or vinyl. As guests arrive, they ask one another about jobs and families. How is your mother doing? Where are the kids tonight? The same kind of questions any group of people who are at ease—even affectionate—with each other would ask.

A woman in her mid-thirties wears black jeans, cowboy boots, and nothing else, calling attention to her strong back, taut waist, and full breasts that sway seductively as she accompanies her conversation with extravagant hand gestures. A fortyish woman in a black rubber corset and very high heels sweats heavily. Jill asks if she would like to change into something more comfortable, but she declines. An hour or so into the evening, after the crab puffs, mini-cheese balls, boiled shrimp, and fried wontons have been consumed, people begin to form little tableaux, S/M scenes of varying degrees of intensity.

A woman in a leather jumpsuit unzipped to the waist shackles her husband/slave to the wall and applies the cat-o'-nine-tails carefully to his back. The blows are spaced so that he can anticipate them, flinching just before they land. After the tenth, he makes a low growling sound in his throat each time the lash falls. A bald man ties his lady to the whipping post and lays into her with a velvet-covered lash. She responds to every stroke with a grunting "uhn, uhn." Two gay men, more attractive than anyone else in the room, surprise me when the one I was sure was the submissive attaches nipple clamps and weights to his partner, not the dominant I mistook him to be. The submissives are soon covered in sweat, their tense, wet bodies somehow more erotic than they were moments ago.

Other couples follow, taking up the implements cheerfully. The beatings are real, but they are not delivered with anger or passion. Often the technique is impressive. The marks left behind will be few and not long-lasting. The woman under the velvet lash begs for mercy, and her dominant husband tells her she will receive ten more "good" strokes, which she must count.

"One, uhn . . ." she begins, straining forward, away

from the blow applied to her back. After four more strokes to her backside, he moves around to the front of her. She closes her eyes, and he hits her stomach. ''Six,'' she cries loudly, pushing upward from her toes. Nine and ten are applied to her breasts, the last, a light stroke, straight across the nipples. She shrieks. He puts the whip to her mouth. Without opening her eyes, she kisses it. He walks away, leaving her for the time being, attached to the hook, eyes still closed, panting audibly, the muscles in her arms trembling.

Then a lesbian couple assumes center stage. Dressed in identical black leather bras with nipple cutouts and black spandex tights, they kiss before one climbs into the swing. The beating with a braided cat-o'-nine-tail whip begins. Blows, increasingly heavy, land on back and shoulders, buttocks and thighs. Red marks rise up angrily, crisscrossing wildly. At first, the submissive woman's grunts aren't much heavier than those coming from the dominant wielding the whip. Gradually, her grunts grow louder and turn into cries. Each stroke creates a spray from her profusely sweating body. She throws her head back, grimacing in pain as she bites down on a scream, trying hard to control her response. This excites her partner, who brings the whip down again and again, harder and harder, fucking her with the cat-o'-nine-tails, breaking the skin in several places.

I know the whipping will not stop until the submissive utters the safeword or begs for mercy. Then it will not stop immediately. The dominant will strike her a few more times, to ''stretch her limits,'' before *lovingly* removing her from the swing.

The crab puffs feel queasy in my stomach. I look away.

Everyone is focused on the two women. Even the lady disciplined by the velvet whip has turned her head awkwardly around to watch. I have heard many S/M participants say lesbians do it harder. These lesbians certainly do. Why? Are they overcompensating for societal perceptions of women as the gentler, weaker sex? Or is it pure machisma? If I faint, will I be letting down my sex? There are no sounds in the room now but the grunts and cries of the two participants, the slash of this one whip, and the collective heavy breathing of the audience.

After a few more minutes, Gary rescues me by asking if I would like to see the rest of the house. Followed by Jill, the hostess, we slip out of the dungeon, Gary holding my hand, rubbing his thumb across my wrist. Jill shows me the numerous framed photos of her children, pretty blondes. In the master bedroom, I see an antique rocker with cane back and seat and curved arms, much like the one I have at home, the rocker in which I rocked my baby many years ago.

"We're like a family, this group," the hostess says to me. "There are a lot of good people in loving S/M families."

This is not the first time I have heard S/M groups described as "loving families." A dom in Manhattan, a woman whose smile is so thin and cruel it reminds me of a butter knife turned on edge, told me, "There are many good folks in the S/M family." Until now, I have thought the words had no more meaning than they do when coming from the lips of a callous employer insisting, "We're like a family here."

"My mother rocked me in this rocker, and then I rocked my children in it," the hostess says.

I want to know what kind of biological families produced the members of these families, people who equate the giving and receiving of pain with love. In sharing pain and humiliation, their own and others', they feel in the bosom of their families once again. No one else looked away when one lesbian beat the other. They watched.

Chapter 8

Who's Really in Charge? Topping, Bottoming, Bottoming from the Top—and the Switch

NEW YORK CITY

"I won't be topped from the bottom."

Over the conversational din surrounding me, I hear the comment made by one middle-aged man in a black leather cap talking to another middle-aged man in a black leather cap. They are standing a few feet away, discussing the power issue. "Topping from the bottom" means the submissive is really controlling the scene by setting the limits beyond which the dominant will not push. Sadomasochists discuss the issue as often as women in consciousness-raising groups in the late Seventies talked about who changed the baby's diapers. (Mama did, but she seethed with resentment. Who's on top in an S/M relationship is more open to debate.)

"This confuses me," I say to my companion, George, my guide to the East Coast scene. "If dominants pride themselves on respecting their submissives' limits, then isn't the bottom always the top, so to speak?''

"Ah," he says, "but a good dominant knows how to stretch those limits, taking the submissive a little further than he or she thinks is possible, and then maybe going a little further than that the next time or another time. The top should be the top.''

After several months of talking to the players, I have grasped the fact that S/M is about power—or *control,* the word of their choice—not sex. If a submissive does want to have an orgasm, something that dominants rarely have during a scene, he or she must beg for permission to come. In real sex, especially good sex, control shifts easily back and forth from one partner to another. You are on top. By mutual consent, you roll over, shift positions. He is on top or at the side or behind you. In real sex, you do not beg for permission to come. He may, in fact, beg, ''Come for me, baby, please come for me,'' because he so much wants to see you have an orgasm. I have never been with a man who didn't delight in my orgasms. In real sex when it is good, there is no game plan. S/M, however, is a negotiated power exchange. There is always a game plan. If you think bridge is boring, or too complicated, don't try this.

George, who warms quickly to the subject of control, promises to explain ''topping from the bottom'' later. He wants me to look around the room and tell him what I notice. We are at the book party for *Different Loving,* held at the Manhattan S/M club, Paddles. I look around the room as instructed.

Different Loving is about The Scene, written by members of The Scene, for members of The Scene. The authors and the lifestylers they quote bask in a self-acceptance, an

I'm Okay, You're Okay for the truly kinky—which is understandable. They have been labeled "weirdos" and worse by families, neighbors, and friends.

Gloria and William Brame, the authors, occupy a raised dais with a few hundred copies of their book—dust jacket, black. William, a large man, wears black leather pants and shirt. Gloria, a small woman, wears a black leather dress. They are talking to Constance, the owner of Dressing for Pleasure in Upper Montclair, New Jersey. Constance is everywhere, knows everyone. I have declined George's offer to introduce me to Constance, fearing she will remember me as the woman who made an appointment to interview her, then failed to show. Constance, in heavy makeup and the ubiquitous black clothing, looks fearsome, like a Mafia godmother or a dom. I can see her using the same heavy pressure on the whip as she does the eyeliner. Is Constance beyond turning a writer over her knee?

On the big-screen TV to the left of this trio, a video is playing. A masked man whips a woman tied, arms above head, to a post. No one is watching. The room is filled with perhaps two hundred people, at least half from the publishing industry or the media, many expressing disappointment at finding no free food. Others, like George, are Scene members. Maybe twenty are guests invited by Constance from her mailing list, good customers who "play" but keep the S/M aspect of their lives tucked away in the bedroom closet. At least 80 percent of us are wearing black. This is New York.

"What do you see?" George asks after I've made a visual circle of the room.

"A lot of black. The floor is black, the walls are black,

the clothes are black. And it's dark in here.''

"Okay, but you don't see much dark skin do you? How many blacks do you see?''

Aside from the gorgeous young editor from *GQ* magazine, I see no blacks. Not one.

"You won't see many blacks or Hispanics in The Scene," George says. "If they do come in, they come in as dominants. Do you know why?'' He doesn't wait for me to consider a reply. "The more powerful a person is during the day, the more submissive they want to be at night. How many powerful black men do you know?''

George has made a social observation, not a racist comment. A Texas dom said the same thing in a more interesting way: "I don't see many blacks or Hispanics. I figure they get humiliated enough in real life out there. Why do they need to pay me to humiliate them?''

"Control," George says. "It's all about control. That's why you're going to see more successful white men into S/M than anybody else. Minorities don't have enough control in the world yet to come looking for this.''

I wander away from George and ask everyone with whom I converse, after the amenities: Who's really on top, the top or the bottom? I get different opinions. These people don't even agree on what the words mean, much less who is which.

Defining the terms is not easy in S/M. Some prefer D&S, for dominance and submission, to S/M, which they reserve purely for the giving and receiving of pain.

"The connotations of S/M are loaded," explains William Brame. "People confuse sexual sadists, who seek romantic fulfillment with consenting partners, and criminal sadists, who inflict pain on victims, nonwilling partners. There are no victims in S/M. A lot of participants prefer to use D&S, because that is a more clear picture of what is going on.''

The picture may not be so clear to people outside The Scene. What is the difference between a top, a dominant, and a sadist? *Is* there a difference?

''A sadist gets into inflicting pain and will do that with anyone who is willing to be hurt,'' explains Janine, who calls herself a ''dominant.'' She says a dominant ''controls the submissive's pleasure.''

'' 'Top' is another word for dominant,'' says Jeff, a bottom. ''I prefer the words 'top' and 'bottom' because I don't like to think of myself as submissive. I like to be the bottom, which is different.''

How different?

''A submissive is like a slave. His limits are set by his dominant or master. A bottom takes the whip or the hand, but his limits are respected by the top.''

While getting a consensus on definitions from S/M players is difficult, most do concede there are varying levels of dominance and submission. At the extreme end, the slave will do anything the master or mistress wishes him or her to do. The slave does not have the right to stop his own punishments. On the opposite end, the bottom or submissive enters into an arrangement with the top or dominant with the understanding that the scene will be designed and controlled from the bottom, the ''now you hit me this way'' school of play. In between are varying degrees of dominance and submission.

"People who top from the bottom are really kinky sensualists who get their thrills from taking a little heavier stimulation than the average person," George says. "They aren't serious players. They're having fun making the top think he's the top when he isn't."

Kinky sensualists. I like that term. It seems to describe aptly those couples for whom S/M is an occasional erotic game, meant to intensify, not replace, sex.

Who is on top?

"The dominant, because he or she doesn't lose control," a middle-aged man in a gray suit says. "No orgasm. That's total control. The bottom or the submissive begs to come. My little submissive is creaming in her pants, dying to come halfway through the scene. I'm cool."

"She wants to know who's on top," a young man calls out.

"The bottom," a shapely redhead in leather hot pants and halter says. "She gives up her power. She's really in control. The top doesn't take the power."

The little knot of people around me grows to include a couple introduced as Bill and Nadine. She calls the power issue "disturbing," while he says it's "confusing." I coax them off to the side.

"Power is the worrisome concept in all this," she says.

"In S/M, you are addressing the issue," he says. "The rest of the time couples don't deal with it. They argue about whose turn it is to pick the restaurant."

"Who's on top?" I ask them.

They say in unison, "We switch."

* * *

Nadine and Bill live in a very upscale New Jersey suburb, where huge sprawling homes have been built on large landscaped lots, creating almost total privacy. One cannot see a neighbor's driveway or deck except in winter when the trees are bare. He is a successful entrepreneur, she a corporate attorney. Both in their early forties, they have an eleven-year-old daughter. Eager to talk about something else after dropping the word ''switch,'' they give me the thumbnail sketch.

''This is not something we talk about to other people,'' he says, nervously swallowing from his glass of beer.

''What else have you written?'' she asks me, but she is looking at him, her eyes telegraphing uncertainty about how much they should disclose.

Slender, not over five-foot-nine, well-groomed, wearing a white shirt, maroon patterned tie, and charcoal gray suit, he is as blandly attractive as a Ken doll. She is wearing four-inch black heels and stands a few inches taller than he does. Dressed in—what else—*black,* a fitted, sleeveless linen sheath, she exudes pricey beauty: blond hair, expertly highlighted and cut in a blunt, chin-length bob; hazel eyes, accented by deftly applied cosmetics; a diamond engagement and wedding ring set that would attract attention at Trump's Plaza. I see the tiny scars behind her ears when she pushes her hair back with one hand. A facelift already.

Together, they are sexy. When she puts her hand on his arm, they both seem to get an electrical charge from the connection. Discreetly glancing downward, I note his erection. He could not possibly be sexy without her, but with her hand on him, he is. What the right woman can do for a Ken doll.

"Constance personally invited us," she says.

"You know Constance well?" I ask.

"She's been very helpful to us," he says, "in offering instruction and support as well as product information."

"Yes," Nadine says, sipping from her white wine, then smiling widely. "So we wanted to come. It's interesting, isn't it?"

This small talk goes on for another five minutes. I am suspecting they will never say anything more useful than what they've already said when he suddenly confesses, "We switch because that's the only way we can do this comfortably. We are both more excited about being submissive than dominant, but we're also both afraid of being too submissive too often. Neither one of us wants to be the kind of person full-time submissives invariably are. Sometimes it takes a while to get back to yourself after playing as a submissive. If you did this all the time, would you ever get back to yourself?"

"There has to be equality," she interjects.

"I am mostly aroused by bondage," he continues, "by being bound. When I was a little kid, I used to spend my allowance on detective magazines. I wasn't interested in the crimes. There were always pictures of people tied up, mostly women, but men, too."

What they do together isn't as kinky as some things I've seen in mainstream movies. A little light bondage, some spanking. No dripping of hot wax onto the nipples. No steel handcuffs. She spanks him with a bedroom slipper, a soft leather flat. He prefers to use his hand on her. Sometimes they make love to each other while wearing nipple clamps, and the dominant turns the screw of the clamp when the submissive of the day is close to orgasm. They own a soft leather whip, which, she says, "is more for effect than anything else. His hand on my butt hurts more sometimes than the whip across my back. It's a sexy idea, though, being whipped. Submission is a sexy idea.

"When we were first married, I read a scene in a historical romance novel. The hero whipped the heroine, who was then his servant. He pulled down her dress and gave her a dozen lashes. Later, she fell in love with him and he with her. They got married. I read the whipping scene over and over again and used it in my fantasies when we made love. But I didn't have the courage to tell him how much this fantasy excited me until after we'd gone into Dressing for Pleasure on a whim looking for, I don't know, body paint. Weren't we looking for body paint, Bill?"

"Something like that, something to get us out of the rut sexually," he agrees. They laugh. He puts his hand on her back, gently draws her a little closer to him. Her breast grazes his side. "We were looking for this all along, weren't we, dear?"

They "play" two or three times a month, seldom more often, and only when their daughter is spending the night with a friend. Their "toys" are kept in a combination-lock safe at the back of her walk-in closet behind a row of long gowns. The play often leads to intercourse and always orgasm for both.

"Sometimes when she is the bottom, I make her swallow," he says. "That's the only time she will." He blushes. "Then I eat her out until she comes, which doesn't take long."

Susan Crain Bakos

When the talk turns from spanking to orgasms, she begins looking around the room, perhaps for someone to whom she must say hello, though that seems unlikely here. Her face relaxes as she spots a young couple she recognizes and waves them over. Too polite to leave me standing alone with my notebook, she wants to pass me along to someone else.

"Alexis and Chad," she says. "They're coming over. You must talk to them. We don't know them really, except for seeing them at a party Constance gave."

After they make the introductions, Bill and Nadine walk away. I watch them move through the crowd, his hand still on her back. Talking about their sex life to a stranger excited them. I imagine his hand sliding up her thigh as soon as they are seated together in whatever vehicle will take them home.

"Who's on top?" I ask Alexis and Chad. They both say he is.

Switching is common for three reasons. First, there are more submissives than dominants, which means a lot of people will have to give to get. Second, most people who play don't get into S/M beyond a superficial level, where it is easier to slip into, and back out of, roles—top one night, bottom the next. Third, they can have the thrill of assuming or relinquishing power, without being stuck with the power imbalance over breakfast. Switchers say there are different pleasures in each role, but being dominant requires the most work and responsibility.

* * *

"I have never switched," Chad says. "I am a natural dominant. Alexis is a born submissive. We don't have any role conflict. We know who we are."

He puts his arm protectively around her and pulls her close to him. I wouldn't be surprised if he called her "the little woman." She is, in fact, a very little woman, a mere five feet tall, without the five-inch heels that keep her tipped precariously forward. Her feet seem to be pointing straight down into the shoes. She's wearing a strapless black rubber dress, a truly ugly garment, which flattens her small round breasts. In another dress, she would be lovely. Her hair, long, bleached blond, is almost as big as she is. He is well over six feet tall and sports his own long mane of bleached blond hair, cut closer to his face on the sides and top. In different clothing, they could be former high school sweethearts, he the captain of the football team, she the head cheerleader, back in town for the homecoming game.

Like Nadine and Bill, Chad and Alexis are a sexy couple, the kind of people you know enjoy marital relations often. They touch each other with the ease and assurance of lovers who know they give the other pleasure. Kinky sensualists? George's definition seems to apply.

"If you are the dominant, you decide how the scenes will be played," I say, making the question a statement to see if one of them will challenge it. They both do.

"Oh, no," she says, leaning into him. "It's not like that at all."

"No," he agrees, "it isn't. She's my darling little submissive, but I would never push her further than she wants to go. She lets me know how far she is willing to go. She is really calling the shots. I love her, worship her, adore her."

"I don't understand," I say.

They look at me with a mixture of pity and amusement. Why don't I get it? She is topping from the bottom and he loves her for letting him think he's the boss. Alexis plays the role of traditional wife, in a rubber dress. She is Donna Reed, Harriet Nelson, June Cleaver, the little woman who lets her husband think father knows best.

"When the submissive is topping from the bottom," George says, "her limits aren't getting stretched. It's a static relationship with the bottom in control."

"Is that bad?"

"I wouldn't put up with it from a bottom," he says, shrugging.

The masked Pony Boy, the paid entertainment, asks me if I would like to climb up into the saddle on his back and take a ride, but I decline. I rode Pony Boy at another party a few years ago and ran my stockings on his saddle. He plunges a few feet into the crowd and persuades a young female publicist to ride. She takes off her pumps and hands them to an associate before hitching up her skirt and climbing onto Pony Boy's back. The flash of her thigh as she mounts him is erotic.

"Are you a hard master?" I ask George, who, in his sixties, frequently travels the Eastern seaboard to attend parties of various social groups or conduct private sessions with women who want to submit to him.

"I can be a brute," he says, laughing. I don't doubt he can be. George, who has been married to the same woman for forty years, has grown children and several grandchildren, ranging in age from six to sixteen. He traces his interest in S/M to the teaching nuns who smacked his hands with rulers and dragged him by the ears when he was naughty. George's wife is a dominant, too.

"In the beginning of our relationship, I tried to dominate her," he says, "but that didn't work. So she dominated me."

"You are her submissive?"

"Yes. She's a professional dom, though she has only a few select clients. We have to be careful about what we do because of the family, especially the little grandchildren. Our children know what we do. They are very supportive."

"But you are a dominant with other women?"

"Yes."

"This isn't a problem between the two of you? Nobody gets jealous? She doesn't mind when you go off to play with women in other cities?"

"She always tells me to have a good time."

"How would you handle someone who's topping from the bottom?" I ask.

"I would take her further than she wanted to go, and she would thank me for it."

Some weeks later, George invites me to brunch to meet some members of Black Rose, the S/M social support group in Washington, D.C. Several tables have been pushed together to accommodate the group at LouLou's restaurant on M Street. It is the least congenial and definitely most paranoid collection of S/M aficionados I've met. George and I are early. As the others arrive, he introduces me. Some refuse my hand. Some grudgingly take it. A man in an official Black Rose logo T-shirt asks if we've met.

Before I can answer, a scrappy little woman behind him says, "Have her turn around. See if you recognize her ass."

To amuse myself, I try to guess which are dominants and which are submissives.

"The red-haired woman with the crewcut. A dominant lesbian?" I whisper to George, the only person other than his buddy, Art, who seems willing to say more than hello to me. Art wants to talk about his therapy, which "isn't working."

No, a lesbian switch.

The guy with the weak chin next to me, a submissive?

No, a switch.

The tall energetic man at the end of the table, a dominant?

No, a switch.

Are you beginning to see a pattern?

I get only one right. The big fat guy, the Major League umpire deep into conversation about staging a scene, is a dominant. The man with whom he is conversing is a firearms expert. Here is the scene the two men plan to stage the next weekend:

A member of another social group in a nearby state, a man, avidly desires his dearest fantasy enacted. He wants to be hunted down, nude, by men shooting at him. He will dodge the bullets until he can run no longer and collapses in a bloody, bullet-ridden heap.

He has the scene scripted. Floors and walls will be covered with plastic. A cassette of a film about the St. Valentine's Day Massacre will be popped into the VCR in the background to set the mood. Bottles of ketchup will be spilled on the floor. Nude, he will run back and forth, dodging bullets, until he falls. Then a dom will slap several pounds of hamburger on his chest and back, grinding the meat into him with her heels.

The group is ready to accommodate him, but they don't know how to shoot without doing some real damage. The firearms expert suggests red-paint pellets shot from paint guns.

"They're going to leave some real welts," he says. He, the umpire, and George chuckle merrily.

Later, I ask George why anyone would want to be hunted down and "shot"—and what was the meaning of the hamburger?

"I don't know," he says. "I don't get it, either, but my wife has done the hamburger routine with him in other scenes. For several days afterward, she can't look at ground beef or meatloaf."

What has this got to do with sex? I ask. George laughs.

"He never switches," he says, indicating the umpire, changing the subject.

I got one right.

Part 3
Getting It Your Way

Chapter 9

Finding a Partner

NEW YORK CITY

Pam met her first S/M partner almost ten years ago at a meeting of the New York City S/M social club Eulenspiegel Society. Sitting in the shaded courtyard of a tiny restaurant close to her apartment on the Upper East Side, she smiles, remembering him. Her smile is a huge dark red gash across her stark white face. Pam is dressed in a Morticia Addams costume: long, sheer black clingy dress with floating sleeves, black high-heeled wedge shoes with open toes, toenails polished to match the lipstick. The whole outfit is topped by a huge, floppy brimmed black crocheted hat. She wears big oversized black sunglasses. A self-described "former anorexic-bulimic," Pam dresses to emphasize her gauntness. People at surrounding tables sneak glances at her. She is so eccentric that they stare at her, obviously trying to figure out who she is. Surely only celebrities are this bizarre.

"He was the one attractive man there," she says of her first liaison. "European. Tall. Handsome. Most of the men at Eulenspiegel meetings are not attractive." She makes a face. "I'm being kind when I say that."

"She's right," says Janet, a business consultant. "A lot of the men in The Scene don't think they need to wash their hair on a regular basis."

Janet looks five to seven years younger than thirty-five, her age. Petite, with fine brown hair cut in a gamin style, she wears oversized black-framed glasses, and dresses in classic clothes. Her black leather outfit, when she wears one, is a suit. She was involved in an S/M relationship for six years with a man she met in the traditional way, at happy hour at Bennigan's.

"He helped me to discover my submissive side," she says, lighting a cigarette, which she will extinguish after one puff. "He hugged, caressed, and kissed as much as he spanked, whipped, and tied me up. The man treated me like a princess. When it was over between us, I was so lonely. I didn't know how I would ever find something like that again. My clients are conservative. I couldn't be seen hanging out at leather bars."

Pam says, "Well, you could, but not in that little coat-dress."

Janet smiles insincerely. Without being able to see past Pam's sunglasses into her eyes, I know what she is thinking of Janet. I can see into Janet's eyes. The feelings are reciprocated. They don't like each other.

"Anyway," Pam says, "I had on a leather skirt at my first Eulenspiegel meeting. He was very much into The Scene, though he acted like he wasn't. But why would he be there if he wasn't? I was dominant. He was very submissive. We had a brief relationship. Then he went back to Europe.

"He sent me a ticket, and I went to visit. He convinced me to switch, and he was one of the best dominants I've ever known in my life. I'm a Gemini, so I can switch. My nature is to experience both sides. He was fantastic as a dominant, because he was capable of being so submissive. I was in love with him for three days.

"The big problem with him was he needed extreme pain—needles and pins and pain and torture—to get off sexually. I didn't want to do that. But, overall, it was a fantastic experience." She pauses for a swallow of tea. "Now that I'm into my forties, I seem to attract the very young men who want to be spanked whenever I go to meetings. That can be fun. Some of them have gorgeous, fantastic butts."

What about the personals? I ask them. Have they found partners through answering or running ads?

Pam finds them "largely impersonal." Janet has answered some ads, with disappointing results.

The club scene? It frightened Janet. She went to the Vault one night. The only person who spoke to her was a man she found "so creepy, I wouldn't have been surprised to see his picture in the paper with the caption 'Crazed Sex Killer/Cannibal Arrested.' " Then, while on the Metroliner, first class, between Philadelphia and New York, she overheard two women talking about an S/M social group. The group was PEP (People Exchanging Power), started by Nancy Ava Miller.

"I found an ad for it in *Philadelphia* magazine," she

says. "I decided to give this a try, because I'm in Philly a lot. Ruining my professional image in Philadelphia wouldn't be as bad for me as publicly disgracing myself in New York. I haven't found the man yet, but I'm learning a lot about S/M, meeting other people like me, and having some experiences I would never have otherwise. How else can a woman get tied up and spanked in a safe environment?"

Pam says, "There are always ways to do that. Tomorrow night I am meeting a new man. I answered his ad in *New York* magazine. We've talked on the phone for hours about our fantasies. We are going to meet in the front row of a movie theater, after the houselights go down; and we'll both be wearing dark glasses.

"I like drama. Theatrical touches make an encounter so much more sensual, don't you think?"

"I thought you considered the ads 'impersonal,' " Janet says.

"This one was different. It spoke to me."

If it's hard to find a suitable partner for sex or a relationship within the vanilla world most of us inhabit, imagine how much harder it is for people like Pam and Janet to find someone to love, or whip. The available pool of like-minded partners is smaller. Few S/M aficionados, cross-dressers, foot fetishists, or bisexuals are comfortable in being open about their needs and desires with someone new. Many, in fact, live in long-term marriages or other relationships with mates who do not know their fantasies and sexual predilections. Fearing rejection, they keep silent.

How can they find partners?

If they are men, they can buy one.

Men, particularly married men, often pay prostitutes or dominatrices to service their needs. The doms I've met all have regular clients who've been married ten, fifteen, twenty years or more without telling their wives about their secret sexual desires.

Both sexes use the personals in mainstream publications, particularly city magazines and the free weekly papers in major cities, and esoteric newsletters, magazines, and journals, such as *The Spanking Times; In Step* (foot fetishists); *Horny Housewives, Coeds, and Couples* (swingers); or *Diaper Pail Fraternity* (diaper wearers and those who love them). These publications have bigger circulations than you might think. A newsletter aimed only at gay foot fetishists has over eight hundred subscribers. The pansexual *S/M News* has a mailing list of seven thousand—and three or four times that number of newsstand sales.

Some people, more comfortable with limited public exposure in their quest for partners, attend meetings of social/ support groups such as Black Rose in D.C., Eulenspiegel Society in New York City, the Janus Society in Los Angeles and San Francisco, or Chicagoland Discussion Group in Chicago. Some of the groups have a substantial membership. Janus Society, for example, has over a thousand members. Nearly every sizable city has a group, and they too advertise in the city magazines.

The listing for Black Rose in *Washingtonian* magazine reads: "The Black Rose, Dominance & Submission. A sincere, caring support and discussion group, featuring education, speakers, workshops w/focus on safe, sane, and consensual relationships. Confidential."

Members of social groups can place ads in their own newsletters and those of other groups', too. An ad, whether appearing in a mainstream publication or a newsletter, can be quite specific about the advertiser's sexual bent. Clayton, a foot fetishist, ran an ad in a conservative city magazine last year in which he said, "I desire to worship at the feet of a strong woman."

"Of the forty or so respondents, nine got it," he reports. "Two were professionals. Seven is still a lot for something this esoteric by mainstream standards. The other thirty thought I was just an uncommonly devoted guy."

Happily, he has settled into a relationship with a woman who understands and accepts his fetish. He pays for her expensive pedicures three times a week, buys her the finest shoes and stockings, and takes her everywhere she wants to go.

Why is she so happy to settle for having her instep licked and her toes sucked in lieu of genital contact?

"She's never had an orgasm," Clayton says. "We don't think she is capable of having one. She gets a lot of pleasure out of satisfying my needs. And she gets sensual pleasure out of having her feet worshiped.

"The ad route may be easier for men," he concedes. "Women have to be careful because they are more vulnerable. A submissive male could probably get himself out of a dangerous situation with a woman, while a submissive female might not have the physical size and strength to do that. With a man, submission seems more a choice to me than it does for a woman. Some men might not let her go back on her choice."

On the other hand, a woman in search of kink will attract a lot more responses from her ad.

"I advertised in a little newsletter for a man with a strong hand," says Denise, "and I got close to one hundred responses. A lot of them had money and were willing to spend it. One man flew me from San Antonio, where I live, to San Diego for dinner—after one phone call. He was very nice, a perfect gentleman, but not who I wanted."

She did find a man among the hundred, and they have been together for three years.

"We should do the clubs together," Pam says. Surprisingly, Janet agrees.

Going to an S/M club in search of romance is risky—and something few women do, though they get in free or at a fraction of the cost to men. For protection, I take along Rod, a male friend who stands six-foot-three and weighs around 225 pounds. To our disappointment, he refuses to wear a slave collar. He does agree to wear the outfit Pam has put together for him—a borrowed leather vest, no shirt, his black jeans, and boots.

When we enter the Vault, Rod whispers in my ear, "It smells like sweat in here."

The sounds of grunts, groans, moans, sighs, and sobs fill the air, sliced periodically by the whistle of a whip. A woman wearing garter belt, black stockings, high heels, a leather collar, and a leather waist cincher is lashed to the wheel. She has two long slender needles pierced through the nipples of her lush breasts. They glint wickedly in the dim light. Sweat pours off her body. Her short brown hair is plastered like a cap to her head. Red lines across breasts, belly, and thighs indicate a very recent whipping. She is breathing heavily.

I have seen needles inserted into nipples before, but Rod hasn't. He stands transfixed for a minute. Pam, Janet, and I sense that he's going to pass out. With Janet shoving from behind, Pam and I each take an arm and drag him to the bar. He orders a double vodka and swallows it in one gulp.

Standing at the bar, we see two unaccompanied women—a zaftig blonde and a brunette as thin as the emaciated model on that month's cover of *Bazaar*. They are dominants in search of submissive men. We know this because each carries her own whip and has a "Don't fuck with me" stance that would guarantee her safety on the subway to the Bronx at midnight.

"Do you meet a lot of guys here?" Rod asks the blonde, giving himself away.

She laughs at him and turns so her shoulder juts into his chest, forcing him to step back. Within ten minutes, she has at her feet a slender young man clad in tight leather pants and boots, no shirt. As we talk to the brunette about her preferences in men, the submissive is licking the blonde's not particularly clean boots.

"I like guys who will give me their credit card numbers so I can order things over the phone," the brunette says. She will not tell us her name.

"That's always good," Pam agrees, while Janet maintains a disapproving silence.

Rod arches his eyebrows significantly at me. One of his gripes about the women he meets is that they are interested only in a man's net worth.

"I had a slave who gave me an American Express card

in my own name," the brunette says. "But his wife found out and canceled it."

Most of the women in the club are accompanied by their masters or leading their own slaves on leashes, but there are two small groups of women bunched together at opposite ends of the bar. I introduce myself to the first group, European tourists in their twenties, sophisticated, nonparticipating observers of The Scene. They have been to clubs in Amsterdam and Hamburg.

"How does the Vault compare?" I ask.

The participants here are more self-conscious, they tell me, and less skilled with the whip—and the club smells worse, "like pine-scented cleaner."

"There is a good energy," says a German woman, whose father was a black American GI. "I always like the energy Americans bring to their pursuits."

The second group of women are novices and S/M wannabes who have come with a leader, a mistress long in The Scene, on a tour provided through Eulenspiegel. They refuse to talk to us. The mistress gives me her card and offers me a 10 percent commission on the initial session with any client I send her way.

"I've seen that nerdy-looking guy before," Pam says, pointing to a man standing hopefully beside the wannabes. "He's always hanging around the fringes of the action, but he never does anything."

"A voyeur," Janet labels him.

"You'd think he'd find something more exciting to view," Rod says. The shock of seeing people in chains, on leashes, under the whip has worn off, and he has noticed nobody is actually having sex. "Why didn't you tell me there was no sex?" he says irritably.

After an hour or so, we move on to other clubs, where we see more chains, whips, leashes, and paddles—and more single men than single women. We put the ratio at somewhere between fifteen and twenty to one. On my way to the rest room at Paddles, I overhear one man tell another he is planning to run an ad in *The Village Voice*.

"Ads are scary," says Janet.

Janet, Pam, and I are again discussing the difficulty of finding a partner.

"You can't be sure you aren't going to end up with a nutcase," Janet says. "I answered an ad in *Philadelphia* magazine from a man who said he had a 'strong, forceful personality' and was seeking 'a compliant, obedient woman.' These are code words for dominant and submissive. I thought I was getting someone who was familiar with The Scene.

"He didn't have a clue, but he almost raped me on our one and only date. What a jerk. So what are you going to do?" She lights a cigarette, inhales, blows a puff of smoke, grinds the cigarette into the ashtray. The three of us are sitting in Houlihan's inside New York's Penn Station, thirty minutes before our train to Philly. "I'm trying to quit, so I make myself light up again for every puff. I have so much trouble doing something like this, quitting smoking, for myself, though I can intellectually understand why I should. You'll think this sounds nuts, but I could do this, stop smoking, or anything, if I were in a relationship with a dominant man who told me to do it."

"I understand it," Pam says. She puffs at her own cigarette. "My date wasn't so great, either. The man I met through *New York* magazine, remember? He was butt ugly."

"Maybe we'll meet some interesting men in this group tonight," Janet says hopefully.

Hundreds of social groups with a kink connection flourish in this country. They are somewhat like the support groups dedicated to alcoholics, drug addicts, overeaters, and sex addicts. Everyone is focused on a single aspect of life, the prism through which they see all reflected. The members tend to think most of the rest of us should be there, too. When I wrote features about Alcoholics Anonymous, Love Addicts Anonymous, and Alanon several years ago, I was struck by the fact that no one ever said to a first-time visitor, "Well, maybe you really aren't an addict or a codependent." S/M support groups operate from a similar premise: There's a little leather in everybody.

Some groups are more narrowly defined than others. Bound by Desire in Austin, Texas, is for women only. Bondage Buddies in San Francisco is limited to gay men interested in bondage. The Kuaigan Hunt Klub for the Advanced Arts in Toronto offers "weekly erotic-costumed and sensuous role-playing adventures" *only* for the "attractive, generous, clean, creative, cheerful, and classy." You must submit a photo and letter of introduction before you will be told when and where the meetings are held.

There are groups for everyone, singles and couples into swinging or S/M, foot fetishists, or gay foot fetishists only—in fact, for fetishists of every stripe, from the Diaper

Pail Fraternity, for men who wear diapers, to the Girth and
Mirth in San Diego, for fat men and the women who want
them. PEP, with branches in several cities, the Black Rose,
descended from PEP, Eulenspiegel Society, and others are
pansexual, open to kinky men and women—gay, straight,
and bisexual. Activities include guest speakers, live dem-
onstrations, potluck dinners, group discussions, slave auc-
tions, play parties, and subgroups geared to special
member needs, such as dominant women/submissive men.
I attended a Chicagoland slave auction where a slender
young male submissive was purchased by a hefty forty-
year-old woman new to The Scene. For $450, he was hers
for the night, and she looked capable of giving him a very
long night. At a July meeting of Eulenspiegel, the topic
was "Putting on the Pressure: Clips, Clamps, and Other
Devices," with Mistress Morgan live onstage, clipping and
clamping her slave in over fifty places on her breasts, un-
derarms, and genitalia.

What do the clubs really do? Primarily, they make the
members feel better about themselves.

"I'd known I was like this [into S/M] since childhood,"
one man told me. "I didn't think anyone else was. I was
ashamed. Then I found Janus and now I'm proud of my
lifestyle."

According to their organizers, the groups provide a net-
work of social support; educational information on how to
practice S/M safely, including techniques and safety tips; a
venue for meeting new partners and other social contacts;
and a means of becoming politically active, which is important to only a small percentage of members. The majority, however, fear that high visibility as an S/M

spokesperson could lead to arrest or legal harassment.

In 1990, the Washington, D.C., chapter of PEP officially changed its name to Black Rose, because they feared founder Nancy Ava Miller's activism could lead to trouble for them. In a letter sent to her, they said the name change was not meant to be taken as an attack on her. They thanked her for starting the group and bringing people together.

"The board felt I am likely to end up behind bars because I am so public," Miller says. "They changed their name to disassociate themselves from me and to create a giant moat around themselves in case I do get into trouble. I am aware that some people have been sent to jail for S/M involvement and others have lost loved ones, jobs, community standing. I still believe the safety of all S&M-ers lies not in isolation, but in unity. We live in dangerous, intolerant times."

Most who join the social groups want to protect their privacy. Many would never identify themselves publicly with other practitioners of kinky sex if they weren't so hungry for acceptance, instruction, friendship, and partners.

"The groups give you a sense of social support you can't get anywhere else," says a woman who recently joined Baltimore PEP. "We owe Nancy Miller a huge debt. She has brought S/M out of the closet and made it accessible to regular people. For the first time in my life, I feel like I'm not alone. I'm with people who say, 'It's okay to be kinky.' Everyone there is kinky."

"I joined a group for the educational aspects," says Dave, who has a longtime partner. "The deeper we ventured into S/M territory, the more instruction we needed.

You can do a lot of damage to flesh with a riding crop unless you know how to use it.''

A lesbian member of a ''butch leather'' group who pride themselves on ''playing harder'' than other S/M-ers says, ''We are like a tribe. In tribes, the wisdom is handed down verbally from one to another. The wisdom in our tribe is about how to do it and how to do it safely.''

An occasional male visitor to Eulenspiegel meetings says, ''This is a way to meet partners. It's hard for a dominant man to find a submissive woman outside the ads, the clubs, and the social groups. I find there is less pressure to get into a scene right away if you meet through a group. You can take the time to talk and get to know each other. When I go into a club, I feel like I should pick up a whip. I've paid the admission fee. All around me, things are happening. The last time I went to Paddles, I hadn't taken a swallow of my drink before a woman came up to me and asked if I would tie her to the wheel and discipline her.

''And ads can lead to disappointment. A lot of women don't look as good as they think they do.''

A man who travels widely and belongs to several clubs on the West Coast says, ''The best parties are private. You don't see the things at clubs you see in private parties. I was in Boston when a master had a fatal heart attack while whipping his slave. One of the men was well connected politically. He was able to make the right phone calls and keep it quiet. What an adrenaline rush! In Atlanta, I watched a fantasy castration scene. The man wasn't actually castrated, of course, but they spent two hours playing with him tied down to a hospital gurney. Every time they put a knife against the base of his cock, he lost his erection.

You don't see such detailed, prolonged acting out of private fantasies in nightclubs, because they take too much preparation.''

There are more men than women at group functions—so many more men that no group charges women who attend social activities, while men pay anywhere from a few dollars to thirty-five or fifty dollars. Gaining admittance at the door probably won't be as difficult as learning where most of the doors are. Eulenspiegel gives the times and location of meetings on their prerecorded message tape. To learn the location of a PEP meeting, you must dial a series of numbers and listen to recorded messages that explain the group and promote a package of material on S/M available by sending a check for $16.95 to Nancy Ava Miller in Albuquerque. After three or four messages, you get a number that connects you to a real person, a master or mistress. He or she will give you directions to the next meeting. For the novice, this byzantine process is a good introduction to S/M, the game of rules.

Janet, who calls herself "Janie" here, introduces me as "Susan, who is interested in learning more about S/M," and introduces Pam, at her request, as "Ivanka." We have brought a box of Carr's assorted biscuits and two chunks of cheese—a sharp cheddar and a smoked Gouda—purchased at a 30th Street Station deli, as our contribution to the "munchies" at this Main Line home. "Ladies," who pay no admission charge, provide the food and beverages. The huge pine common table, used as a coffee table, holds crudités and dip, bowls of nuts and chips, plates of homemade brownies and chocolate-chip cookies, and a basket of perfect fruit. We have our choice of bottled water, coffee, tea, soda, juices. No alcoholic beverages are served at PEP gatherings. To me, though, it seems exactly the place where one could use a glass of wine, if not a scotch and water.

"It violates the 'safe and sane' credo," a woman explains, referring to the S/M axiom of "playing" safely. "You can't think clearly if you use alcohol or drugs. There should be no mixing of mind-altering chemicals with S/M."

I can see her point. Would you want the person sticking needles through your nipples to have a shaky hand?

Moving around the room clockwise, people introduce themselves with a first name and a brief description of what they like to do. "Hello, I am Betsy, a submissive, I like to be paddled." "I'm John, a switch with a special affinity for tight bondage." "I'm Kevin, a submissive cross-dresser who likes to be spanked through my panties." And so on through nineteen men and eight women, including Joyce, who "will pee in a man's mouth if it's really important to him." Ivanka/Pam announces she will do brown showers (defecate on someone), but I think she is trying to one-up Joyce, who spoke right before her. Four people "pass." I am one of them.

A perky ex-cheerleader type in her late forties, the group leader whose highlighted blond hair is shaped in short wings framing her face, introduces the speaker, a therapist who discusses relationship issues for S/M practitioners. He hints that he is involved in sadomasochism himself. Dominant, I guess, but you know how good I am at picking them out. He probably switches or wears diapers that his mommy/dom changes.

People have questions. Will my dominant's self-esteem be crushed if I ask to handle my own checkbook? a woman asks. Possibly, the male expert says. Another female participant asks the group member if she has considered how much the "low-level pitch of dissension adds to the erotic tension" between her and her dominant. Shouldn't she sustain the tension by allowing him to hold the checkbook, which makes her tense? Heads nod in agreement. They are female heads.

More questions. They are mostly of the "who does the dishes after everyone is untied" variety. A couple, married parents, worry about keeping the kids out of the playroom. Single men want to know how far to go with a new partner and how soon to go there. A married woman in her thirties wants to know if she should tell her seventy-year-old mother she's S/M. The consensus is no, she shouldn't. ("What, are you crazy?" Ivanka/Pam says. Janet, blushing, frowns at Ivanka/Pam.)

After the speaker has finished and gone, the group leader announces it is time for refreshments and "general support and group sharing."

"I'm having a problem with my boyfriend," says a woman in her late thirties. "He wants me to wear my nipple clamps out to dinner. I know they show through my clothes, and I just can't feel comfortable doing that."

"What has comfort got to do with S/M?" an older man asks.

A good question. I look around the room and realize the single men are mentally planning their moves on the single women. Janet makes eye contact with the man who asked the comfort question. He is in his forties, graying, but lean and appealing in a heavy silk black shirt, sleeves rolled up above the wrists, snug black jeans, and expensive soft black leather loafers, no socks. His eyes run up and down her body. Is he imagining how she will look with arms raised over her head, breasts vulnerably uplifted? She looks at me, eyebrows slightly raised, asking for a silent opinion. I shrug noncommittally. He doesn't look like he'd torture her to death on the first date, but what do I know? Do I want her calling me next week to tell me the man I approved beat the shit out of her? No. Ivanka makes a gagging gesture, finger to open mouth. I think Ivanka may be annoyed that Janet has caught the attention of the most attractive man in the room.

Janet goes home with him that night, leaving me and Pam, who is still calling herself Ivanka, to take the late train back to New York without her. I worry about Janet. What if he's a crazed whip master who scars her for life? Ivanka reassures me that "his vibes are wholesome."

Two months later, Janet has his initials tattooed onto her left buttock—and says that they are "in love."

Chapter 10

S/M for Sale: The Doms

"Some great 'fantasy' girls, but the Scandinavian Ava
is full of herself."

From a review of Ava and
her services in *The New York Sex Guide,*
a tabloid covering the sex-for-sale scene

NEW YORK CITY

"Lower your eyes, slave, and keep them down," Mistress
Renee says to Robert.

The quote is running through my mind as I watch Mistress Renee seize control of Robert, her client, in the entryway of her Upper East Side apartment. Doms are, by definition, full of themselves. They have to be. If you are a woman alone in a room with a man who is paying to be dominated, you need more than a good whip hand to put your power over on him. You need Attitude with a capital A.

"Mistress, may I speak?" he asks in a soft, obsequious tone of voice.

Robert is in his late thirties, over six feet tall, and conventionally handsome, with a strong jawline, dimpled chin, thick and healthy salt-and-pepper hair. A lock of the hair falls across his forehead as he stands, head bent down, eyes on the toes of Mistress Renee's combat boots.

"Do you have the tribute?" she asks, extending one black gloved hand.

Without looking up, he takes three crisp hundred-dollar bills from an inner pocket of his suit jacket and hands them to her. He knows I am in the room behind Renee. He has been told that being watched by another woman is part of his humiliation for the day.

"Go to the interrogation room and take off your clothes," she tells him. "Wait for me there."

Head down, he walks back toward the small kitchen. Renee unzips a pocket on the short leather pants she's wearing and stuffs the bills inside. Her waist-length leather halter top also has a zipper, which she pulls up to hide her cleavage. She adjusts her cap, a copy of the headgear worn by Hitler's Nazi troops.

"Showtime," she whispers.

I follow her into the kitchen, where Robert, naked, is waiting, eyes on the white tile floor. He has a nice body—strong buttocks, flat but not hard stomach, long legs more muscular than his arms—a jogger's or runner's body. His erect penis, projecting at a ninety-degree angle parallel to his body, indicates how aroused he is at the prospect of spending forty-five minutes in Renee's kitchen playing captured Jewish resistance fighter to her Nazi storm trooper. Robert, by the way, is not Jewish, but Renee is.

"This is Robert's favorite game," she told me over the phone when we set up this appointment.

"Why?" I asked.

"I don't know," she said. "Maybe he had a Jewish nanny when he was a little boy."

I've talked to doms from all over America and some from Europe who were visiting New York or L.A.—their expenses paid, of course, by American clients who are willing to spend thousands of dollars in airfare and hotels to be whipped, caned, or otherwise disciplined by the best in the world. Take away their riding crops, leather, and eyeliner though, and you have women who look like other women. Some have good, even great, bodies, while others are, frankly, fat or flat-chested without benefit of push-up bustier. Many are older than the average call girl, as old as fifty, possibly older. Sans costume and makeup, they look unremarkable. In full regalia, they are commanding, powerful, often more darkly beautiful than you would believe possible having seen them before the transformation.

Renee orders Robert to sit on the straight-backed chair in the middle of the kitchen, under a single low-hanging light bulb. She fastens his ankles, protected by the socks he hasn't removed, to the chair legs with leather shackles and pulls his arms together behind the chair, binding them with leather cuffs lined in soft white cotton. He can't go home to his wife with reddened wrists.

"You will answer my questions about the location of the

troops," she barks, slapping her riding crop hard against a rear leg of the chair for emphasis.

Constantly moving, Renee continues her monologue in this vein. Putting one foot far ahead of the other, she stomps and struts around her prisoner, piling verbal assaults on top of him. She calls him "a kike asshole," "a cowardly piece of shit," "slime," "excrement," and more. Sometimes she strikes the wooden chair and sometimes, far more softly, the flesh of his thighs, stomach, chest, and shoulders. He winces under each blow, though none leaves a mark. Then, eyes shut tight, mouth held in a grimace, he twists his head from side to side. Sweat breaks out on his brow, above his lip, on his chest. Drops of lubrication appear on the tip of his penis. He is highly aroused.

"I will tell you nothing save my name," he gasps after the fifteenth blow.

This is the code phrase they have arranged in advance as Robert's way of letting her know he's had enough of the whip and would like to move on to the next stage, electrical genital torture.

She pulls an instrument that looks like a long, thin dildo from a cabinet drawer, touches it to his nipple, and pushes a button on the end. Reacting to the shock, he pushes against the back of the chair, tilting its legs forward. One comes down on the toe of Renee's boot.

"You will pay for that, kike slime," she hisses.

I know what is coming next. So does he. Our eyes are on his penis thrust proudly forward from his body. She takes the wicked little tool, pushes it against the flesh between the base of his penis and his testicles, and hits the button. *Bzzt.* He cries out.

After a half-dozen more shocks to nipples and testicles, he mutters through clenched teeth, "You aren't going to get anything more out of me," his signal that he's reached his limit.

She replies, "All right, then. I'm sending you back to your cell. Next time I will break you."

When he is released from his bonds, he kneels in front of her. She asks him to turn so his cheek is placed against the floor. He complies.

She rests one foot on his face and says, "You were a good boy. Do you have a meeting this afternoon?" She turns to me and says, "Robert is a partner in his firm," by way of explaining, I suppose, why his meetings require that he not be redolent of sweat.

Somehow he manages to say yes with his face squished between her boot and the floor.

"You may use the bathroom to freshen up before you go," she says and removes her foot.

"He likes to be a hero," she confides while he is in the bathroom. "In his scenes, he never breaks. If he had to beg me to stop, he would never come back. Other guys love to beg."

After Robert leaves, Renee opens a bottle of Cabernet Sauvignon and pours us each a glass. She takes off the combat boots, unzips the leather top to the point where she can comfortably breathe, and curls up on the sofa, which unfolds into a bed. Her eight-by-ten-foot bedroom is filled with S/M equipment. She is particularly proud of the stout wooden X frame secured to one wall—built for her by an adoring slave. A series of leather straps along each leg of the X permit her to fasten men of any and every size to the apparatus.

"In my own life, I was assertive, but I never felt dominant until I got into S/M," says Renee, who at forty-six sees only a few regular clients in her apartment. The doormen, who know what's going on, are well compensated. "I always felt manipulated by men, controlled by men. I fell into S/M in my early thirties through a couple I met at Plato's Retreat. They used to have an S/M night once a week. I dressed up and went just to see what it was all about, and I met this couple. I am bisexual. She turned me on more than he did. They were very involved in S/M. They took me from Plato's to the Hellfire Club, which was a very famous S/M club at the time and a much rougher scene than the clubs are now. I saw a woman hanging up by her wrists. Men were doing these interesting things to her, torturing her nipples, putting dildos in her vagina and asshole, whipping her. This was very erotic to me.

"At first I was submissive to this couple. Then, with other partners, I switched. I discovered I liked being dominant. The first time I beat some guy's ass, I was wearing a tiny black miniskirt and a little white angora sweater, and I was loving every minute of it. This nice Jewish girl from Long Island, and I was loving every minute of this. When my career in music wasn't going anywhere [Renee had a single on the Billboard chart in the late Seventies], I was looking for something to do. Waitressing seemed to be the only option. Someone suggested I apply at one of the S/M houses. I put off doing that until I was seriously broke."

She stops her story to answer the phone and schedules an appointment for a client. They briefly discuss the scene. He wants to be Spartacus on the cross.

"I was a natural," she continues her saga. "After the first week, I thought: I'm getting paid by these assholes to beat them up. This is fabulous. What a great way to get out your anger and aggression. This is the perfect way for me to have a relationship with a man. An hour or two and they're out of my life. No emotional attachment."

Renee's apartment is only blocks from the brownstone "house" where she worked for almost a decade. An S/M house is run by a head dominatrix rather than a madam. Ostensibly, genital sex is not on the menu of options for a client who can choose to dominate a submissive, be dominated himself, have a switch session, or a fantasy scene, typically involving foot fetishism or crossdressing. The prices begin at approximately $100 per half hour of domination, with the more elite houses charging $200 and more. Submissives command higher fees, starting at $125 per half hour and escalating to $250 and more. Tipping is not expected by the house. Sessions last an hour and more.

According to Renee and other women who've worked in the houses, some "girls" do choose to masturbate or fellate the clients after a session for a tip that goes directly into their pockets. Occasionally a girl may even have intercourse with a man, usually a regular client who tips well.

"For a while, I worked as both a submissive and a dom in the house," Renee says. Her auburn hair, facial features, and curvaceous body give her the appearance of an actress or an older model. "I took a lot of abuse," she says. I believe her, but her body doesn't show the wear. Even her back, exposed by the halter, is smooth. "Most guys are just into the idea of sadomasochism. They don't hit that hard. But occasionally you have someone who beats the shit out of you. I've had bruises. I've had excruciating sessions of nipple torture, when the guy hung five-pound weights off my nipple clamps and then swung them back and forth. You can't imagine how much that hurts. The other girls don't tell you anything, they don't tell you about the bad asshole clients. I had one guy, Eddie the Hairbrush, who beat my bottom with a wooden hairbrush so bad once I couldn't sit down for days. My ass was black and blue all over. His deal was that if you let him go as far as he wanted to go, he tipped you a hundred bucks.

"But I could make several hundred dollars a day, and that's what I was into for a while. Maybe I needed the pain to work through where I was at in my life. There's a place where pain turns into pleasure. It's a strange sensation. That's the dangerous thing about S/M.

"Also, it was easy sometimes to be a submissive. I didn't have to do the talking. I wasn't in charge. Nothing was up to me, which was a relief after having several dominant sessions." After she'd been in the house for two years, however, she stopped acting as a submissive. "I couldn't deal with it anymore. I just worked as a dominant."

Many clients came to the house with prepared scripts, down to the dialogue—a level of control they wouldn't be allowed to exert over the prima doms, such as Taurel, San Francisco's Cleo Dubois, or, for that matter, any woman listed in *The Domination Directory International*. These ladies take a man's input, then do it their way.

"I don't think there are many true male submissives," Renee says. "A lot of men think they are, but when push comes to shove, they want to tell you exactly how they plan to submit."

"What about women?" I ask. "Are there many true submissive women?"

"Some are, some aren't, but more women are than men, I think. I've been truly submissive with a few men. I wanted to prove to one man how much I loved him, so I let him take me way beyond my limits. I wouldn't do that again. I'm at a different place in my life. Emotionally, I'm healthier. My self-esteem is higher. But it is incredible the orgasm you can have after this much pain. When you finally come, you're like vibrating all over. There is nothing like it."

Renee gives me her book of photos to examine while she humiliates a client over the phone. He is calling from a large Southern city, where he is chairing one of those ubiquitous private sector conferences about environmental issues. The photos are of Renee in various outfits from classic leather-garbed dom through governess in discreet gray dress and glasses. Each photo is accompanied by a one-page synopsis of a fantasy script. New clients can have an hour's consultation with Renee and her book for a flat one-hundred-dollar fee.

"I want you to go to the nearest pharmacy and buy the biggest box of maxipads you can find," she tells the man on the phone. "Don't let the clerk put them in a bag. Carry them back to the hotel and stand in the lobby with them for ten minutes before going up to your room. Be sure the label is exposed. Don't try to hide it.''

''Is he really going to do this?'' I ask after she hangs up the phone.

''Who cares?'' she says, shrugging her shoulders. ''He gets off on humiliation more than pain. He might. It all depends on how much power I have over him. It's hard to gauge that long distance, when they aren't quivering at your feet.''

The client who wants to be Spartacus calls again to switch his appointment because he has a scheduling conflict.

''Do you think the modern S/M house is a very different place from the religious houses of old?'' I ask Renee, who is well read in philosophy, religion, and ancient history.

References in classical literature linking pain and pleasure often have religious overtones. In *Confessions,* the eighteenth-century philosopher Jean-Jacques Rousseau admitted his lifelong craving for the whip, which he traced to childhood punishments, whippings meant to curb his sensual and sexual awakenings.

''I don't know, but I do know there is a big difference from one house to another here. You should visit Ava Taurel. She runs the classiest operation in the city. She's also a sadist. I don't inflict pain. I supply it on demand. She inflicts pain. I've seen her in action. Her submissives adore her.''

''Why do you think so many men want to be abused?''

''They're such controlling assholes in their real lives, they need to set aside a few hours every month to pay for their behavior. Otherwise, they would be consumed with guilt. My clients run their offices and their homes like little dictatorships. They don't want anyone who really knows them, like the wife, kiddies, and secretaries, to see them with their guard down. They're emotional sickos.''

"Did you leave the house after ten years because you felt emotionally healthier?'' I ask Renee.

"Oh, no, feeling healthier came after I'd been out awhile. I left because I fell in love with one of my submissive clients. Very big mistake in business.''

Could she fall in love with Robert?

"Robert's not a submissive. He likes to pretend he is.''

"The scene in Europe is much more sophisticated than it is here," Mistress Ava Taurel tells me.

Ava presented a paper on consenting sadomasochism at the prestigious AASECT (American Association of Sex Educators, Counselors, and Therapists) meeting in Denver this year. She is the most respected dom on the East Coast, possibly in the country. We are sitting in her office in a residential hotel on the West Side of Manhattan. The office is part of a complex with rooms in two buildings, known to the IRS as Taurel Enterprises. This is a legitimate business upon which she does pay taxes. She advertises in *New York* magazine, *The Village Voice,* and the Yellow Pages. "Escape from the usual—explore your unobtainable dreams,'' the brochure promises, with "social companions who enjoy the art and psychology of fantasies." There is no genital or oral contact between the mistresses and the clients.

"We make this very clear," she says. "No prostitution.

I do not want to come into conflict with the law. Also, you understand, the dominatrix is supposed to be the unattainable dream, the woman the submissive cannot have. She is never seen naked by him. That's part of the power. If this client could have intercourse with me, I would lose my power over him.''

Ava has dismissed her slave girl/administrative assistant for the day. (''This is my slave girl. She was given to me by Xaviera Hollander [aka the Happy Hooker, the first celebrity hooker and author of the book by that name] at a party in Amsterdam. I held her over my lap and spanked her while I was being interviewed over WNBC Radio.'') Ken—a client turned friend—has been invited by Ava to participate in my interview.

''There is much more sophistication in equipment and clothing in Europe,'' she says. ''Here you have mistresses discussing their submissives as 'jerks' or 'assholes.' They seem to be in contempt of men who want to submit. European mistresses take pride in their work and respect their submissives. Everything is so commercial here, everyone is in such a rush to get the next client's money.''

Ava's client book includes more than two thousand names, men willing to pay three hundred dollars an hour for a session, preceded by a fifty-dollar consultation fee. Most won't see the Scandinavian mistress herself, but one of her ''companions,'' six striking mistresses and one submissive, picked from a book to suit the desired scene. The companions have been trained by Ava and other experts, such as the male-bondage authority who taught them how to make perfect knots. The clients are professional men, with lawyers making up the biggest category, followed by bankers. She knows this because she keeps computer records, with breakdowns by professions, marital status, sexual variations, zip codes, and so forth. Ninety-five percent are married. Academics and journalists are at the bottom of the list. (''And I have only one FBI agent. Can you imagine? They are so paranoid of discovery.'')

''Why do men really come here?'' I ask.

''Some men have these special needs. They can't get them met at home. Very few wives will accept their needs and try to accommodate them. If they did,'' she says, laughing, ''I would be out of business.''

Some men want to worship the Queen of Sheba. Others want to be womanhandled by the mistress of a prison camp. A client might want a schoolmistress to cane him or a nurse to administer an enema. Ava runs the session only if she is intrigued by the client or if ''something highly technical is involved, such as a complete submersion in latex with double inflatable hoods and breathing tubes.'' Only the British ask for that.

''Rubber bondage has hardly been heard of in New York,'' she says. ''Everything began in Britain. I buy my bondage equipment there. England supplies to France and Holland. Now there is also an excellent tradition in Hamburg, Germany. The Heli Krohn Institute has more equipment than one can imagine. There are wonderful mistresses in London, Hamburg, Switzerland, and, of course, Amsterdam, even now in Paris.''

After our interview, Ava is meeting three friends for dinner: the ubiquitous Constance of Dressing for Pleasure and two Frenchwomen, an erotic writer and a dom who arranges extravagant S/M parties in Paris for wealthy American clients, some expatriates, and some who fly over for the festivities. Ava has just returned from Mexico, and future travel plans include S/M parties and balls in London, Hamburg, Switzerland, and Paris, then back to New Jersey for the Halloween gala thrown by Constance, the premier party in this country. Her publicity credits range from *Geraldo* to a Learning Annex class ("Become a Dominatrix, for Fun, Love or Profit"), which was attended by reporters from newspapers and *Redbook* and *Vanity Fair* magazines. She is truly, as her PR material claims, an international dom.

She also considers herself a therapist.

"People come to me and they have guilt about their sexuality," she says. "They need a place to take their guilt and be made to feel better. This is what I do." She gestures toward Ken. "This is why I wanted you to talk to Ken, so you would get a better idea of what I do."

Most therapists would probably consider therapy the place where patients come to find the source of their guilt—with the goal being eliminating it from their lives or at least reducing its hold over them. In Ava's brand of therapy, the client's guilt is alleviated by the acting out of the S/M ritual. Maybe they do feel better for a while. But the cycle of guilt, punishment, redemption goes on.

"I don't agree with your article at all," Ken says, smiling tentatively. "I want you to see the other side."

The article to which he is referring, about male sexual fetishes, appeared in *Journal* and "stunned" Ava when she read it. I'd interviewed wives who suffered their mates' fetishes for shoes or lingerie, some couples who had, through therapy, largely overcome the man's dependence on a fetish for arousal and ejaculation, and the therapists who had helped. The average woman would be dismayed to discover her husband considers her feet the only truly erotic part of her body. Ava believes she should get pedicures and enjoy.

"Your article was one-sided," Ken says.

Shy and diffident toward Ava and me, he is six-foot-four, twenty-seven years old, a bodybuilder enrolled in medical school. I can see why Ava found him intriguing enough to handle his sessions herself. I cannot, however, see him in pantyhose, which he loves to wear while worshiping her feet.

"The women I interviewed wanted more from sex than having their feet rubbed and kissed," I reply carefully. "Surely you can understand why they would?"

"There is another side," he says, glancing frequently at Ava as he talks.

He seems nurtured by her, though she does not seem capable of casting benevolent glances. Her face is almost masculine—the detective-novel cliché "strong-jawed and steely-eyed" applies—while her figure, clad in an ordinary black dress, is matronly. She is the mother of a twenty-two-year-old daughter and grandmother of a cherubic blond baby girl. ("Look at this photo. See how the light falls on her head. Isn't she wonderful?") In publicity photos, Mistress Ava is dressed in thigh-high black leather boots and a black leather corset; the matron has disappeared.

"I was embarrassed about who I am until I started seeing Ava," he says. "She's helping me to feel okay about what I want. Articles like yours are harmful because they make men like me feel bad."

Susan Crain Bakos

He has a long way to go toward full self-acceptance, Ava says, but she is helping him. And he looks beautiful in his teddy, she assures me. Would I like to see? He blushes.

Having passed on the opportunity to see Ken in his teddy, I am flipping through the current issue of *The Domination Directory International* as I wait for Ava to take me on a tour of the fantasy rooms. "The Source for Meeting a Mistress!" "Direct Contact Ads—Cover to Cover!" "Real Dominatrices from the USA, Canada & Europe!" "Specific Wardrobe & Equipment Details for Each Advertiser!" All for only ten dollars.

Ava's listing is on page 56. She has two photos, one in a Swiss garden, leather booted and dressed in a short leather tunic. In the other she wears a shapeless rubber dress with leghorn sleeves and elegant high-heeled sandals. "Exclusive Consultation or Appointment with Ms. Taurel May Be Possible If You Comprehend . . . •Advanced Bondage •Artful Foot Worship •True & Total Servitude •Advanced Rope & Rubber Restraint •Strict Discipline •Crossdressing."

Across the page on 57, Cleo Dubois is a fearsome sight. A hefty woman with very large breasts, she looks somewhat like Roseanne Barr in leather. Mistress Anika, a Canadian on page 55, has the most chains. I would be surprised if Mistress Rayne from Georgia on page 48 is actually a woman. The ad for Lady Cassandra of San Francisco on page 16 features a blond nurse wearing a surgical mask and two rubber-clad creatures, gender indeterminable, in gas masks. Cybelle, San Francisco, page 19, a specialist in age play and total transvestite transformation, is

184

shown administering a bottle to a blond woman in romper suit and looking haughtily away from a man who is dressed in little-girl clothes, wearing heavy makeup, and holding a shoe. I recognize the man beneath the paint: her life partner. Robin Byron, worldwide outcall and New York dungeon (meaning she will travel anywhere or you can come to her place), page 23, is an absolutely stunning blonde.

"It's an interesting publication, isn't it?" Ava asks from the door. "You can take it with you. I have another."

Page 11, Diva, L.A., cone-shaped bra. Is this where Madonna gets her wardrobe ideas?

The rooms are either spartan, clean, and mirrored, or as dark as the dungeons they are meant to be. Some clients prefer the dungeon atmosphere. Others want to be spanked in women's clothing with the sunlight streaming into the room because they enjoy the possibility of discovery by someone with binoculars in a neighboring skyscraper. There are beams and shackles, bondage tables with cutouts in the chest and genital areas so a client, lying on his stomach, can have nipple clamps and testicular weights applied. The hallways contain overstuffed closets and cabinets filled with women's clothing in men's sizes, whips and other hitting and bondage paraphernalia, needle-lined jockstraps, and personalized enema bags for use in the age of AIDS.

As she pulls out items for display and explanation, Ava tosses in words of advice: You must be careful not to hit a man wearing a needle-lined jockstrap; occasionally check a man wearing a gas mask for trauma and heat problems; when using a cane, make sure the submissive's buttocks are clean to avoid smears on the equipment. We move to the final room, which contains a mechanical hoist, the kind garages use to remove car engines.

"Some clients like to be left to dangle," she says.

"Don't some clients want to have orgasms?" I ask.

"Oh, yes, some do. Some are happy to be told they may not relieve themselves, because they will go home and have passionate sex with their wives. Others beg to be allowed to ejaculate."

"Do you let them?"

"Sometimes, if they are particularly good clients, I may let them ejaculate into a handkerchief."

"What happens if a man gets so excited he can't control his response?"

"Well, if he is going to do this without permission, he is going to lick it up."

I take Ava out for champagne. She has offered to show me genital bondage, where a rope is tied around a man's testicles, somehow separating the two, and then around his penis, with knots tied every half inch into which numerous sharp objects can be inserted. I have declined. We talk about her life.

Fluent in English, French, German, Spanish, Russian, and the Scandinavian languages, better traveled than the average diplomat, and possessed of impressive business skills, she could do something other than torture genitals for a living, couldn't she?

"I love what I do," she says passionately. "When I give seminars, women ask me how much money they can make.

I tell them that you have to choose this for a lifestyle first, then you become a professional.''

Before "discovering" the S/M subculture on a trip to New York City when she was thirty-five, Ava was an au pair, model, dancer at the Folies-Bergère, cancan girl in Canada. As a sixteen-year-old, she thrilled to *The Story of O.* At first she practiced S/M for fun. Then she realized she could make a living at it.

"I am a true sadist. I love inflicting pain," she says, her eyes glowing fervently. "No matter how successful the business might be, I still do it for fun. I love black men. They are my secret passion. I love chewing on black lips. I am seeing a black man now, and I am trying to make him submissive. The other night I blindfolded him, and later he was so angry, so enraged, that he raped me. I loved it. Today I was pushing him in the park to run harder and longer when we were out for a jog. He told me again that he was so mad he felt like raping me."

"I'm told there aren't many black male submissives."

"No, there are black mistresses, but very few male submissives. You see why I want to do this, don't you?"

We order another round and she gets back to the subject of business. What she wants, she says, is to have an operation on par with the best European establishments.

"In this country, the best places are private. I have been to private homes, mansions, where the submissive male has enough money to let the mistress equip the playrooms however she pleases. I have seen some wonderful private places, equals to the establishments in Europe. This is what I want to bring to New York, and I will, because I am passionate about what I do.

"The important thing to me is to reach the submissive's vulnerability. When a man can become vulnerable through submission, he is beautiful to me. It gives me a thrill to see him this way.

"Do you see the difference between the doms in American houses and the way I work?" Ava asks me.

Yes, I do. If a man really wants to feel the burn, he should call Ava.

Part 4
Other Kink

Chapter 11

The Video Revolution

The two men are gasping. The woman, her mouth filled with a penis, is moaning. They are naked, stretched across a long sofa in a tableau worthy of the *Kama Sutra.* A muscular man with thick brown hair is sitting at one end. He is stroking the genitals of the woman, slender, pale, and delicate-looking, as she kneels between the two men. The third player, a tall, slim blond man, is stretched out on his back, his penis in her mouth. They shift positions slightly. The muscular man inserts his penis into the woman's vagina.

The phone rings in my room at the Adam's Mark. I press the pause button and pick up the phone. I have stopped these three on the downstroke, her long hair just beginning to fall forward. What this video lacks in production values—professional lighting, makeup, and a director to arrange the limbs more artfully—it makes up for in energy and immediacy. They are real people. And you are there while they Do It.

Have you ever glanced at your neighbor's bedroom window and wondered what is happening behind closed shades?

When video cameras became affordable, the average person could become a porn star, if only for a very limited audience—people like you who have wondered just what the Smiths do in bed. The technology that took porn out of the sleazy movie houses and put it into the bedroom VCR made the next leap possible: Mr. and Ms. America taping themselves making love. Many couples who would be too embarrassed to have an X-rated roll of film developed have put a video camera on a tripod in the bedroom and discovered that the presence of its watchful eye made the sex hotter.

Maybe you have recorded your lovemaking and played the tape while making love again. Would you show this tape to someone else? Would you let another person handle the camera, to increase the number of angles from which your couplings could be viewed? And would you make copies of these X-rated videotapes and sell them to strangers?

You are appalled by the idea? Oh, really?

I put down the phone. My friend Kate is on her way over. We are going out to lunch. But first she wants to "peek" at the amateur videos piled on the desk in my room.

The threesome have moved from the sofa to a bed. From a sitting-straight-up position, she lowers her body down on the blond's erect member. Once he is inside her, she leans forward on her elbows so that her body is almost parallel to his on the bed. He fondles her breasts, taking a nipple in one hand and squeezing it lightly between his fingers. She shivers with pleasure. From behind, the muscular man grasps her shapely buttocks and pushes the head of his penis against her anus.

"Why would anyone want to do that on camera?" asks Kate, who, like several of my old friends, still lives in the St. Louis area where I grew up.

"I've no idea," I reply glibly, but something in her questioning green eyes makes me reconsider. She thinks I have some idea, doesn't she?

Is what these three are doing so very far removed from what I have done, writing about my sex life for publication? Would the average person catalog her sexual exploits for *Cosmopolitan, Playgirl, Forum*? Would she describe taboo anal sex experiences for the readers of this book? Why do I do what I do? Would she make love in her bedroom, the windows covered only by hanging plants? I am a bit of an exhibitionist, someone who enjoys shocking or titillating others. Furthermore, I believe the average American *needs* a sexual shock now and then as an antidote to Puritanism.

Again, Kate asks, "Why would anyone want to do that?" as she is glancing from the screen and perusing the stack of literature from amateur porn companies.

"For the same reason you're going out in a dress that reveals your cleavage."

"I might expose my cleavage, but I wouldn't go that far," she retorts, pointing to an ad for *Naughty Nurses,* in which "Laurie and Sylvie double-team their friend in the doctor's office, and tongue every square inch of his body in eye-popping close-up action."

I wouldn't go as far as Laurie and Sylvie do, either. Kate wouldn't go as far as I do, writing about my sex life. The question is not How? but How far? Few people haven't dipped their spoons into the forbidden carton of Häagen-Dazs chocolate ice cream. Maybe you stop with a spoon, I with a quarter of the carton, and someone else when the flatware hits the cardboard bottom. If we say we simply don't understand how she ate the whole thing, we're probably kidding ourselves.

At Kate's request, I pop in another cassette. She fast-forwards through the introductory clothed scenes to the naked action. A slender woman with full hips kneels on the bed and leans forward, weight on elbows. The two men—both short and slim but well-endowed—assume positions behind her, one crouching over her, the other kneeling behind the first. Somehow they each manage to insert their members into her anal opening without working up a sweat. She, however, is bathed in sweat, gasping, tossing her head from side to side, and clutching wads of black satin sheet in her hands.

"Oh, yes!" she cries, then grunts fiercely as the men begin to move in sync deep inside her.

Kate and I sneak glances at each other, each trying to ascertain if the other is aroused.

The literature advertising Video Alternatives, an amateur adult video sales company in St. Louis, is not attractive. The illustrations and descriptions of the products are likely to produce giggles or embarrassed winces from anyone who possesses an erotic sensibility. American porn is more offensive to taste than morality.

"There's something wild going on at the No-Tell Motel tonight . . ." is the blurb for *The Long and Tall of It,* a one-hour-and-thirty-five-minute production selling for thirty dollars and featuring Brian and Cherry meeting on a blind date. She, at six-foot-two, is the tall of it. He, no statistics given, is "a little on the short side." The description promises the viewer will see Brian "smothered with Cherry's huge, hot breasts." Obviously this couple did not ponder The Question: *How soon in a new relationship should we have sex?*

This Butt's for You features four "passionate interludes with young, sexy couples . . . if you like backdoor action, you'll especially love watching Kellee give her man his twice-a-year treat!" Ninety minutes for thirty dollars.

The cheaply produced fifty-page catalog with a bright yellow cover is printed in black and white and copiously illustrated with photos of the "real people" who have sold the rights to their X-rated home movies. The pages are filled with women who have bad hair—long, teased, permed, highlighted, and hot-rollered. Breasts list downward more often than not, heavy and pendulous breasts. Where are those Frederick's of Hollywood push-up bras when we really need them? Tan lines beg the reader to color in bikinis over veins, stretch marks, and overgrown pubic hair. If the difference between real people and centerfolds is a combination of body makeup and airbrushing, a photographic technique for improving upon nature, *vive la différence.* The blonde on page 5 with the toothpaste-commercial smile held inches from an erect penis has good hair, blond and smooth—but she's wearing a whole tube of mascara on her lashes. A makeup artist could have turned her into a true porn star. I look at these photos and understand why the great strippers of old, Sally Rand and Gypsy Rose Lee, always left a little something to the imagination.

There are few photos of men. Male sexual organs, unless they are large, are not seen, though female genitalia, often with labia parted suggestively, is on display. We're told on page 10 that Don, the "new neighbor," has a "huge, black cock," but to my disappointment it's covered by a white female leg draped over his lap. To see more, perhaps one must order the adult video sampler, "a full two hours of uncensored XXX-rated highlights from every video that we offer" for twenty dollars—"fully refundable!" or purchase price applied to first order.

These real people appear to be in their twenties and thirties, with a few exceptions. Kitty, star of *Kitty-Kitty Bang-Bang!* and *Kitty's Bachelor Bang,* looks forty or more. She is "our buxom beauty who likes to get fucked as hard as possible by as many men as possible as quickly as possible." Sound like fun? The unnamed big mama, star of *Cum to the Mountains* may be forty, too. This video, shot at a swingers party "just as it happened," features "good titty-fucking . . . big boobs, big big fun." Forty minutes for twenty dollars.

I am flipping desultorily through the catalog and promo material before my meeting with Suzy Wahl, aka Kim Scott, her video name. Suzy and her husband, Robert, own Video Alternatives. She has appeared on numerous talk shows, including *Geraldo, Sally Jessy Raphaël, Maury Po-*

vich, A Current Affair, and *Real Personal,* as both a spokesperson for the company and a defender of First Amendment rights. Following her arrest for making amateur videos, she campaigned for the job of police chief in Lake Saint Louis. She may have lost the election, but she's won the national media skirmishes.

After her appearance on CNBC's *Real Personal,* host Bob Berkowitz told me, "She is the most polite, unassuming, down-to-earth, soft-spoken woman . . . so typically Heartland, in the best sense of the word. I couldn't believe she was in the porn business after I met her."

Suzy, in her thirties, has short blond hair, big blue eyes, a creamy complexion, and winning ways. You would have to try not to like Suzy. Clothed, she looks wholesome. I wouldn't have been shocked to hear that she was once Miss Dairyland or Miss Midwestern Farm Products or the face on a soap carton. Even the long fingernails add to her image, their incongruity emphasizing her healthy beauty, the way Cindy Crawford's mole makes her seem all the more perfect. Undressed and on-screen, Suzy has large breasts with only a slight sag, a trim waist, lean hips, long shapely legs, and a nice, high firm butt. She is more appealing than anyone else in the Video Alternatives catalog. Her best-selling videos feature Suzy alone, masturbating in different settings. A hang gliding scene has a stirring climax—Suzy's hand pressed to her genitalia, mouth open wide, head thrown back in triumph as she appears to reach orgasm seconds before she reaches the ground. Too bad more housewives next door don't look like Suzy.

* * *

Susan Crain Bakos

If you believe her, she was inspired to make and distribute her own videos by some kinky strangers who responded to an ad she'd placed soliciting their do-it-yourself projects.

"My husband and I got into this business by accident," she says, sitting with her knees together, her hands in her lap. "About six years ago, we started distributing amateur videos, things like how to fix your bike or tune up your car. We started getting all these erotic videos in the mail. I thought, 'Well, this is interesting. I could do this.' And we were in business."

"What made you think people would be interested in buying homemade erotica when the market is flooded with products featuring women without stretch marks and men without pimples on their butts?" I ask.

"That's the appeal of the videos," she says earnestly. "A woman who might be put off by professional videos looks at the women in these and doesn't feel intimidated. Their nail polish isn't perfect. They have panty lines. They don't have perfect bodies. She says, 'I could do this, too.'

"She's willing to try some of the things her husband wishes she would try, like oral sex, because she sees a woman who looks like her doing it on-screen and this woman is having a great time. In professional videos, there is a barrier between the actresses and the female viewers. That barrier is beauty, the slick kind of beauty, not natural beauty."

I mull this over. You don't see ugly women in mainstream movies, either. Did that stop women of all ages from identifying with Julia Roberts in *Pretty Woman*?

"Most of our videos feature married couples, and they aren't nineteen-year-olds," Suzy says.

198

"But are they forty-nine-year-olds?" I ask. "Do men want to see forty-nine-year-old women who aren't Raquel Welch naked?"

"We have one video with a couple in their sixties." She rushes past age to the next subject. "In groups or with new partners, our people practice safe sex. We encourage safe sex.

"They are real people getting together and having a good time, not actors pretending to come. People are tired of leaving sex to the experts—the actors and the therapists."

For the jaded and bored video customer tired of watching the same old stars, the amateur cassettes offer something new—not perfect, but different. The price probably doesn't hurt, either. Professional videos typically start at $59.95 and go up. Nothing in the Video Alternatives catalog lists for more than $30.00. A lot of men like those big droopy breasts anyway, don't they?

Suzy unabashedly admits she "may be a bit of an exhibitionist." She's not alone. The amateur video segment of the X-rated market is growing rapidly, fueled by the exhibitionist fantasies of ordinary people. How else can you have sex in public with reasonable safety?

"This is like putting the letters in *Penthouse Forum* on video," a male collector of amateur videos explains. "It's real. Kinky reality, but real. When I was in college, my girlfriend sent a snapshot of me to *Playgirl*. I was wearing unzipped jeans. My cock was pulled out and held in my hand. I had a good erection. The way she photographed me made it look bigger, badder. They published my photo. Let me tell you, that was one of the highlights of my college career.

"You think I wouldn't get a rush if someone shot a video of me in my best-ever sexual performance and I knew women all over America were watching me come in the privacy of their own bedrooms?"

That "rush" must be reward enough for the participants who seldom make more than two or three hundred dollars on the sales of their tapes, unless they become amateur stars like Suzy.

"People don't make the tapes for the money," she concedes. "They aren't going to get rich doing this. They can either sell us the rights for a cash fee or agree to a 15 percent commission on all their tapes sold. Either way, it figures out to two to three hundred for an average video. By taking the cash up front, they get all their money at once. We do have some people who do well, maybe making into the thousands rather than the hundreds. If you develop a following and have several tapes in the catalog, that can happen.

"But people aren't doing this for money. They are excited at the thought of anonymous viewers watching them have sex. I've had couples tell me that making a tape and selling it improved their sex life a hundred percent."

The amateur video business is fairly new. What happens when this couple who gets excited about anonymous strangers watching them discover that their teenage children's friends are not so anonymous viewers? Or what happens when they get divorced and the new spouse happens upon the old tapes?

"Well, it's a concern to some people," she admits. "They wonder what if the boss or my sister-in-law or somebody else sees this. If you are bothered enough about being seen by these people, then you don't get involved in videos, do you?"

Suzy isn't "bothered" because she believes sex is good, clean, healthy fun. Unlike some other amateur porn distributors—particularly Video Sophisticates U.S.A. in Los Angeles, the producers of the double-anal-penetration video that held Kate and me spellbound in my hotel room—her company doesn't handle tapes on S/M or other topics associated with the dark side of sex.

"I'm very feminist," she says, "and there are things we won't do because of how I feel about them. No pain, bondage, humiliation. No rape videos, even though rape is a common fantasy. The fantasy rape might be acted out lovingly by a husband and wife, but we would never sell that tape, because some viewers could take it the wrong way. We are very, very careful about women not being degraded, exploited.

"I see our mission as part of the sexual revolution. Sex needs to be out in the open. Parents have trouble talking about sex. Some of them even fight sex education in the schools. We are a Puritanical culture, and we have turned sex into something dirty, which it isn't and shouldn't be.

"Maybe we wouldn't be reading about priests who got away with molesting little boys for years if sex was more open."

Suzy's belief in her mission seems sincere. She also likes to make money. In addition to selling tapes, Video Alternatives has several 800 numbers offering services (for

customers only) ranging from Kim Scott's daily recorded
message (three dollars per minute) on some aspect of making your own video to advice from several "counselors,"
including Heather, who has appeared in *Las Vegas Reunion,* Annie, the astrologer, and Johnny, the man with the
answers for straight, bi, and gay men.

Today's message from Kim concerns finding "talent."
She advises would-be producers to contact college drama
departments among other places. But don't bother looking
for stars among exotic dancers. The bouncers will toss you
out. And the "ladies" make a great deal of money, more
than you can pay them for making a tape.

"They'll think you're just another jerk trying to get a
date," Kim warns.

The rewards for Suzy are obvious. Why would a couple
like Paul and Jennie film and *sell* their own "erotic out-
door sex-capade with their best friends?"

SOUTH COUNTY, ST. LOUIS

"It was Paul's idea," Jennie says. "I had some resistance."

"She said, 'You're full of shit. You're sick. You're
crazy,' " he says, laughing and poking a finger in her ribs
to tickle her. "That's 'some resistance.' "

"I'm not a prude," she says defensively, swatting his
finger away. "I liked watching the amateur tapes. I was
afraid of making one. What if somebody you know, but
don't want to know you would do this, gets his or her hands
on your tape? My mother didn't speak to me for three

weeks last year after I said the word *fuck* in her house. You see how far I've come from her, don't you?''

Jennie, twenty-seven, and Paul, twenty-six, have been married five years. They are a typical couple from a small Midwestern town. Tall and slender, with a droopy mustache and shaggy brown hair curling into his shirt collar, he manages an auto body shop and bowls in a league. A bank teller, she is a medium in every measurable area, brown-eyed, with brown hair worn in the long and overprocessed style. They wear Nikes, jeans, and matching red T-shirts with the emblem of the baseball Cardinals. Their parents are regular churchgoers, hers Methodist, his Unitarian, but Jennie and Paul rarely attend services at either church.

''You don't get any more normal than we are,'' she says. ''We have a shaggy dog and everything.''

''First I got her to play around with the camera,'' he says, explaining how he brought Jennie from No Way to autographing copies of their tape for their closest friends. ''I told her to shoot me first, getting undressed, playing with myself. When she felt comfortable, I shot her stripping.''

''Just stripping at first,'' she says. ''He agreed to stop when I said, 'Stop.' He honored his agreement, and he let me buy all that great new underwear at Victoria's Secret.''

''She realized how hot she looked stripping when we played back the tape,'' he says. ''We played that tape several times over a few weeks before she said, 'Okay, I want you to shoot me masturbating.' ''

''We agreed every tape we made was my tape,'' she says. ''I kept them in my old jewelry box, which looks like a pirate's chest, under lock and key. He didn't know where

Susan Crain Bakos

I hid the key. If he had ever taken charge of a tape, I wouldn't have trusted him. I wouldn't have gone any further with this. He kept his word every step of the way."

"She suggested making another tape," he says. "We kind of went from there. After we had six tapes, she was into it."

"They were still my tapes," she interjects. "He kept his word about not pushing me to send them in. One night we had our best friends over for dinner. Everybody got drunk. I put on the tapes."

"They wanted to make one, too. We kind of went from there."

Two weeks later the two couples went to a cabin in the woods, had sex with their best friends, which they had never done before or since, and took turns recording the event using S-VHS for a sharper picture. They'd agreed that all four had to be enthusiastic about submitting the tape to a distribution service or club. One negative vote would have meant the tape hit the campfire.

How did they get their friends to play along?

"Oh, that was the easy part," he says. "They've got tapes of themselves, which they show at parties. Every time she gets drunk in front of company, she puts a tape in. We call him The Tongue."

"We thought we were too hot to burn in the campfire," Jennie says, laughing. "I doubt if we will ever do anything like that together again. It was wild. I still can't believe I had my mouth on her pussy while she had my husband's cock in her mouth. You see this in videos, but you don't think you'll ever do it yourself. The camera helps you get

204

rid of your inhibitions. I know it sounds crazy, but it's true."

"She didn't have an orgasm during the filming," he says. He puts his arm around her shoulder, pulls her to him, and kisses her cheek. "But she did later, when we were making love alone in our own bed."

"There was too much going on," she says. "I couldn't come, but at least I admit it." She casts a meaningful glance at him.

Is she insinuating, perhaps, that she suspects the other woman in the foursome of faking?

"I won't say," she says demurely.

If Suzy Wahl is the beauty next door in an upscale suburb, Jennie is the girl next door in a tract housing neighborhood. She and Paul were high school sweethearts. They broke up, dated others, went back together two years later after running into each other at the Jaycee Days summer carnival on Main Street.

Maybe some amateurs think they are going to be the next Traci Lords or Ginger Lynn—or even Kim Scott. Jennie doesn't. She and Paul have made a second video for distribution, shot by their friends, the costars of the first one. Theme: lickin' and suckin'. They may do one or two more before Jennie becomes pregnant with their first child, an event planned for next year. He would like to film her initiation into anal sex. She hasn't consented to either the initiation or the filming—yet.

"I can't see doing this as a mother," she says. "But I know I am always going to be glad I did it when I could. These are memories. Someday we'll be eighty or ninety and giggling over our fuck films."

"It's exciting to watch ourselves fucking on film and know some strangers in another city might be watching us at the very same time," he says. "This has added a lot to our marriage. I'm proud to be married to a girl who is sexually adventurous."

According to Suzy Wahl, this desire to see and simultaneously be seen is the primary motivating factor for ordinary people who become, if only for ninety minutes, porn stars. She's learned a lot about what people want and why they want it from answering the phones. Some of the calls to the 800-number advisors are from women who want to make a tape but are having trouble overcoming their inhibitions. Other women are curious about bisexuality. They want to know if they should make love to another woman to sell a tape. Questions like that lead Suzy to speculate some people use the tapes as an excuse for trying something new, especially female bisexuality.

"I had never made love to a woman, but I had some curiosity about it," she admits. "I made a tape. You can satisfy your curiosity this way. For some people, the tape is the excuse they need to jump into something different."

Male callers most often want to know how they can get their partners to participate. Suzy's advice sounds like the method Paul used to get Jennie involved: Give her the camera and have her shoot you. Then, when she feels comfortable, you shoot her. She gets to keep all the tapes. I suspect Paul got his plan for convincing Jennie to make a video from Suzy's 800-line advisors.

"We started the 800 line because we discovered so

many men wanted to talk when they placed their orders," she says.

The second most-asked question by men is: What kind of tape should I make?

"Oral sex is very popular," Suzy says. "That's always a safe bet.

"Our best-selling tapes now are interracial—black man, white woman. I am not completely comfortable with that. It seems like domination to me, but women tell me it excites them. And white men like it, too, which surprises me."

I raise an eyebrow at the clearly racist remark, but Suzy presses on, oblivious to the implications of what she's said.

"But you have to be careful about saying that over the phone. You don't know how people feel about race, or even what race they are when you can't see them."

Back at the Adam's Mark, I compare Suzy's list of video hits to the best-selling tapes at Video Sophisticates U.S.A., an amateur video club with European and U.S. membership. VS best-sellers feature double and triple penetration.

"When you realize that the young girl from Des Moines (tape #SV-31) who takes two cocks up her ass at once is a receptionist for a law firm, it adds a new dimension to your sexual pleasure," the promotional flier promises. Or how about the young blond housewife (tape #SV-45) experiencing "triple penetration by three dicks stacked up"—of, one presumes, the vagina?

VS is a club rather than a mail-order company. Members, who don't have to submit their own tapes, receive the "confidential" members phone book, the Sophisticates photo album containing over 230 photos from European and U.S. members, and the club newsletter, all for fifty dollars. If their photos are selected for the book, they are paid twenty-five dollars—and one hundred dollars for videotapes. A highlight from their catalog is *Kinky in Kokomo,* boasting "bizarre penetration" with kitchen utensils, sporting equipment, and so on, and wild group sex, featuring "golden showers" and "brown showers."

Under law in this country, commercial bondage tapes can show no penetration or ejaculation shots. By operating as a private club in which videos are "traded," not sold, VS gets around the law. Bob and Vicki Halloran, who own the company, are particularly proud of their "European-style product" as well as their European members.

I call them at a prearranged time for an interview. Lying on my bed, surrounded by real-people porn, I ask them how big are those kitchen tools. They tell me to use my imagination or send for the video.

"This trend of amateur video started in Europe," he says. "In countries where porn has been legal and accepted for some time, the consumers of adult entertainment got tired of the commercial products. A small group of adventurous couples got together, started a club for making and exchanging videos of explicit sexual nature—and, there you are.

"A trend was started. We're proud to be part of it."

The Hallorans follow up our phone conversation a week later by sending me a lot of material under a cover letter, signed "Yours in Pleasure, Bob & Vicki," with the same upwardly slanted flourishes a Bible Belt couple might use in signing "Yours in Christ."

A kitchen-tool video is enclosed. Anal and vaginal penetration with wooden spoons, spaghetti servers, spatulas, handheld mixers, and other items. Should this be categorized under "erotica"—or "Believe It or Not"? Before accepting a dinner invitation at the home of a new acquaintance, one might want to ask if the kitchen tools are ever used for any other purposes. And if so, do they own an autoclave sterilizer?

Chapter 12

Fetishes

WASHINGTON, D.C.

"You face the corner, foot slave, you stay in the corner, foot slave, until I *let* you worship my feet!" Mistress Zena commands, removing her red blazer as she speaks. Her voice makes me think of heavy silk, of sheathed claws, of subtle power. "You are not worthy to worship my feet, are you, slave?"

"No, Mistress Zena, I'm not," replies the "foot slave," mock cowering in the corner of his splendid office.

"You're going to be good now, foot slave. You won't embarrass me in front of my friend."

He is just a man, average height, average weight, expensive haircut, manicured nails, somewhere in his forties—wearing a black silk jockstrap and nothing else. Blazer removed, Zena, a beautiful black woman, is dressed in a black knit catsuit that hugs her firm body attractively. She wears shiny vinyl thigh-high boots and heavy silver hoops

211

in her ears. After tossing the jacket across a chair, she pulls a suede flogger from her shoulder bag. Striking the flogger against the corner of the foot slave's massive teak desk, she hands me the bag. I walk to the opposite end of the room and sit down on the comfortable and equally tasteful gray leather sofa to watch her perform.

"Foot slave," she says in a low, growling voice, like honey over pebbles. She draws the flogger gently across his shoulders. He sucks in his breath. "Have you been good this week? Have you done the things Mistress Zena has told you to do? Did you send your secretary flowers for being so nice to me?"

Zena has told me she insists he give his secretary and the receptionist frequent gifts of flowers, perfume, and candy because they treat her with such warmth and courtesy when she makes her weekly visit to his office. What do you suppose they think is going on? I asked her.

"Oh, hell," she said in an affected Southern accent. "They think I'm his nigger call girl. They think I'm suckin' or fuckin' him in here. They surely don't think he's kissin' my feet."

"Yes, Mistress, I did that, I did everything you told me to do."

"Are you a good foot slave?" Again she draws the flogger across his shoulders. He shivers. "Well, are you going to answer me?" She swats him lightly across the back. "Foot slave, you aren't going to lie about how good you've been, are you?"

"No, Mistress Zena, I can't lie. I am not worthy."

She takes several steps backward away from him and stands with her feet apart, one slightly ahead of the other, arms akimbo. The room is quiet. His calls, including those from his wife, are held during Zena's visits. The windows are shut against the Connecticut Avenue traffic. There is no sound except the swishing of the flogger—and her voice, strong, cultured, commanding, assured.

One kneeling naked man has begun to look pretty much like another to me. But the doms each have their own theatrical style. Zena, who specializes in foot fetishism, has panache. She commands worship rather than fear.

"Turn around and crawl over to me," she coos. He crawls toward her without looking up and stops an inch or so shy of the toe of her right boot. She lifts her foot until the toe is under his chin. Now I notice his erection. "Lick," she says, putting her foot back on the floor.

He applies his tongue to the shiny vinyl in long, broad strokes as if he was cleaning her boot.

This foot slave's wife does not know about his fetish. And if she did, would hers be the boot in his face now? Few wives can happily accommodate a man's fetish, which is why many men pay doms to do so. The average prostitute may be no more familiar, or comfortable, with foot fetishism than the wife. Doms, however, know the territory.

Zena says there are four types of fetishistic behavior: worshiping, in which the man is content to lick and kiss feet, both shod and not; sucking, in which he licks the soles of the feet and sucks the toes; walking and stomping, in which the dom, wearing heels, walks and/or stomps on various parts of his body; and acting out the giantess complex.

According to Zena, a man who has the giantess complex, which is unusual, wants to pretend you are the giant and he's the midget and you're stomping him to death. "Not many of my clients want that," she assured me.

Watching the foot slave progress upward with his tongue along the sides of Zena's boots, I decide he's easy to peg. A worshiper.

Zena has a few clients like this one who pay her $235 an hour to come to their exclusive offices, rather than her dungeon, where she makes them strip naked and worship her feet while their secretaries hold all calls. Most want a stocking that she's worn all week as a parting gift. She leaves them with the desired stocking, wrapped tightly around their testicles, and the admonition to leave it in place until they go home.

"I keep the stockings in my running shoes to pick up the right ambience," she told me on our way to this office. "I'm not going to wear them all week." She laughed. "That's a professional secret."

Nearly all her clients are married. None of their wives knows about their foot fetishes. Like most doms, Mistress Zena does not have sexual contact with her clients. She sends them home in a state of arousal. Most of these men are capable of having sex only after a session with Zena.

"Now smell my feet," she orders. "Rub your nose in them and really smell them."

He is on his knees. She is sitting in his chair. He has removed her boots and placed them lovingly on his desk. From across the room I can hear his ragged intakes of breath as he smells deeply and longingly of her feet.

"Now rub them," she says.

Zena has slender feet with long toes. Except for the

slightly shorter baby toe, each one is the same length as her big toe. ("Fetishists love long toes.") She has twice-weekly pedicures. Each night before going to bed, she works Vaseline into the soles of her feet and then pulls on white cotton socks. She never goes barefoot. ("I keep my slippers by the bed. If I wake up and they aren't there, I yell at my lover and ask her to bring them to me. She's always up first, because she has a job.") Zena may be thirty-five, but her feet are baby soft. The nails are painted a rich red. These are feet worthy of worship.

He moans occasionally while rubbing her feet. Though his penis is now hidden from view by the desk, I can read the sexual excitement on his face. When she's had enough of the foot rub, she shoves one big toe gently into his mouth. He makes a muffled cry, the sound of a man who has just entered a woman he desires. She allows him to suck for a while, then pulls the toe out. For several minutes, he licks and sucks her toes, gasping, panting, and moaning as if he were having intercourse with her.

"I want to rest awhile," she says, pulling her foot away from him.

The look on his face makes me uncomfortable. Naked longing, a desire so strong it almost cannot be held in check. I look away from him and study the Southwestern art, the photos of blond wife and little blond daughters, the glossy leaves of carefully tended plants. She lets him worship again for several more minutes, but I do not watch.

When it is over, she ties the stocking around his testicles and murmurs something low to him as he puts her boots back on her feet. While he remains kneeling, she puts on the red blazer, takes the envelope containing three one-hundred-dollar bills from his desk, and signals for me to join her at the door. The secretary cheerily wishes us a nice day.

We are alone in the wood-paneled elevator, so Zena says, "His wife will get laid tonight. He'll come through the front door with a hard-on." Anticipating my question, she says, "He'll take that stocking off in the office. He keeps them in his bottom left drawer, locked."

Fetishists are shyer about discussing their lives and desires than S/M participants are. None of Zena's clients wants to meet privately with me, though this foot slave said he would if she commanded him. To find someone more willing to talk, I have to go all the way to Cincinnati.

CINCINNATI, OHIO

After collapsing onto my bed in the Holiday Inn in Cincinnati, home of the American Foot Fetish Society, I call my own home and check my answering machine. Fourteen messages, including three from the man I call the Penis Fetishist. Every time I leave town, he clogs up my machine with long messages, which all say more or less the same thing: He wants me to come to California at his expense and measure him. This is never going to happen.

The Penis Fetishist is well known in the sexual underworld. He runs ads in personals columns in sex magazines, newsletters, and tabloids. And he is a member of a club exclusively for men with large members and the women who want to love them.

"Looking for women to measure my huge ten-inch dick.

Plenty of fun to follow your tape against my flesh.''

Much depends on your idea of fun. Many lucky respondents have been sent first-class round-trip tickets to California, where they soon discover this penis-obsessed man measures a standard five inches, flaccid, which he apparently always is while in the presence of willing women with tape in hand. The more derisive, even verbally abusive these disappointed women are toward him, the more excited he grows—or so the women say. (''Humiliate him long enough and he almost gets an erection.'' ''You can't be mean enough to him. When I discovered that, I turned sweetly understanding. He asked me to leave.'') If they hang around his estate long enough, he calls another man, someone from a stud service, presumably, who possesses the inches he covets for himself, and he watches while the stud and the woman have sex.

This man is totally focused on penis size. He cannot get or sustain an erection unless he is in the presence of a large penis. Nor, apparently, can he ejaculate without having one in the room with him. His path toward sexual gratification is more convoluted than that of the typical fetishist, but he has a lot of money, which allows him to take the slow road. He can afford the ads, plane tickets, champagne and caviar, stud service, and lavish parting gifts to women, meant to buy their silence.

Fetishism, the dependence on an object or body part for arousal and ejaculation, is one of the most common sexual compulsions and an almost exclusively male phenomenon. Although no one knows why, foot and shoe fetishes are among the most prevalent. Other fetishes are for lingerie—including unwashed panties—long hair, and garments made of rubber or leather, either worn by a woman or by the man himself. A man never has a fetish for a woman's vagina or labia or clitoris.

While most men have individual sexual preferences—like women with blond hair or pretty feet, or women wearing lingerie—they can enjoy sex without these things. In our culture, large breasts are admired to the point of being almost a cultural fetish. In Japan, the nape of a smooth, long neck is desirable. Some African cultures prize large buttocks. Men in these cultures may admire and desire the ideal body parts, but they can settle quite happily for the woman they love, whether she comes so equipped or not. A man with a fetish cannot settle happily. He must have this part or this thing, however nonsexual it seems to the rest of us.

When I was a columnist at *Penthouse Forum,* I was astonished by the number of letters from men who masturbated by rubbing rubber bathing caps across their penises. They considered the hated headgear from my childhood swimming classes *sexy?* I was dumbfounded by these men and by the men who wrote requesting my used panties.

The fetishist reduces a woman to a part, or sometimes less than a part—to an object worn. The body part may be anything except the female genitalia. The whole point of fetishism is to direct the erotic impulse away from the genitals and onto another (safer?) part. Some experts believe the fetishist is terrified of women or of female sexuality. Some speculate he develops a fetish because he cannot relate to a woman as a whole being. He needs emotional distance from his partner to feel safe. By never really making love to *her,* he maintains the distance. This inability to get close keeps him locked in a sexual pattern of compulsive fetishistic behavior. In certain African and Native American cultures, a fetish is a sacred object or artifact, a talisman with spiritual power. The worship of a foot or a golden length of hair can be a way of putting a woman on a pedestal, objectifying her as a sacred, rather than profane, object—another distancing maneuver. For centuries, men have elevated chosen women to this level. The fetishist takes women to new, more unattainable, heights when he replaces intercourse with fetishism.

I thought about this view of fetishism as I watched a pivotal scene of the film *The Age of Innocence,* based on the Edith Wharton novel of the same name. Daniel Day-Lewis, playing the male lead, fell at Michele Pfeiffer's feet and kissed her shoe, then wept with his face pressed against the shoe. The lovers were, of course, fated never to consummate their union. She remained, for the rest of his life, the perfect woman he could never possess. (Meanwhile, his wife bore his children, nursed his illnesses, and so on.) Like the fetishist, he has, in this relationship, saved his beloved from lust.

Whatever his psychological motivation, the fetishist cannot make love to a woman without the presence, either physical or imagined, of the fetish. Young men may be able to sustain the illusion of "normalcy" in lovemaking by using a fantasy, reinforced by private play with the object or photos of the body part. Older men require the physical reality.

As any man ages, he requires more sexual stimuli to become aroused. As the sexually obsessive man gets older, he generally needs more of whatever he really likes and cannot make do with anything else. At this point, his relationship with his wife may fall apart. That's what is happening to Ryan, the man I've come to Cincinnati to meet.

"We haven't had sex in seven months," Ryan says. "Lisa [his wife] wants to have another baby. How can she have a baby with me when I can't make love to her?"

Ryan and Lisa, both thirty-five, have been married for ten years and have a seven-year-old daughter, Liselle. He has a growing pediatrics practice; she is a successful freelance commercial artist. They met when they were both attending New York University in Manhattan. On the outside, they appear to have everything—from matching Mercedes to an annual vacation in the south of France. Who would guess that what this lean and fit thirtysomething couple doesn't have is a sex life?

"In the early days," he says, "I was able to have reasonably good sex with her. She didn't know I had a foot fetish. I knew I was a foot fetishist when I was in high school. I stole a pair of my girlfriend's ballet slippers and masturbated by rubbing them across my penis." He runs a hand nervously through his thinning blond hair. "I'm not proud of this. I know there's something basically wrong with me.

"Whatever it is, I was able to hide it successfully for years. I made love to Lisa's whole body, kissing and caressing every part of her so that she didn't notice I kissed her feet. She wore the black stockings and high-heeled shoes I asked her to wear. My obsession with feet was safely tucked inside my own head.

"I have fetish magazines, but I keep them at the office. I

have never kept anything like that at home. Fetish magazines came between me and Suzanne, the woman before Lisa, whom I would have married if she hadn't found my collection.

"Suzanne had a key to my apartment so she could let herself in if I was going to be late. In those days I was going to school and working two part-time jobs. One night she was snooping around and found my collection of magazines. I'll never forget how I felt when I walked through the door and saw them spread across the floor. She was standing at the window, righteous tears in her eyes, arms folded across her chest, looking at me like I was some kind of psycho.

"She asked me to explain. I tried, and I never saw her again."

The number of publications aimed at fetishists is startling to the uninitiated. I've found over two hundred without half trying. When America's most famous foot fetishist, Marla Maples's publicist, Chuck Jones, was arrested in his office in 1990 after stealing several pairs of her shoes, copies of the glossy *Spike!* were also carted away by the police and held as evidence. One officer, who told me he'd prepared himself for photos of men kissing, sucking, and licking women's feet and shoes, was profoundly shocked at some other pictures—of women standing on men, pressing their high heels down hard into nipples and genitals. "What has this got to do with sex?" he asked me.

Some foot fetishists are content to lick, suck, and kiss, but others have interests that include crushing, trampling, stuffing (her foot is rammed into his mouth), and giantess fantasies. Foot-fetish "zines" seldom show a woman above the knee and frequently picture the woman's foot standing on the man's face or some other section of his anatomy. The publication *In Step* features a regular column, "The Giantess Speaks," which is illustrated by a cartoon drawing of a spike-heeled giantess stomping on a miniature man.

"It's too bad that the laws of physics and biology prevent giant women from ever really dominating little men!" one reader wrote the giantess.

She replied, in part: "Some time ago the Watusi, the tallest people on earth, were mortal enemies of the Pygmies, who are the smallest people on earth. . . . The Watusi conducted a ceremony called 'maribu butu,' literally translated as 'the tread of the elephant.' In the maribu butu ritual the Watusi humiliated and denigrated the Pygmy captives [who were then] given over to the tallest Watusi maidens, who trampled them to death."

To a foot fetishist, this is pornography. A woman who stumbles upon such materials in her lover's apartment might consider them proof of insanity.

"After I lost that important relationship over the magazines," Ryan says, "I never kept any in my home again. Lisa had no idea anything was wrong with me. I began having sexual problems with her a few years ago, but she blamed herself. She thought I was losing interest in sex because she wasn't sexy anymore. She joined a health club, had a makeover, bought a fortune's worth of new clothes and lingerie. I was finding it increasingly difficult to keep an erection with her. I'm a doctor. I should have understood why.''

Like most men, Ryan found his sexual responses changing somewhat after thirty. The average man begins to require more tactile stimulation, more fondling, kissing, and caressing. Ryan needed more of Lisa's feet. He couldn't tell her that, so he came up with a solution, similar to the one another husband might find for his own sexual malaise. While his neighbor might have an affair to rekindle latent sexuality, Ryan got a job as a clerk in a shoe store two nights a week. He told Lisa he was volunteering at a city shelter.

''She thought I was going through some kind of spiritual crisis,'' he says. ''She was worried, but she thought it would pass. I thought if I could get aroused by women's feet at the store, then I would be able to go home and make love to Lisa. It worked. We had a sex life again. She was so glad about that, she didn't nag me about the shelter anymore.''

Then her cousin came into the shoe store and saw Ryan at another woman's feet. She reached the obvious conclusion: Her successful relatives were on the financial skids. The rumor made its way back to Lisa, who was horrified.

''I had to tell her everything,'' he says. ''She was stunned. Lisa had never heard of a foot fetish. I give her a lot of credit. She tried to understand. When I refused therapy, she tried to go along with my desires. She got pedicures, let me focus erotic attention on her feet. Lisa gave it everything she had. I didn't control myself. When I ejaculated on her foot, she got hysterical.

"She said, 'That's it. You have to get this taken care of right now.' "

He considered seeing a dom, but rejected the idea.

"I couldn't see myself using a prostitute," he says. "Now I wish I had. Maybe things wouldn't be in the mess they're in."

His marriage is "shaky" in his estimation—and "almost over," according to his wife. While she will not agree to meet with me, she does consent to a phone interview. I call her, as instructed, from a pay phone in a restaurant while Ryan waits at the table.

"I've set a deadline of six months," she says in a soft voice, teary at the edges. "If he hasn't sought professional help by then, I have to leave. Last week I caught him in the bathroom fondling our daughter's feet. I can't stay with him under these conditions."

"I wasn't fondling Liselle's feet," Ryan protests. "I was drying her off after her bath. She was wrapped in a big fluffy bath sheet. I used a smaller towel to dry her hair and then I dried her legs and feet with it so she wouldn't drip.

"Lisa went ballistic on me. She said a seven-year-old could dry herself, that I shouldn't be in the bathroom with her ever, that I was using her bath as an excuse to play with her feet." He runs his hands through his hair again. "I would never abuse my daughter. I would never do that. Doesn't Lisa know anything about me after all these years?"

After being confronted for the first time with his sexual secret, the wife or partner of a fetishist could feel as if she's never known the man, couldn't she? Through my own interviews with men, conversations with doms, and research for a magazine piece on sexless marriages, I have become familiar with the behavior pattern. Predictably, most men with fetishes do not tell their wives and typically have a lot of trouble performing sexually as they age. I suspect that a good percentage of male sexual disinterest is rooted in fetishism.

When a man appears to lose interest in sex, his partner blames herself. She thinks he's grown bored with her or has been turned off by her aging body. Is she likely to think he has a secret fetish for feet or latex or lingerie? No. Is he likely to overcome his shame and break his longstanding silence to confide in her? No. Will she reject him if he does? Probably.

The hundreds of men who belong to the American Foot Fetish Society, formed in 1990 "to promote foot worship as a lifestyle," have "proudly claimed" their fetishistic behavior, according to president Bill Volkart. Membership includes the right to subscribe to the newsletter and one free ad for men, and a free subscription and unlimited free ads for women. The women listed on the AFFS membership rolls are mostly wives accommodating their husbands. Few single women, except doms, actively seek out the fetishists by placing ads in their newsletters.

One who does, a 250-pound woman in her forties, says, "I may be fat, but I have beautiful feet. If a man wants to worship my feet, okay. How many dates do you think I'm going to get otherwise?"

The magazines and support groups work to make their readers and members feel good about their fetishes. Some men do. Many men do not. Ryan is far from a ''proud'' fetishist. Why doesn't he get help?

''I don't believe there is help,'' he says. ''I've read about treatment programs for people like me. I'd probably have to go to Baltimore to the sex disorders clinic. It's a risk for someone in my profession. And there's no guarantee they could change me sexually after I risked my reputation to get into treatment.''

Ryan cannot identify a causal factor in his childhood for his behavior as an adult. He does, however, associate early memories of women's feet with sexual arousal, lending credence to the fetish theory developed by psychiatrist and researcher Alfred Binet: Fetishism is acquired largely through association. If a boy has an erection at the moment he is focused on a woman's foot, he will always associate the female foot with sexual arousal.

''My parents were emotionally cool toward each other and toward me and my brother,'' he says. ''There was no abuse, physical, sexual, psychological. At least none that I can remember. And I have tried to engage my brother in conversations about our childhood to see if he has any memories. I'm sure he doesn't. He never seems to get what I'm trying to ask.

''I do remember being a little child, so small I was crawling on the floor. I remember crawling under the table when my mother and her friends played bridge. I know I was aroused by them. I remember their feet in high-heeled shoes. Sometimes one of the women would kick off her shoes. I remember those feet in silky stockings, the way they smelled, and the sound of one foot rubbing against another.

"Have you ever noticed that women tend to rub one foot across another after removing their high-heeled shoes?"

I've heard similar childhood erotic memories of feet from other fetishists. Yet every man was once a child who crawled at women's feet. Why do only these few men find feet so entrancing?

Why feet?

Some men insist their fetish is no different from another man's preference. The breast is the most frequently mentioned, and derided, preference.

"There's no difference between my finding a foot beautiful and another man finding a breast beautiful," insisted a Chicago attorney I interviewed. "Our culture finds the breast acceptable, that's the only difference. Do you think the average American male could make love to his wife if she had her breasts removed?"

Another man asked, "Why not feet? It's the first part of a woman's anatomy we really get to study, isn't it? When I was a little boy, I used to get erections smelling my mother's feet. I think that's normal."

Why feet? Why a fetish of any kind?

"If you knew that, I suppose you wouldn't have one," a man whose fetish is rubber said. "I suppose you would choose to be like everybody else, because it's easier. I asked my mother once if she put rubber sheets on my bed when I was a baby. She said she didn't. I think she must be mistaken. Why else rubber? I don't know. I didn't tell her why I asked the question, by the way."

* * *

On the plane from Cincinnati, I scan a stack of fetish zines, books, and newsletters.

"Nowhere are the sacred and profane more intimately intertwined than in the realm of fetishism, whose linguistic identity itself originates in the religious and whose practices often involve elaborate, sometimes ecstatic rituals," opines one windy and enthusiastic observer of the fetish scene. I am reminded of a favorite saying of the twentysomething crowd: Get a life!

In *Leg Show*, a kneeling man is tonguing a woman's calf. In a rubber zine, a man recounts his early experience with his sister's bathing cap after she left him alone with it in the baby pool. The orgasmic moment of putting on his first corset is recalled by a man in a zine for men who wear corsets.

The promotional package for Diaper Pail Friends, "world's largest adult baby-diaper club," contains an order list for true diaper stories, including "Diapered and Humiliated," and "Aunt Mary's Baby," in which aunt turns eighteen-year-old nephew into the baby she always wanted. Scanning the list, I see this aunt-nephew syndrome is common. For the diaper wearer who prefers to pretend he can't yet read, the video *Turned into a Baby* promises: "You'll thrill as the woman forces Lee to wet his pants right in the middle of a busy restaurant. . . . In one of the most exciting scenes ever filmed, you'll watch as the woman changes his wet diaper right on the floor of a public ladies' room."

These diaper men are, by anyone's standards but their own, *strange*. One man tells of wearing his diapers to work because he loves the feel of their bulkiness and the freedom to urinate whenever he pleases. Another describes the excitement of wearing to the grocery store his diaper with garter belt and stockings under his baggy trousers. Both men marvel that "nobody notices" how they look. Does anyone get close enough to notice? Could the faint odor of stale urine be keeping observers at a distance?

I put the diaper fetish material at the bottom of the stack. The foot zines represent the largest category of publications aimed at fetishists. In one, a foot fetishist describes playing with the neighbors at age four and having another boy "knock me down, kick off his moccasins, and rub his feet in my face. At that moment, I knew this was what I wanted for life."

Several zines contain editorials expressing cautious optimism about the growing acceptability of fetishistic and other outside-the-mainstream sexual practices.

"Fifty years ago, even less, a man would forfeit his right to be sexual rather than try to fulfill his needs," one opinion writer says under the heading "The Door to the Shoe Closet Is Open a Wedge."

Jamming the whole mess of paper back into my flight bag, I notice the man seated across from me eyeing me curiously.

"Excuse me," he says. "Haven't I seen you on *Geraldo* or somewhere?"

A week later I have a message from Ryan on my phone machine. He and Lisa are "negotiating a possible truce" in which she will consent to his seeing a dom once a week if that will permit him to be sexually active with her again.

"Should this work, we will not divorce but have another baby, instead. Do you know any doms in this area who specialize in foot fetishes? I don't want to go to just anyone."

I call Zena to see if she knows someone in Cincinnati. She doesn't, but promises to put out feelers. Meanwhile, she will send him one of her videos if he would like.

"There aren't many good foot fetish videos," she says. "A lot of men spend ninety dollars on a video that contains a minute or two of foot fetishism. I saw the need, so I began making my own." In the background, her lesbian lover is reminding her they are late for a dinner date with another couple. "Have to go," Zena says. "Let me know what happens with this guy. I feel sorry for these guys. What they go through . . ."

And the wives? I can't help but silently ask. What they go through . . .

Chapter 13

Gender Bending

"I went through the hair-removal process once," Carl confides. "Waxed from neck to ankles, even my pubic hair. That hurt. Removing the pubes wasn't necessary, of course. I just wanted to feel what women feel when they shave their pubis for a lover."

Carl is a thirty-five-year-old heterosexual investment broker. We are sharing cappuccino and brownies in the café of the Angelika Theatre on West Houston following a showing of the film *Orlando,* which was adapted from the Virginia Woolf novel of the same name. Midway through the story, Orlando, the hero/heroine, wakes up to find her sex has changed.

"Same person, no difference at all. Just a different sex," s/he observes.

After our snack, Carl and I are going to his private class at Miss Vera's Finishing School for Boys Who Want to Be

Girls. There are similar classes or private instruction for crossdressers in major cities all over the country. Carl has been trained in the arts of makeup, hair, and wearing panty hose in Philadelphia, Los Angeles, Chicago, and San Francisco. According to Carl, Dean of Students Veronica Vera does it best. Today he will be shaved, waxed, coiffed, corseted, and layered in makeup while I watch.

"Her finishing school is the most fun," he says enthusiastically. "She has this wonderful theatrical flair. I got better makeup tips there than anyplace else, too."

Carl truly looks androgynous.

The word *androgynous* was overused in the Seventies to describe David Bowie, female models with no hips and wispy short hair, and clothes marketed to either or both sexes. That word always brought to mind the effeminate boy, not so much sexless as presexual. For all of Jagger's writhing on stage, and presumably off, he didn't project the aura of a potent *man*. Only the lips and tongue promised adult joys of sex.

Carl is not an effeminate boy. He is a sexual chameleon, capable of being erotically appealing in the guise of either gender.

"There's no place in the world for someone like me," he says, grasping his coffee cup in a firm, masculine way. "Crossdressing is more open and acceptable today than it ever has been. But the accepted crossdressers are flamboyant entertainers, not real people."

By the Eighties, androgyny was passé as a marketing tool and drag queens soon were to become hot. Chicago's Chili Pepper, for example, appeared on every major talk show more than once. Dustin Hoffman's character was "a better man as a woman than he'd ever been as a man'' in the blockbuster movie *Tootsie*. Madonna learned how to vogue from RuPaul, the crossdressing singer, and other boys who want to be girls—a subculture made human for a wide audience in the 1990 documentary *Paris Is Burning*.

In the Nineties, crossdressers and lesbians are on the media *in* lists. The 1992 hit movie *The Crying Game*, featuring a love story between a straight man and a crossdressing man, pulled off a neat crossover trick of its own by drawing an audience greater than the anticipated bicoastal art-house crowds. Bisexuality, as long as it is female, is even hotter, but even lesbians are in. Lesbians have made the cover of *Newsweek*. The President of the National Organization for Women, Patricia Ireland, has admitted publicly to having a female lover and a husband. Gender bending in our time celebrates the woman, not the boy. Carl is right.

"Did you make her?" he asks. He inclines his head slightly toward an overdressed woman—man?—at the counter waiting for her café latte. When a man is dressed as a woman, the politically correct pronoun is *she*. "I think she's pretty good. I haven't noticed anyone but me make her. I think she's passing. If she got past those teenage girls, she's good. Teenage girls don't miss much. They're always looking at other women, sizing them up, checking their makeup."

"Passing," going unnoticed—or better yet, admired as a woman—is the cherished goal of crossdressers. They want to move among people while dressed as a woman without collecting startled looks or denigrating stares from those who know what's under their makeup and wigs. In a sophisticated city like New York, where you have to be very good not to be made, the average crossdresser considers himself a success if the person who makes him doesn't register a response beyond the brief glint of recognition as their eyes meet.

Everyone who lives below 23rd Street in Manhattan has a crossdresser in their neighborhood, if not their building. Joanna is the TV (transvestite) in my building. We have chatted amiably at the mailboxes or waiting for the dryers to finish in the laundry room. Once her long blond wig fell forward when she was pulling towels from the machine. I looked away. And once, when she was in full drag, she got into a pitched battle with the superintendent on the street outside the building and forgot to control her voice, which in its natural state is deep and full of bellows. Mesmerized, I watched the confrontation from my fourth-floor window as blasé New Yorkers strode past without giving them a second glance.

In the Angelika café, I check out the transvestite Carl admires walking with her café latte to a table across the room from ours. She is close to six feet tall with large hands and feet, but she moves as easily in three-inch heels as most women do. The blond hair is clearly a wig. But nothing about her is jarring. She could walk through a crowd without everyone looking for her Adam's apple.

"She's good," I tell him. "Are you that good?"

"Better," he says, smiling hugely. "Darling, you should see me in my little black sequined number." He stretches his arm toward me, bends his wrist, wriggles his hand. "To die for," he says, emphasizing the words, camping and vamping happily.

"I'll bet you are," I tease, giving him a head-to-toe appraisal, which he clearly enjoys.

At five-foot-eight, with natural blond hair, slender hips, no belly, small facial features, and a light growth of facial hair, Carl seems made for women's clothes. That is obvious, though he's dressed in a classic white cotton-knit Izod pullover, tucked into chinos, and Top-Siders with no socks. Casual menswear.

"I'm a perfect size eight," he says. "How many women can say that?"

"What about the other girls at Miss Vera's? Do they look as good as you do?"

"See for yourself," he says confidently, "but I don't think they do. No. Miss Vera herself whispered in my ear that I'm the prettiest."

The flippant attitude disappears when I ask him, "How long have you been crossdressing?"

Recalling Mommy's reaction to his love of women's clothing saddens him.

Crossdressing is acceptable if you're a star like RuPaul or hang out with the avant-garde. In middle America, where transvestites remain more closeted, they are still largely regarded as those freaks who appear on *Donahue* a couple times a year. Your grandmother knows who they are, which doesn't mean she wants to know one, and especially she doesn't want to know *you* are one. As a society, we don't seem to realize we're discriminating when we accept women in men's clothing but not men in women's clothing. Since Katharine Hepburn switched to pants in the Forties, no woman has been ostracized for wearing them.

When Diane Keaton wore baggy, layered menswear in *Annie Hall,* she launched a trend. Did Dustin Hoffman start any fashions dressing as a woman in *Tootsie*?

Most people still wrongly assume all transvestites are gay. Gay "drag queens" typically dress to lampoon both femininity and straight attitudes about homosexuality. The overwhelming majority of TVs are heterosexual. Even if they sometimes make love while wearing women's lingerie, they have sex as men. Like the majority of men, they consider intercourse the primary method of lovemaking.

Why would a straight man want to dress in women's clothing?

Dressing in women's clothing is a form of fetishistic behavior. Men who crossdress become sexually aroused by the donning of female apparel, makeup, and wigs. As with other fetishes, no one knows exactly why. Experts postulate that the transvestite may have become sexually aroused by women's clothing, lingerie, or makeup as an adolescent and continues to associate arousal with these items. Some men who are aroused by these items are content to see and feel them on women. Others, transvestites, need to wear them.

"It expresses my feminine side, which is there, whether I wear lipstick and a bra or I don't," one man told me. "I believe everyone has a masculine and a feminine side. In most men, the feminine side is smaller than it is in me."

"I love the feel of makeup on my skin, silk and satin against my body," another man says. "Women's things are more sensual than men's, and I am a sensual person."

The word *transvestite* is derived from the Latin *trans* (cross) and *vestire* (to clothe), but it was first used in deink

scribing members of Berlin's gay subculture in the early twentieth century. Those men, largely club performers, dressed as women. Crossdressing has existed in many cultures through history. The Cheyenne called their braves who wore the feminine version of animal hides *berdaches* and thought them to possess love magic and great powers of healing. In our culture today, crossdressers are either elevated to celebrity status or treated as objects of amusement or scorn.

"It's hard not to laugh at a big man in a silk teddy, unless you're crying, that is," said one woman who called off her impending marriage when she caught her fiancé wearing women's lingerie. Another woman in a similar situation called off the wedding *and* went back to his apartment the next day, using the key she still had, and set fire to his trunk of women's clothing. His artworks and a small, highly prized collection of first editions also went up in smoke.

Some fortunate TVs do have wives who accept their second natures. In these relationships the amount of time a man can spend dressed as well as how much money he can spend on female clothing and accoutrements is often negotiated. One woman told me she could "live with" his dressing no more than once a week. Another said the cost of his "female obsession" bothered her more than the fact of it.

"He always wants new things," she says. "I don't understand why he can't be satisfied with his wardrobe the way it is. After all, he doesn't wear these things out of the house. If I stayed home all the time, I wouldn't need many clothes at all."

Some wives will also let their crossdressing husbands wear lingerie while making love, at least part of the time.

"This is a turn-on for him, not me," one wife explained. "I let him wear his girly things during sex sometimes. There are things I like which he doesn't like as much, such as cunnilingus. We trade sexual favors."

One couple sent a photo of the two of them together. His wig was styled like her hair. They wore the same black dress and black pumps and pearls—and flashed identical smiles. "Can you tell who is who?" was scribbled across the back. They did look very much alike, the resemblance heightened by the shadow of a mustache above *her* upper lip.

Another woman, a wife of ten years who discovered her husband's other side when she caught him hand washing his silk panties, told me: "I'm glad we're the same dress size. It could be a lot worse. We have so much fun together, I can overlook this."

"I started dressing in my mother's clothes when I was three or four," Carl says. "The nanny thought it was cute. My mother didn't, so I had to have everything off and back in her closet before she came home from work. She got home before my father did. It was unusual to have a working mother in those days, and mine was an executive. I liked her evening things the best. She had some great silks, dresses made from lengths of fabric she and my father had brought back from a trip to India.

"I can almost taste how good they felt when I close my eyes." He shuts his eyes, licks his lips, smiles enigmatically, then opens his eyes again. "I can also remember the feelings of shame and guilt washing over me. Shame is a physical sensation. I knew this was a wrong thing for a boy to do because my mother found it distasteful, not bad, really, but *distasteful.* She looked at me with that mouth-full-of-lemons face whenever she caught me in her clothes.''

Like most crossdressers, Carl fought the urge to don women's clothing as he grew up. In high school, he occasionally wore his mother's clothes when both parents were out for the evening. One night they came home early, forcing him to hide her outfit in his closet and jump into the shower to scrub off the makeup as they were coming up the stairs. That was the last time he wore his mother's clothes.

"I still wonder if she suspected,'' he says. "I couldn't replace her silk evening pajamas until the next day. Did she notice they were missing? Did she ever smell me on her things? Mothers can smell their offspring, can't they? I'll never feel completely comfortable with her, because I'll always wonder if she knows.''

During his four years at the University of Michigan, Carl didn't crossdress. Like many transvestites, he tried to rid himself of the habit as another person might try to stop drinking or using drugs. This is part of a shared behavior pattern, the part called "purging,'' when the clothes and makeup are thrown away and the man does everything he can to prove his manliness.

"I lifted weights,'' he says. "I fucked a lot of women. I even participated in a group sex orgy.

"Then, when I was living alone for the first time in my life, I started dressing again. I felt guilty, lonely, and ashamed. When I dressed, I would get real high. Then, later that night after I'd put the clothes away—and I kept them under lock and key—and washed the makeup off, I felt sick to my stomach. I was a pervert. That was what I called myself then. But I couldn't stop.''

Though he would like to be married and particularly wants to have children, Carl has remained single because he has never met a woman he trusted enough to tell his secret.

"I imagine sometimes when I am with a woman what it would be like to open my trunks and show her my things,'' he says. "In my fantasies, she would clap her hands and say, 'How lovely. Will you wear them for me?'

"In real life, she would run out shrieking into the night—and call my boss the next day with a full report. Hell, she'd probably call Mom, too.''

Carl came out for the first time as Carole at the International Foundation for Gender Education "happening" held at the Philadelphia Hilton & Towers in August 1993. In preparation for the event, he'd taken several classes in different cities, beginning in March in Los Angeles. ("I was visiting my mother and her new husband when I saw this ad for makeup lessons for men. Oh goddess, I don't mean for my poor mother to be such a big part of this story.") In the seminar "Hair Removal A to Z" he met Lisa (Leonard) who told him about Veronica Vera's finishing school, the "most important contact" Carl's ever made.

"I learned a lot at the happening,'' he says. "Most transvestites fight their desires and try to reform until they're somewhere between thirty-five and forty-five. Then they say, 'Oh, hell, this is part of me,' and learn to deal with it. I met some men who had thought about killing themselves. One guy did try to take his life after his girl-friend left him when she caught him wearing her under-wear.

"I was one of the few guys who had never gone out in public dressed. At the happening, they told me that I couldn't count dressing up at home. I had to go out on my own for the sake of my self-esteem. I don't know if I ever would have done that without Miss Vera's help."

Veronica Vera is one of the few women in this world who does clap her hands and say, "How lovely. Will you wear them for me?"

I met Veronica during my *Forum* days when she was about to marry her best friend, a gay man dying of AIDS. He wanted a wife to take home to meet his family, and he did not want to die alone. A charming, intelligent, and compassionate woman, she's acted in a dozen or so X-rated films, produced and directed a few more, once posed for Robert Mapplethorpe, and testified at the Meese Commission hearings on porn. At another point in her life, she traded over-the-counter stocks. Together with her best friend, performance artist and former porn star Annie Sprinkle, Veronica has dabbled in various forms of sexual transformation, such as teaching classes for women who want to look like porn stars in the bedroom. In the finishing school, which she always calls "the Academy," she's found her true calling.

With long, thick brunette hair falling to her shoulders and ample cleavage spilling out of whatever gold lamé or leopardskin or hot pink dress held up by spaghetti straps she happens to be wearing, Veronica looks younger than her forty-six years, a glamour queen of indeterminate age. She also looks like the kind of woman a man who wants to look like a woman might choose for a role model. This is fortunate, because many of her students leave the Academy bearing more than a passing resemblance to Veronica through the miracles of makeup and long dark wigs.

"As many as five percent of American men are, or want to be, crossdressers," Veronica says with authority. She is preparing for a private class with Carl, his second, in her studio apartment on Eighth Avenue in the Chelsea area of Manhattan. "There's a need for the Academy. Men don't *just* want to dress. They want to look good as women."

Veronica charges three hundred dollars for her private class, which includes instruction on dressing, sitting, standing, and walking like a woman and a makeup lesson from Paulette Powell, the dean of cosmetology. There are cheaper group sessions and some expensive extras, including a day of "photo therapy" with Annie Sprinkle for a thousand dollars, and a two-thousand-dollar weekend excursion into femininity, which entitles the man to do shopping, lunch, dinner, and clubhopping with Paulette and Veronica. He, of course, picks up the tabs, though Veronica may treat him to a drink or two. All fees are paid in cash—*new* bills—handed over to Miss Vera in crisp pink envelopes.

"I do grant partial scholarships to men who are willing to clean my apartment," she says. "They get to wear a French maid's uniform while they work."

She started the school in 1990 after a male friend asked her to show him how to be a woman.

"He spent the whole weekend dressed," she says. "We did everything together. I taught him how to buy makeup and lingerie. I took him to be waxed. It was so much fun, I knew this was what I wanted to do next."

She put an ad in *Transvestian* magazine promising to help men "experience the sensual pleasure of their femme-selves." In the first two years, more than three hundred men, largely between thirty-five and forty-five, have responded. Approximately 80 percent of them are straight *and* happily married and have included such diverse types as highly placed corporate executives, policemen, and construction workers. A few, she says, have brought their wives. Most, she concedes, try to keep their "femme-selves" hidden from their wives or girlfriends. They are limited to clothing that covers their chest and leg hair, because waxing is out of the question.

"I find when a man approaches forty, he no longer fights his desire to dress," she says. "And like women who are aging, he is concerned about finding ways to look more attractive, more youthful."

"More attractive to other men?" I ask.

"Well, that's what being a woman is about, isn't it?"

"Why would a straight man want to be attractive to men?" I persist, because this is the question that has not been satisfactorily answered by the men I've interviewed.

"Some men do tell me they're straight in the real world, but when they dress, anything goes. There isn't a clear line between gay and straight. You remember the Kinsey scale, don't you? He thought there were degrees of homosexuality, starting at one end with the totally straight person and going to the totally gay person at the other end, with a lot of gray areas in the middle.''

"Do those men in the gray area have sex with other men when they're dressed?''

She shrugs eloquently.

"I have no desire to have sex with another man,'' Carl insists.

He is sitting between me and Veronica, his candle shaped like a woman in hand. Veronica sends all her students to Magickal Childe, an occult supply store in Chelsea, to buy a woman candle ($1.75), which is lit at the beginning of the "ritual of transformation.'' The candle is blue, contrasting nicely with the dean's hot pink decorating theme. Photos of men dressed as women are everywhere. A florid and fetid incense is burning. The place smells like the vestibule of an Indian restaurant.

"Two men at the happening talked about having sex with men when they were dressed,'' Carl says. "Only two. One guy said it had always been his fantasy to be picked up by a man in a bar. He went home with a guy he met at a TV bar in Los Angeles. He said it was a disaster. His fantasy of a female with a penis turned out to be the reality of this hairy, sweaty man. Luckily, the other guy was just as disappointed as he was in reality.

"The biggest fantasy for most of these guys was having a woman accept them the way they are. Everybody wants to curl up in bed with his wife, both of them dressed in satin nightgowns.'' He smiles ruefully at me. "I know what you're thinking. 'In your dreams, bozos, in your dreams.' ''

* * *

I stay for the private session, which begins with Carl on his knees. He lights the candle while pledging to "dedicate [himself] to releasing all of the female energy inside [him]." Veronica touches him on the head and calls him Carole.

"Carole, I want you to strip and put on these black panties," she says.

I can't help but notice how exceptionally well endowed Carole is as she steps into the black silk "cheaters panties," a cross between a G-string and an elasticized jockstrap, meant to bind the male genitalia to the body.

She arches her eyebrows coyly when Veronica says, "Miss Carole's so excited about getting dressed, isn't she?"

There is simply no way around it. Carole will have a bulge.

Veronica massages Carole's body all over before performing the hair removal with safety razor, electric razor, and depilatory cream. Carole, now smooth from cheeks to ankles, showers and returns in a black silk nightgown over her panties. She sits obediently still while Miss Paulette does her makeup, beginning with heavy pancake foundation. Too much iridescent blue eyeliner for my taste. Clear red lipstick, very nice. Next come the undergarments—a padded black lace bra, garter belt, and stockings. The wig the three select is long and blond. When Carole puts it on, the transition is nearly complete. I have to glance down and check the cheaters panties to be sure Carl is still there.

Carole has brought her own clothes, which are more tasteful than the selections in Veronica's TV closet.

Dressed in a simple black knit dress—long sleeves, square neck, knee length, with front slit—and three-inch black pumps, Carole is a stunner. I look for the bulge, but it's barely discernible. The dress forms a soft gathered V in the pelvic area, directing the eye downward to the legs, and Carole has a great set of gams.

"What do you think?" she asks. "Would you make me on the street?"

No, I wouldn't.

"I'd kiss you, but we'd smear lips, darling," she says, throwing exaggerated air kisses my way instead.

A few weeks later, Carl and I meet again for cappuccino at the Angelika café, where he has just seen *Orlando* for the second time. His hair is growing out.

"My chest itches," he complains. "I've thought about keeping it shaved, but if I do that, I can't date women. There's a woman I'd like to take out. I'm just waiting for my hair to grow back in."

If he finds a woman who will accept his crossdressing, would he like to make love to her in drag?

"I don't think so. My ultimate fantasy is the two of us dressed up and doing the town together as girls. We would flirt with men. Maybe we would pretend we were sisters or lesbian lovers. Then we would come home together. I would take off my clothes. We would shower together and have incredibly hot sex.

"But you never know. I might someday want to make love in drag. Now it would be enough to be accepted and loved by a woman while in drag."

Chapter 14

When One Is Never Enough

TEXAS

The condoms are served on silver trays with the appetizers. Lead crystal bowls hold latex condoms, lubricated and nonlubricated, ribbed, and multicolored, in regular and magnum sizes. There are mint-flavored condoms, French ticklers, and condoms treated with nonoxynol-9, thought to aid in preventing pregnancy and the spread of sexually transmitted diseases (STDs). Each bowl holds a different kind of condom. Skewered shrimps, strips of pâté on thin slices of baguette, chunks of fruit and cheese on toothpicks, and other hors d'oeuvres are on the trays, radiating from the condom-filled bowls like spokes in a wheel.

"No lambskin," the host, a wealthy entrepreneur, whispers in my ear. "Lambskin is not effective against STDs."

This is a safe-sex party. With few exceptions, the guests look like they've been participating in multipartner experiences long enough to remember when cocaine, not condoms, was distributed on trays along with the crackers and caviar and cream cheese—perhaps even long enough to remember when marijuana and Gallo hearty burgundy were passed around, sans benefit of silver trays or hired waiters.

Welcome to an orgy in post-AIDS America. If you were expecting sleek, glistening, young bodies and juicily interacting body parts, you're going to be disappointed—though most of these people *have* held up very well. The annoying guy with the graying beard who won't leave you alone at the hotel bar is here, however, and he's going to take off his clothes.

A few months before this party, I met the host, Greg, at a sex club in New York City, where, for the ninety-dollar admission fee, a couple can have sex with strangers in a public space. One free condom is handed to each couple at the door. No single men are admitted, and the staff seems to spend a lot of time counting and matching heads, making sure even numbers of men and women enter and leave. There are about fifty sex clubs operating in New York City on a quasi-legal basis, about two-thirds of them gay clubs. The authorities know the clubs exist and periodically make noises about closing them, but no one believes that will happen soon—and not at this club, considered by aficionados the best of the heterosexual lot. People who swing only occasionally come here, as do couples who want to do it by themselves in front of an audience. Some of them actually are young, sleek, and glistening.

I had bribed the doorman with a hundred-dollar bill to let me talk to customers in the outer lounge, wood paneled and highlighted by a mirrored disco ball. Couples have a drink here at the bar before going into the "playroom," where clothes are not permitted and clean towels are provided. From the lounge, I could see the hot tub surrounded by floor-to-ceiling mirrors that reflected ten people, one stunning curvaceous blonde under thirty and nine less attractive naked men and women who appeared to be over thirty-five, two of the men about twenty years over. Greg, forty-nine, a big, handsome man, was in the outer lounge with his third wife, Catherine, also big and handsome. They appeared to be a couple who shared enormous appetites for food, drink, excitement, sex.

I asked them the same question I was asking everyone else: Why are you here? The younger couple I'd met before them had assured me, "We're here for a little clean sin. You can pretty much tell when someone has AIDS."

"You meet good people here," Greg said. "No sleaze. These are people with money, with college degrees. We come to New York three times a year and we come here to play. We've always met good people. It's a safe place to have fun."

"How can you know it's safe?" I asked. "You don't know anything about these people, their sexual and drug histories. Good people can have STDs, too."

"We always insist on condoms," Catherine said, pushing her full mane of tawny streaked hair behind her ears with both hands. Her nails were two inches long and painted a frosty coral. I would have bet she's deliberately scratched a lot of backs in the heat of passion with those nails. "But look around you. These aren't drug users. And they carefully screen at the door. There are no gay men. No man-on-man sex is permitted."

Greg and Catherine walked back to the playroom, which they told me was a huge mattress-lined room with a spiral staircase leading to cubbyholes for semiprivacy, "if that's your trip."

After they were out of earshot, a middle-aged man sitting next to me said, "Everybody wears condoms at first. By the end of the evening, they aren't using them anymore. If people look clean, you just don't, that's all."

"Why do you and your wife come here?"

"She isn't my wife," he said, indicating the younger woman beside him. She was a brunette with short, spiky hair, this season's style favored by bisexual women. "But we like it because there's no emotional baggage connected with coming here. It's easy. No emotional strings, only pleasure. Isn't that what everybody really wants?"

I was getting ready to leave when Greg, wearing a towel, came back to the bar and handed me his card.

"If you're going to be in Texas," he said. "Call. We give private safe-sex parties. You should see swinging on the grassroots level."

Now in Texas, I am sitting alone in the media room watching tapes of orgies past when a couple asks if they can join me. They appear to be in their late thirties or early forties. She is tall, almost six foot in high-heeled sandals. He is a few inches shorter. They are tanned and prosperous-looking. I invite them in. On the screen, a man and three women are engaged in four-way oral sex. She sits on one side of me, he the other. Uh-oh. Something about this scene reminds me of the night a couple asked me to dominate them at an S/M club in L.A.

"I love your dress," she says, stroking the sleeve of my black lace minidress. "It's so New York."

"I love the stockings," he says, running a hand down my leg and quickly taking it away. "Black stockings are great on a woman. You know what I hate? White panty hose. You see so many women out here in white panty hose. That's okay if you're into nurses."

Making an attempt to toss her big blond hair, which doesn't toss because of the amount of hair spray, she laughs delightedly at him. I look at her hand on my arm. She takes it away.

"I love your breasts," he says. "You have beautiful breasts."

"How long have you been swinging?" I ask.

"Why don't you take off your dress?" he asks.

"Gene," she chides him. "Is that your idea of subtle?" She lays the hand on my arm again. Her nails are long and lacquered tangerine. A huge diamond sparkles on her left hand. "We'd like you to play with us," she says throatily. "You can't write about this if you don't even try it, can you?"

"It would be like writing about skiing without skiing," he says.

I tell them my publisher has made me sign a statement agreeing not to participate in any of the activities I report.

"Legal reasons?" he asks. I nod affirmatively. "Damn lawyers are ruining the country. Some of my best friends are lawyers, but I can't help it. That's the damn truth. They're destroying individual rights."

* * *

Susan Crain Bakos

According to the North American Swing Club Association, based in California, a lot of swinging is going on at "the grassroots level." There are more than two hundred swing clubs in the country, ranging from small-town organizations meeting in the back room of a bar to New Horizons outside Seattle, a fourteen-acre theme park for swingers, which includes a replica of a turn-of-the-century Texas bordello. The median age of the association's membership is forty-five. The executive director, Robert McGinley, estimates there are three million American swingers—and counting. He insists there's been "a steady increase since the 1980s."

Various newsletters and magazines devoted to swinging put couples in touch with one another through the classified ads, if belonging to an organized club doesn't appeal to them. New York writer Judy Walters, who publishes a newsletter, claims there are "thousands and thousands of couples who swap. It didn't go out of style just because the media stopped writing about swinging."

Swapping, or swinging, is having sexual relations with someone other than one's spouse—with the spouse's active approval. Sometimes the couples do swap partners, going off to have sex in different rooms or meeting at different times. And sometimes the four have sex together. Frequently, small groups of couples have house parties, or private orgies.

In the Sixties and Seventies, swingers and their clubs got a lot of media attention. With the advent of AIDS and the prevalence of other STDs, editors stopped assigning stories on swinging. We in the media tend to forget that people don't stop behaving a certain way just because we stop writing about it.

"Well, what do you think?" Greg asks, indicating his thirty-six guests with a sweeping arm. "Are these good people? You've got doctors, lawyers, dentists—the cream of the crop. Didn't I tell you?"

"Yes, you did," I say, taking a tiny chili cup from the tray of a passing waiter. Too much sour cream. "Are they all married?"

"Two or three are living-together couples, but the majority are married," he says. "Family values." He laughs. His eyes do not laugh with him. Is that why he has no lines around them? "I was a Bush man, you know."

"Second marriages?" I ask.

"I don't know how many are second marriages," he says, a suspicious frown momentarily crossing his brow. "What difference does it make? Are you trying to turn this into a sociological study with a negative conclusion? I like you, baby"—the smile again—"you don't want to do that."

Before the evening is over, I will discover that eleven of the fifteen married couples are on their second—or third or fourth—marriage. Some were swingers during their first marriage, and some weren't. Few believe swinging contributed to their divorce. Greg, for example, says his two marriages before Catherine floundered for more prosaic reasons: They grew in different directions, she spent too much of his money, his kids didn't like her kids, and so on.

"A man is going to cheat," Greg says, guiding me through small clusters of guests out to the terrace, which overlooks an "English-style" garden. In the natural light, I can see the tiny scars at the corners of his eyes indicating he's had them tucked, which explains why the skin around them is so smooth and flat, untouched by smiles. "These days a woman is probably going to cheat, too. Why not do it together? No secrets, no lies, no emotional involvements with other people. Swinging can keep a marriage together."

"You aren't jealous when Catherine is with other men? Do you watch?"

"Occasionally I feel a twinge of jealousy," he says, "but that's good. Jealousy is sexually arousing. Feeling jealous of Catherine makes me horny as hell for her."

I notice his body language. He's standing feet slightly apart and moving his pelvis ever so slightly forward and back again on key words such as *sexually* and *horny*.

"Sometimes I watch. Depends on the scene, on what everybody wants." He takes me by the shoulders and turns me gently so that I am facing the French doors leading back into the house. His hands are strong, his fragrance crisp and citrusy. He is obviously well-endowed beneath the white linen slacks. "See the couple under the Georgia O'Keeffe? Jeanie and Ted."

Leaning intently toward her husband as he speaks, Jeanie is dressed in a brilliant green silk pants suit that goes well with her big head of auburn hair. These women do have big hair, their clothing colors are hot, and their bodies not fat, though not as toned as New York or L.A. bodies. She and Ted both look a well-tended, prosperous forty. He seems annoyed, perhaps with her neediness, which she visibly projects.

"She's a very hot little number, but something of a narcissist," Greg says, leaving one hand on me so that his fingers dangle over the edge of my shoulder onto my back and his wrist lies flat on my shoulder blade. I can feel his pulse. "She only likes to do it one-on-one with the door open so her husband can walk by and see. Not stand in the doorway. That throws her off, his standing and watching. She wants him to be able to catch the occasional glimpse. But she never wants anybody else in on the action. Just her and one man, no women. She won't do it with a woman."

"That's your definition of a narcissist?"

"Sure. Someone who is so into herself she doesn't want to share the action ever." He puts his hand under my chin and turns it slightly. "The woman next to the ficus, Shelley, she is the total opposite: The more the merrier. Shelley likes a bedful, women and men, cocks in her hand, her mouth, her pussy."

"Her asshole?" I ask.

"We don't do that in this group," he says, seeming mildly offended. "It smacks of queer to me."

Catherine sweeps through the French doors toward us, resplendent in sheer white palazzo pants with a multicolored belted sleeveless tunic. She is wearing gold high-heeled sandals, which might look cheap on another woman. They look wonderful on Catherine. Greg doesn't take his hand away from me. If they were not swingers, he would. Then, possibly later, he would slip me his card with his private office number and whisper, "Call me, *please.*" If they were not swingers, he would be cheating on her.

"Are you pointing out the heavy hitters?" she asks him.

* * *

"Heavy hitters" are couples who have sex with other couples as often as they can fit recreational sex into their schedules. If they don't belong to a sizable group such as the one organized by Greg and Catherine, they frequent clubs. The private groups control membership, often asking new members to submit proof they are HIV negative. Some, like a group of twelve couples in Minneapolis, sign a pledge not to have sex with anyone outside the group and to submit to a battery of STD tests, including the HIV test, once a year. Greg and Catherine require only the medical clearance from new members. They say it is "understood" by the membership that everyone will choose other partners carefully and practice safe sex at all times.

Given their level of promiscuity, the swingers I interviewed are not very well informed about STDs. Over 90 percent did not know, for example, that chlamydia, the number one STD in this country, is carried by one in three sexually active adults, is asymptomatic in the majority of men and women, is the leading cause of infertility in both men and women, and can be transmitted through foreplay and oral sex. A condom is not 100 percent effective against the transmission of it or *any* STD.

One group of San Francisco swingers did pass the STD quiz almost unanimously with perfect scores. At their safe-sex parties, the players rarely have intercourse, even with condoms. Wearing plastic gloves, they masturbate each other. Kissing is not allowed. Oral sex is performed on condom-sheathed penises or vaginas covered with dental dams (protective plastic sheets). Most of the party goers are voyeurs. They merely watch the few who choose to masturbate each other.

Groups like Greg's discourage the presence of "tickets," onlookers who have no plans to participate. Occasionally, a member may choose to sit out the action, but not often. ("Sometimes if a woman is having a heavy period, she won't want to do anything, not even suck dick," Greg says. "PMS, maybe? But she comes along so her husband can eat some clean pussy.") At the clubs, however, watching from the sidelines is more common. As many as a third of the people who pay to get in a club on any night may choose not to play.

"I'd say everyone in this group is a heavy hitter," Jeanie tells me proudly.

We are standing outside a bedroom door and chatting while two naked couples are "getting some action" on the king-size bed. Black satin sheets have slithered to the floor, where they lie like pools of bayou water. The fragrant mélange of blended expensive perfumes, sweat, and latex wafts toward us. A blonde with good legs kneels at the side of a man, his penis in her mouth. He massages her breast with one hand and fondles a younger brunette's genitals with the other hand. The fourth player, a man, is entering the brunette from behind. I cannot tell if he is wearing a condom, but the man receiving fellatio is not. I don't know who is married to whom.

"Do you like to watch?" she asks me. She likes to watch. Her eyes dart back and forth compulsively between me and the bed. "It's better than a movie, isn't it?"

The man having intercourse with the brunette grasps her hips firmly in both hands and thrusts vigorously. She braces herself with both arms and pushes back against him with equal vigor. The blonde seems to move her mouth up and down the other man's penis in the same rhythm.

"How long have you and Ted been part of the group?" I ask.

"Two years. Ted met Greg through business about four years ago." She looks at the bed. "Greg said he had a feeling we were the type, but he had to wait until he knew Ted better to ask."

Again, she casts her eyes toward the bed. I suddenly realize by the inflection in her voice and the look in her eyes when they settle on him that the man with his hands in two women is her husband, Ted. I hadn't recognized him with his clothes off. As we watch, he begins sucking the brunette's nipple. A drop of sweat rolls down her breast into his mouth.

"Some people would be offended if you thought they were swingers and they weren't," Jeanie says. "Ted and I have never been part of a group like this before. We used to be occasional swingers, going to a club if we were in L.A. or New York or hooking up with a couple we met while traveling or whatever. We like this much better. We know the people and trust them. When you hook up with strangers, you have to be careful.

"We met a couple through a personals ad we answered in *Screw* once. They were crazy—well, anyway, he was. He wanted to fuck Ted in the ass. Well, you know what that means. Of course, Ted would never, under any circumstances. Here we were with this couple in our house, which is like Greg and Catherine's home, very isolated. This man was drinking and we were terrified he would rape my husband. Well, they left, thank God, but it could have been terrible.''

''Whose idea was it?''

''Whose idea was what?'' she asks, her eyes again focused on the bed, where the four are changing positions.

''To try swinging the first time.''

''Oh, it was his. I was lukewarm to the idea.'' She brings her eyes back to me. ''A lot of women here will tell you it was their man's idea, if they're being honest. I don't think women are likely to be the ones who initiate swinging. You write for the women's magazines. You know what I mean. Women have enough trouble initiating sex with their own husbands in their own bedrooms.

''Ted suggested we try it. I was nervous about it. I knew he and his first wife had split over sex. He was seeing someone else and she caught him. In the back of my mind, I thought I'd keep him if I did this. I was also really nervous about having sex with men I didn't know. Would they be turned off by my body? It isn't perfect. You expect your husband to want you anyway, but will somebody else's husband want you?

''He was like a little kid, the way he kept asking me to try it. Finally I did. And do you know what? I had a great time. It was fun. I'm still not as uninhibited as most of the other women. I don't want to do a foursome like this.'' Her eyes are back on the bed. Ted has entered the blonde, who is lying on her back, legs bent at the knee and open wide. She grasps his buttocks, pulling him deeper inside her. He yelps enthusiastically. ''Not now,'' Jeanie says. ''Maybe someday I will. I've learned never to say never. You just don't know.

"There's something you should know about most of these women," she says, lowering her voice. "They swing both ways." She inclines her head in the direction of the bed, where the blonde is screaming, *"Oh, God, oh, God, yes, yes yes, I'm coming now."*

"Those two, they're bisexuals, not that I care, but I'm not. That's why I like to do it with only one man at a time. If you get into a foursome, you're going to have some woman's mouth on your body."

We stand by the door long enough for the four people on the bed to change positions several times—and for the women to have at least one orgasm each. They remind me of a kaleidoscope, shifting into new patterns, none more pleasing or less so than the one before or the one after. The blonde is triumphantly astride Jeanie's husband, masturbating herself with one hand as she rides him, when I walk away, leaving Jeanie to watch alone.

Later, the two women who were on the bed with Ted invite me to share a joint with them in one of the six bathrooms. Nora, a lanky brunette in her late thirties, sits on the toilet seat. She lights the fat joint, inhales deeply, and passes it to Jerrilyn, who is occupying a velvet-covered bench. Jerrilyn is also in her late thirties. Nora's thick pubic hair is matted. She is blissfully unashamed of her nakedness, but Jerrilyn, whose body is compact and taut, is less comfortable. She pulls a green bath sheet around her after passing the joint to me.

"You should use the bidet," Jerrilyn says to Nora.

"I should have used the condoms," she retorts, and they both laugh.

The bathroom is larger than a typical Manhattan studio apartment, done in green, gold, and black. The marble shower, green shot through with black, could accommodate four adults. Plants hang from the ceilings, nourished by huge windows and two skylights.

"This is Greg's bathroom," Nora says. "It's his decorator's idea of manliness. What do you think?"

"His decorator should know all about his manliness," Jerrilyn jibes.

"Do you feel funny going to parties like these and keeping your clothes on the whole time?" Nora asks. "I would feel really out of it."

"A writer who wrote about swinging for a city magazine in the late Seventies told me she couldn't resist participating in the action then," I reply.

"And, of course, there was Gay Talese," Jerrilyn says, referring to the author who sampled some of the sexual practices he chronicled in *Thy Neighbor's Wife*.

"Maybe I'm naturally more inhibited," I say.

"I had trouble letting myself go in a swinging setting for a while," Jerrilyn says, nodding sympathetically. "My husband wanted to do it. I was really curious about what it would be like to be with a woman, so I went along. At first I was going through the motions, faking orgasms. I got Nora and her husband into this group, because, quite frankly, I wanted to have sex with Nora, if I was going to do it with women."

"I faked, too, when I was new at this," Nora says. "The thing about faking is by throwing yourself into the acting, you eventually turn yourself on and get into it for real."

Jerrilyn nods. The joint goes around again. They tell me

about their first husbands, a construction worker and a policeman, who were both boring and bored by them. After the divorces, Jerrilyn supported herself and her two children as a cocktail waitress by night and attended college during the day. Nora, who became her best friend after the two met at a nursery school parents' night, worked a variety of jobs while earning her MBA. They were together when they met their second husbands at a wine-tasting party hosted by Jerrilyn's pediatrician, who'd promised to introduce the women to some eligible men.

"I had to make things different this time," Nora says. "I think Jerrilyn would say the same thing." Jerrilyn nods in agreement. "This time around, we caught the brass ring. We're going to keep these guys happy. And aren't we lucky that seeing us have a good time in bed with each other makes them happy?"

"What do you think of Catherine?" Jerrilyn asks, perhaps to change the subject, but more to the point, I suspect, perhaps because Catherine is the true center of this group. She is avidly desired by more of its members than Greg is.

"Catherine is charismatic," I say.

Robert McGinley, the executive director of the North American Swing Club Association, estimates that 50 to 75 percent of women swingers are bisexual. Bisexual contact among women is encouraged in swing groups and clubs. (Watching two women make love is a top male fantasy. *Penthouse* pictorials of women together are a popular feature of the magazine.) Male bisexuality, however, is not allowed in the clubs and the majority of social groups.

McGinley says swingers are not likely to get AIDS because "male bisexuality is extremely rare among swingers." When two women in a Minnesota group were found to be HIV positive last year, he said publicly that both women had had contact with bisexual men "outside the group." In other words, they would not have become infected had they played within the confines of their own group.

"I abhor the term 'safe sex' because it implies there's something unsafe about sex," he says.

As long as only women switch, swingers believe, everyone will be fine.

"What did you think of Jeanie?" Catherine asks.

We are reclining in wicker chaises outside on the terrace. The night air is soft and cool, not chilly, but she's loaned me a silk shawl in case I need it. Behind us, the house is alight and filled with sounds, quiet jazz, the low buzz of conversation, occasional moans and grunts, punctuated by one male voice or another saying "Yes, baby, come" or "Yes, baby, I'm coming."

"She's lovely," I answer.

"Uhm," Catherine says. "She needs to loosen up, but I don't think she ever will. Greg says he'd love to see Jeanie make it with a woman, but I tell him, no way, dream another dream. She's scared. Do you think that means she's a secret lesbian?"

"Have you made it with another woman?"

"Sure, plenty of times. Why not? It's just another way to feel good." She stretches her arm across the space between us. Her hand does not reach my arm. "Look, I play sex the way I play tennis, hard. I work up a sweat. I can play just as well with a woman as a man."

"Then why be married?"

"Why not be married? Being married to Greg is the best of both worlds. Do you think I could have all this without him? I have a great life."

We sit in companionable silence for several minutes before Greg joins us.

"I've got videos of the day's action," he says. "I think you should come inside and look at it. This is what swinging is all about. I've got some great stuff on tape." Catherine and I get up to follow him inside. "I'm going to set you up in the media room, then I have to take care of Jeanie."

He turns to Catherine and makes a face, the same face I've seen on husbands at other parties when they had to spend some quality time deep in conversation with in-laws or her business associates. She laughs, a big tinkling laugh filled with herself.

"Jeanie likes him best," she says.

"Do you mind?" I ask.

"Why should I?"

Catherine pats his rear affectionately as he walks away toward Jeanie, who is waiting for him, her arms open, her lips wet and parted.

Chapter 15

Body Piercing

LONG ISLAND

"I had my navel pierced five times before it took," Lauren says matter-of-factly, as if repeating the cycle of piercing–infection–rejection of piercing–piercing is something worth doing, like taking the bar exam, until you get it right or run out of tries. "You can see where it didn't take," she says, pointing with a long magenta nail to the raised scars etched into her belly button. The scars surround the gold ring in the piercing that finally "took."

Her belly is round and firm, a little on the heavy side. Stretch marks, like iridescent road maps, indicate the history of its ups and downs. Stray wild black hairs on the lower part match the hair on her head.

"Navels are tough," Blade says. He is the piercer extraordinaire brought by limo from Manhattan to perform a piercing of the clitoral hood on Lauren's friend Dina. "The navel is one of the most difficult piercings to heal. The

265

ridge of skin is thick and tough. The area gets irritated by clothing. You almost have to do it in summer and be able to spend six weeks in crop tops and bikinis.'' He examines Lauren's navel, his fingers gently smoothing the skin around it as he talks. ''Looks like it's in there pretty good, but you've got a little infection going on around it. See the redness?''

''Does anybody have a mirror?'' she asks.

A brunette with rings through her eyebrows and a fat gold stud in her nose hands Lauren a Clinique pressed-powder compact. Lauren studies her navel. Someone behind us turns the knob of the black halogen floor lamp up to a brighter setting.

''Yes, I see it,'' she says, but Blade has already moved across the room, where he is closely inspecting a young man's pierced nipples.

These piercings appear to be fairly recent. Two thick silver rings are embedded in fat, red, puffy nipples. On either side of Blade are other young men waiting to show the expert their piercings, too. No one in this roomful of approximately twenty people is over twenty-five, and everyone has something other than their earlobes pierced.

''Why do you want a pierced navel?'' I ask Lauren.

''I think it looks hot. It looks sexy.'' She closes the compact, hands it back to the little brunette, and zips up her jeans. ''Even if nobody else sees it, if you know it's there, it's enough. You feel sexy, even if it doesn't show. I like the way it looks. I turn myself on. I want to do my inner labia next, one ring on each side.'' She looks around the room, spots the familiar face, and points. ''My friend Leanne had hers done, no problem.''

"Aren't you a little nervous about having your labia pierced after all the trouble you've had with your navel?"

"A little, but I really want it. I fantasize having my lips done. You could feel them down there all the time. You'd always know they were there. Walking around you'd know." Her big dark eyes, rimmed in black eyeliner, are shining. "You can be one way on the outside, you're this and you're that, the mother of a child, somebody's woman, but you know you have something kind of up there, and it's hot."

Lauren is twenty-two, the mother of a three-year-old daughter, Anastasia, called "Stasia," whose paternal grandparents are baby-sitting her tonight. This is Lauren's apartment, two bedrooms, beige carpeting, Euro-style kitchen and bathroom, with white tile, white cabinet and fixtures in the bathroom, white appliances and cabinets trimmed in a strip of pale wood in the kitchen. Photos of Stasia, a dark beauty with huge eyes and chubby cheeks, sit on the unfinished folding bookshelf from the Barnes and Noble sale catalog, which also holds half a dozen paperback romances and a CD collection. The living room is sixteen by twenty feet, outfitted with a new floral-print sofa and matching chair in shades of green and blue, coffee table and end tables in real oak, her mother's taste.

Lauren's divorced mother, a real-estate broker who earned close to two hundred thousand dollars last year in spite of the recession, bought all the furniture, pays all her bills. Lauren, who does not work, is divorced now, too, from her husband of four years, George, thirty-two, who sends her two hundred dollars a month for their child. She married George because he helped her get off cocaine when she was eighteen, then got her pregnant. She divorced him because he was "boring."

"If he knew about this party, he'd shit," Lauren says. Looking around the room at her friends and acquaintances, she says, "I'm the only one who has *had* a husband and a child." She pauses, assumes a reflective pose with arms crossed over chest, eyes downcast. "I feel like I missed a lot. I mean, like I never had a childhood.

"My mother says I've never had anything but a childhood. She's really on George's side, you know, in all this, not like he needs someone else on his side. His parents think I'm an unfit mother."

Young people are putting holes in their bodies in places their parents never would have considered piercing. If you're over thirty, you probably cannot understand why this fad, which started in the gay S/M community, has caught on with girls, who, nose rings removed, could pass for high-haired mall girls dressed in grunge for a trip into the city—or caught on with boys, who should be dramatizing their rebellion by dyeing their hair purple and green, or something else painless but visually disgusting to their elders. Piercing of anything but the earlobe is painful, sometimes extremely painful. Having been pierced creates new challenges in everyday life, such as chewing food with a tongue bar in place, sitting with rings attached to labia and testicles, walking through metal detectors without causing embarrassing airport incidents.

Why is a generation so interested in body mutilation?

Social commentators are fond of saying the trend began with *Modern Primitives,* a 1989 book compiled by V. Vale anesthesia. I won't pierce somebody who wants to take a painkiller first. You have to feel the pain to earn the piercing. Otherwise, you're walking around with a ring that says something about you that isn't true.''

While most will be content with one or two piercings in places other than their ears, some become what Blade labels ''piercing junkies.'' They get a new piercing to mark a life passage, such as a birthday or the end or beginning of a relationship.

''Some will do it for almost any reason,'' he says. ''Afterward, they point to the piercings and say, 'I did this on the day I realized my father is an asshole.' They tell me they are reclaiming their bodies and their lives for themselves through piercings. One girl got her nipples pierced on her mother's wedding day. It was her mother's fifth wedding.''

He has, for example, a twenty-one-year-old client who has twenty-five tiny rings in the cartilage of her ears, double-pierced nipples—yes, that's two rings on each nipple—pierced labia, clitoris, navel, lip, eyebrows, and tongue.

''She wants a spike through her lip now,'' he says, shrugging his shoulders as if he thinks perhaps she's gone too far. Has she? He shrugs again, perhaps not willing to make that kind of statement for a tape recorder.

''What happens when she runs out of places to pierce?'' I ask.

''Branding,'' he says, surprisingly ready with an answer. ''You're seeing it already on the West Coast. I think

and Andrea June, published by Re/Search Publications, known for high quality paperback books on outrageous subjects. *Modern Primitives* profiled members of an underground subculture—men and women who had been pierced, tattooed, scarred, and branded, often with extreme results. These people, labeled ''body-modification pioneers,'' claimed inspiration from primitive groups, such as the sadhus of India and the Ndebeli of South Africa. The book did get a lot of attention from the avant-garde press.

Only one of the twenty people in Lauren's living room had ever heard of it. It's difficult for me to believe that a significant percentage of the tens of thousands of young people puncturing nose and ear cartilage, lacing their eyebrows and upper lips, and having circles of metal inserted into nipples, navels, and genitalia were motivated by a book that can't be found in B. Dalton or Waldenbooks. Why, then?

''They see it,'' Blade says. ''Axl Rose has a nipple ring. You see pierced body parts on CD covers or the illustrations inside in the liner notes. Some of the men and women photographed with Madonna in her *Sex* book had piercings. The kids come into San Francisco or L.A. or Manhattan from the burbs and they see girls working in boutiques and bagel shops with piercings in their eyebrows, nose, lips. One of the girls who works at the cookie shop in my neighborhood has eleven piercings. It's something that belongs to their generation.''

At twenty-nine, Blade barely belongs to their generation, but his ''aura,'' he says, is ''forever young.'' With strong features and thinning dark hair worn long and slicked back into a ponytail, he conveys authority. His hands, though large, are smooth, soft, and steady, a surgeon's hands, but there is no compassion in these hands or his face. He must get a primal thrill out of inserting needles into flesh.

"And, the S/M connection," he says, nodding his head solemnly. "Don't forget the S/M connection. Even if they don't really know what S/M is all about, they get off on feeling a little pain with the piercings, on thinking they're part of something dark and exciting, they're marked somehow. Piercing is more than rebellion, it's sexual rebellion. Your generation had free love. This generation has AIDS. What are they going to do? Can they outfuck their parents without killing themselves before they're thirty? Not likely, is it?

"They pierce themselves."

Trained at the Gauntlet, Inc., the California-based chain of piercing salons, Blade "freelances," so to speak. A master in the S/M subculture, he has a dungeon in the East Village, where he performs piercings with pain—light, medium, or heavy. A lot of his New York clients are young professionals, lawyers, accountants, bankers, who pay thirty to fifty dollars to get a secret thrill knowing there's something unexpected under their white shirts and blouses while they're walking the corporate lines. He also services a contingent of "frat boys," from New York University, Columbia, and other schools, who "use piercings to get girls and get back at their parents."

"Can you imagine what the folks back home think when Junior is home for the holidays and walking through the house naked from the waist up, his nipple ring winking at them?" he asks, laughing. "It's worth a little pain for the

discomfort it causes the parental unit. A guy can't get Mummy and Daddy with an earring anymore, because Mummy and Daddy have social friends, men, who wear earrings."

Blade also does "scenes," costing one hundred dollars and more, like the S/M marriage last weekend in which he pierced the bride's clitoral hood and the groom's penis.

"I gave him the Prince Albert, which is the most popular penis piercing now. It's done through the urethra at the base of the penis head. It's quick and heals rapidly. Some men say it enhances sexual pleasure for both partners."

"The bride and the groom couldn't have sex that night, could they?"

"Oh, no," he says, laughing hard. "Not for four to six weeks. People who get infected are the ones who don't wait for the healing to be completed before they try it out."

Blade has already discussed Dina's piercing in advance with her, because he wanted to be sure she knew what to expect now and later, as she's healing. He's told her how to perform the aftercare and how long to wait before masturbating or having intercourse. She knows, he assures m "what to look for," so she will call him if anything g wrong.

"You can't emphasize strongly enough that people to go to a piercer who knows what he's doing. Any can put a shingle out. You don't need to be certified b governing board. I sterilize my needles, use them on throw them away. Unsterile needles can transmit hepatitis, and other diseases. I have an autoclave s in the dungeon, and I always use surgeon's glov grins. "I'm like a doctor's office, except for one t'

it's only a matter of time until branding becomes as acceptable as tattooing.''

''Branding,'' I repeat. ''With hot irons?''

He nods affirmatively.

''Isn't that what they do to calves?''

''Same principle, except you make patterns or designs in the skin by layering the brands. You can hear the flesh sizzle. The smell is something, like a charred piece of meat, or some people say like bacon frying in a pan. Maybe it depends on how fat you are.

''Or cutting,'' he continues. ''They mark themselves with knives. A girl who came in the shop last week told me she cuts herself because she lets her emotions run out with the blood. She has knife marks on her thighs and belly. Another girl keeps reopening the same cut. She's built a thick curling scar on her arm.''

Blade excuses himself to prepare for the ritual of the piercing, which, he has acknowledged, will be a ''toned down'' version of the ritual he performs in his own dungeon. Dina wants the ambience of being tortured, some pain, not agony. She wants to show her friends what she can take, and it will be Blade's job to enhance her performance, to lend her true grit. Dina's parents, members of the moneyed artistic community, have homes in Manhattan, the Hamptons, and Paris. They are vacationing in Switzerland, so Dina has told Blade she can ''have marks.'' He has no intention of sending her home with marks, only a new metal addition to her body.

''Leanne wants to talk to you,'' Lauren says, touching my arm tentatively. ''She wants to be interviewed.''

Leanne is standing by herself in a corner of the room framed by two five-foot dracaenas, one on either side. She isn't much taller than the plants, thin and giving the impression of wispiness that is natural, not associated with anorexia. Her light brown hair is teased, sprayed, and lifted around her head, the younger version of the helmet her grandmother may wear. She puts her hand out. There is a small spike running through the fleshy skin connecting her thumb with her the rest of her hand. The area is reddened, inflamed. I steel myself not to wince as I touch the end of her fingers in lieu of a handshake.

"I have thirteen piercings," she says, and she enumerates them for me. Two nipples, two labia, one navel, one nose, one hand, six in the ears. "I want at least that many more."

Why?

"This is my way of being different," she says. I look around the room. *Everyone* is wearing black and is shot full of metal. Different from whom? "I am an individual. I am saying, 'This is my body.' It doesn't belong to my parents or my boyfriends. It's mine. Do you understand?"

"Piercing is symbolic," the slender young man behind me says. I turn to face him. His earlobes are smooth, untouched by the gun, but tiny gold rings outline his eyebrows. "Piercing symbolizes freedom and control to us. Life is dangerous, you know. You could die of AIDS or something. Life is painful. People hurt you and you have no control over what they can do to you.

"I live in the same building as the Japanese student who was killed last year. She was stabbed getting her key out of her purse. She died on the floor of the lobby before anyone could help her.

"I control this, my piercings. I decide when and where and how I am going to hurt; and the best thing is I get something out of my pain. I have these excellent piercings."

He sticks out his tongue at me to display the barbell through it. The silver bell is wet with saliva. White and mushy flecks stick to one end. He must have just eaten mashed potatoes or cream of wheat.

"This and seven in each brow," he says. "That's all I have so far. I plan to do my nipples, navel, and nostril soon." Nipples, navel, and nostril are the three most common sites for nontraditional piercing. "I did an unusual thing, starting with the tongue. I've never met anyone else who got their first piercing there."

Why did you?

"I saw someone on television with a pierced tongue, a woman. I liked the way it looked, the surprise element of it being there when you open your mouth. You were surprised, weren't you? I saw it on your face. You were surprised even here, where you are expecting piercings. And it isn't a gay thing, the tongue."

I turn back to Leanne and ask, "Is that why you want more piercings? To symbolize freedom and control?"

"I guess," she says. "I just like the way they look and feel, and I want more. It doesn't make me a freak, you know. In this society, if I had three hundred pairs of shoes, I would be, like, so excellent. Maybe I would like to have three hundred piercings. It takes more than signing a credit slip to get three hundred piercings. It should say something about a person, being able to do that.''

I circulate around the room, soliciting opinions on the psychology of piercing. Men and women cite the same reasons, freedom—*sexual* freedom—control, to be different, to be part of something, to claim their bodies as their own. Veiled references are made to childhood sex abuse. Have they been abused? No one makes such a claim. Children of our talk show society, they infer that childhood abuse, remembered or not, must be behind everything. And, underlying all, is the theme of machismo or machisma. Yes, it hurts, it hurts good. Real men and women bite down on the pain stick and pierce. Pain is sexy.

"Piercing is a way of connecting to African rituals," says Todd, a pale Nordic blond who could not possibly have a trace of African blood in his veins. "In Africa, piercings are part of certain rituals, which signify becoming a man. Your piercing is like your emblem of manhood."

"Yet piercings are more common in the white community than the black," I point out.

"Well, they have the kente cloth and all that," Todd says. "Blacks don't like it when you wear their cloth."

"There's a difference between people who will pierce only their genitals and those who do their faces," says Kirsten, nineteen. "I've been to San Francisco and seen men and women with so much metal on their faces you can't look at them in the sun. They are making a statement. A lot of people hide their statements by piercing only their nipples or genitals. Those are the S/M types who try to pass for straight in the world. So what if you have pierced labia if your face looks like you could be in the Miss America pageant?''

Blade walks by while I am listening to two boys earnestly explaining why intense parental disapproval has nothing to do with what they're doing.

''I'm part of these kids' fantasy,'' he whispers in my ear. ''I make it happen. I control it.''

About ten years ago, I heard almost exactly the same words from a stripper I was interviewing for an article on the club where she worked. She told me she made and controlled the fantasies of her audience.

''Have you asked Dina why she's doing this?'' Kirsten wants to know. ''I think she's doing it for all the wrong reasons.''

Four heads—two male, two female—nod in agreement. Dina, who means to impress the assemblage with her bravado, is having her motives questioned behind her back. I glance across the room at Dina, a shapely redhead dressed in black leather pants, black leather boots, and a halter affair that looks like the framework of a bra, lifting and exposing her breasts like an offering to the world. She is taut with excitement as she swigs from a can of Heineken. For the past hour, she has been thrusting her breasts out, in case the bra failed to provide enough thrust, in case we failed somehow to get the point.

''What are the wrong reasons?'' I ask.

''She's doing it to please her boyfriend,'' says the Nordic guy enamored of African rituals. ''He's got this idea that having her clitoris pierced will make her his sex slave." All eyes turn toward the boyfriend, a pasty-faced man in his early twenties with lank, greasy brown hair pulled back from his face, who, at five-foot-eight or so, is shorter than Dina. "He talks leather culture, but he isn't really part of it."

"You don't see him getting his cock pierced, do you?" a young woman says, snorting. I wonder: Does snorting make her nose ring tremble? "He wants her to do it to see what it feels like because he's too big a wimp to do it himself."

"He thinks having seventeen rings in one ear makes him a god," Kirsten says. "Fuck him."

As if he knows we're talking about him, he looks across the room at us, then looks away quickly.

The ritual begins. Dina, stripped of all clothing except the leather bra skeleton and black leather wristbands, is tied down to a long folding table that someone has borrowed from his mother's laundry room and brought here in the trunk of a rented car. Her legs are open and up, spread wide, knees bent in the childbirth position. They are trembling slightly. Her nipples are erect, her breathing is shallow. A hanging lamp over her genital area provides illumination for Blade. Her pubic hair is light brown, not red, the color of her hair. We stand around the table, each of us holding a lighted candle.

With a suede flogger, Blade lightly slaps Dina's breasts, belly, and inner thighs. She moans softly. He asks her if she is feeling okay, and she says she is. He puts on a pair of surgical gloves, pushes her labia open, and probes her body until the little pink clitoris is exposed. If your clitoris is too

278

small, you can't have this piercing done. He deftly swabs the clitoris and the hood, the fold of skin covering it, with a cotton ball.

"Don't move," he tells her. "You have to keep still while I'm doing this."

She nods her understanding, and her boyfriend, he of the seventeen ear holes, places his hands on her shoulders and leans over the table to look into her eyes. She flinches as Blade slices the needle vertically through the hood. A drop of blood appears. He follows the needle with a small gold ring, which induces more bleeding and elicits a cry from Dina. Then he swabs the area of the piercing again, and it's over. A few yelps and cheers break the silence.

Blade and the boyfriend unfasten the straps binding her to the table and help her stand.

"Feels great," she says, smiling weakly.

An hour later, she thanks me for coming and says, "It hurts like hell, but I'm glad I did it. I'm throbbing big time down there. I want this. It's something I felt like I had to do for myself. I became a woman today."

I ride back into Manhattan with five people who are going to Limelight to see Genitorturers, a Miami-based S/M band, perform. One of the five is the son of a couple who were at Woodstock. I ask the passengers if they consider themselves sexual outlaws. Cheers, whoops, catcalls fill the air. They do.

They call me the next day to tell me what I missed. The band wore leather masks, multiple body jewelry in their multiple piercings, and little else. A member of the band urinated on the audience. An audience volunteer performed cunnilingus on the lead singer. A woman dressed as a dom ran a spike through her own tongue. (The hole was undoubtedly already there, my informants said.) A penis was pierced on stage. A clitoris was pierced on stage.

And we thought Ozzy Osbourne was wild and crazy when he bit the heads off live bats during his concerts.

How was the music? I ask.

Nothing special, they say.

Chapter 16

Working Within the Kinks

SAN FRANCISCO

"The question is not if it's normal, but if it's a problem," Bernie Zilbergeld, Ph.D., San Francisco sex therapist and author of *The New Male Sexuality,* told me at the beginning of my research.

"Normal" is a statistical term, defining what is typical or average—and defining it by the numbers alone. For the purposes of this book, I considered sex practices "outside the norm" to be those that a majority of people tell researchers and survey questionnaires they do not practice, at least on a regular basis. "Normal" is nonjudgmental. Numbers carry no moralistic connotation. They simply are. If nine out of ten people quizzed like peanut butter, does that make the tenth person immoral? No. His feelings about peanut butter, however, are outside the norm.

Therapists tend to take a nonjudgmental view of their patients' sexuality. They say sex is a problem if it's illegal (exposing yourself in public, having sex with minors), if it's compulsive (you have to masturbate several times a day, which cuts into your job productivity), or if the way you want to have sex creates problems for you and your partner. If you are a foot fetishist and your wife loves having her toes sucked to the exclusion of all else, you have no problem.

The problem with this "no problem" view of sexuality is that it gives tacit endorsement of whipping, mutilation, and relationships in which power is cruelly used, and perhaps abused, under the umbrella of dominance-and-submission "play." Nobody takes a stand against destructive consensual behaviors in the name of sex, except rigidly moralistic critics on the right, the kind of people who may very well be at least partly responsible for the existence of such behaviors in the first place.

"I encourage patients to get rid of the word *normal* and focus instead on what they and their partners want in their sex lives," Zilbergeld told me.

Other therapists echoed his advice. In fact, some of the ones I interviewed, particularly in California, admitted to indulging in sexual practices pretty far outside the norm themselves. A male and female therapist, from different parts of the country, who are in dominant/submissive relationships, each play the submissive role. The man is fairly active in the S/M scene in his community, making him the expert of choice for S/M couples who seek counseling.

Is this a good idea?

I don't think so. Several therapists who would not speak for publication out of fear of sounding judgmental and repressive do not think so. Freed by the shutting down of the tape recorder, therapists typically save their best remarks for the final five minutes when they are showing the reporter out the door.

I went to Isadora Alman, Ph.D.—therapist and author, known nationwide through her syndicated newspaper column, ''Ask Isadora,'' which appears in weekly newspapers such as *The San Francisco Bay Guardian* and *The Village Voice*—because I hoped she might speak more openly. Witty, sophisticated, and very well respected within the therapeutic community, Isadora, in her own estimation, attracts more than her fair share of alternative lifestylers because she is known for her nonjudgmental attitude.

On the phone she told me about a couple who had come to her for counseling. Dominatrices in a lesbian relationship, they had ''issues'' within their working, not their personal, relationship.

''They were fighting about things like, 'You never sterilize the dildos, and I always have to do that.'

''They knew I wouldn't get bogged down in the peripherals. I would see their issues as the same ones of the couple who say, 'You always chew gum when I type,' or 'You never take out the cat litter.' ''

Maybe she just attracts more than her fair share of such types because she practices in San Francisco, where one sometimes suspects an alternative lifestyle would be a heterosexual, monogamous marriage with children.

In the cab on the way to her house, I make a list of questions for Isadora.

Can you be involved in S/M on any but the most superficial level and be healthy?

Could you possibly have a healthy, intimate relationship if you are, or are with, a fetishist?

What about swingers? Piercers? Crossdressers?

Is there a psychological profile for the average cross-dresser—dominant, submissive, etc.?

Can one get into, and then with any degree of ease, get out of relationships like these?

Is the behavior progressive? For example, if he whips you a little bit now, will he progress to whipping you a lot?

How do you treat people in such relationships?

Any idea of how widespread these behaviors are?

And, a question probably no one could answer, why does the dark practice of S/M flourish in this beautiful city, with its spectacular views springing into the line of vision every other time you careen around a corner?

It is an overly ambitious list.

Isadora apologizes for the cat, who climbs up on the big soft black leather chair to sniff me. She offers to lock him out of her office. He kisses me. I tell her the cat can stay. Seated across from me in a matching chair, Isadora puts her feet up on the black leather ottoman between the chairs. She's wearing ballet shoes and comfortable clothes. I'm wearing three-inch heels and a miniskirted suit. I kick off my shoes and put my feet up, too. The cat settles down between us, with one eye on the tape recorder. Isadora is warm, sharp, funny, and she seems like a woman who enjoys sex. I like her immediately.

We talk about S/M relationships first. Is the goal to help people get out of these relationships?

"My goal is whatever their goal is," she says, beginning

in the careful way experts speak for publication. "It's certainly not for me to say what their goal should be. Somebody may say I want to renegotiate my relationship, or equalize it, or we want to play different games, or one of us wants this and one of us doesn't. I need both partners to tell me what they want, to restate their goals, so I can help them focus on what they do want and are willing to give each other. But I don't decide for them what their goals should be."

"What if you're faced with a couple in a heavy S/M relationship?" I ask her. "They tell you their goal is to intensify the relationship. What do you do?"

"If their goal is not something I can support, I will tell them that and suggest another therapist. For example, if person one said to me I want to own person two, not only in the bedroom, but outside, and person two is agreeing with the goal—I would still have to say, 'I can't support this. Let me give you some recommendations of other professionals.' " She pauses. "I wouldn't say, 'This is disgusting stuff and I want no part of it!' "

We both break into peals of delighted laughter.

Isadora is capable of seeing a couple's problem with his foot fetish or her need to be spanked in the same way she sees a couple's problems with how the money is spent or the chores are divided. These are all issues to be negotiated. They have no moral weight.

She doesn't treat people who are involved with illegal activities. People who have, or want to have, sex with children or animals or are flashers are referred to therapists "more cognizant of the law as well as the psychology."

But consensual spankers, dominants and submissives, foot fetishists—all could be her patients.

"I try to put aside the more exotic aspects of the situation, because that really isn't the issue, and get to the basic problem," she says. "Often the problem is finding a partner or getting what you want from the partner you have."

She leaves discussions of what causes a behavior to the Freudian analysts. If I thought I was going to find the answer to the question "Why?" I was mistaken. Perhaps "Why?" is rightly more a journalist's question than a therapist's concern.

"How people got to want what they want is of no interest to me," she says. "I'm not an analytical therapist. I don't feel one has to understand where desires come from to accomplish a patient's goals. Turn-ons are lost in the mists of time. We have no clear way of knowing why. Even if you do know why you are turned on to something, so what?

"I have a dear friend who is attracted to fat legs, thick from knee to foot. In our society, that has never been considered sexy. He thinks he can explain his attraction. His mother, a Polish immigrant, was almost fifty when he was born. His earliest memories are of being an infant, crawling around the skirts of his mother and her friends. He remembers his feelings of excitement being around them, smelling their perfumes, listening to their voices, looking at their fat legs. He's deduced that's where he got his turn-on. Probably, he's right. But maybe his third-grade teacher had fat legs, and he's forgotten. Maybe the Polish women didn't have fat legs as he remembers. We'll never know. So what? If liking fat legs is not an issue for him and he has no trouble finding women with fat legs, what difference does it make why he likes them?''

For Isadora, the basic questions are: Are you okay with your sexuality? Can you find satisfaction? Is what you want within the confines of law?

I tell her about Lisa, married to Ryan, the doctor who has a foot fetish. She wants a baby. They haven't had sex since he ejaculated on her feet. She finds his foot fetish quite distasteful. This isn't a basic question. It is what Isadora terms a ''partner issue.''

What can Lisa do?

Take the issue out of the charged sexual realm. Isadora is speaking in her patient tone of voice. I'm supposed to be getting this by now, aren't I?

''What if you were married to a man who eats only oysters?'' she asks. ''Is that a problem? How does his diet affect you? If you can't go out to eat anywhere with him except an oyster bar, that could be a problem. How big a problem?''

A big problem. A man who eats only oysters would be incredibly boring to me. And what if he ate them raw? The sight of raw oysters turns my stomach.

Lisa wants sex, meaning cunnilingus, fellatio, intercourse. She wants to be inseminated by her husband's sperm during the act of intercourse. Up to a point in their marriage, he was able to give her what she wanted. Now he can't move past her feet. Can she realistically be expected to call this state of affairs a ''partner issue'' and approach it in a nonjudgmental way?

Isadora says she can.

"She's saying, 'I'm not getting what I want.' Can he give it to her? Can she get it elsewhere? Will he care if she has sex outside the marriage? Will she care? What if she has another man's baby? Once they begin to explore their options, they will know what is acceptable and what isn't. Most couples believe everything would be solved if the other one would straighten up and fly right. They have to look at each aspect of the relationship and ask if there is a way to salvage the good.

"It's hard to do these things when sex is the issue. If something else is the issue, couples can more easily see the negotiation. Sex is so loaded. It's easy to make judgments."

I tell her Ryan has decided to see a dominatrix in the hopes he will then be able to have sex with his wife after his foot-worship sessions.

If not a dom, then whom? The more you deviate from society's standards of beauty or standards of sexual behavior, Isadora maintains, the more trouble you will have finding a suitable partner.

"Sex means intercourse for most people, not oral or anal sex or mutual masturbation, but *intercourse*," she says. "Other practices are foreplay or kink. If your idea of sex isn't intercourse as the main event, you will have fewer opportunities for getting your needs met than the 'average' person."

Compounding their difficulties, people with unusual desires are reluctant to admit they have them, Isadora reminds me. How much harder is it to find what you want if you dare not say what that is?

"Few people laugh if you're twenty pounds over-weight," she says, "but if you like to suck toes or wear diapers, yes, people laugh. Who wants to risk exposing himself to such ridicule? Who wants to risk being rejected by someone they care about, someone with whom they want to share a bed?"

Then how do they find partners?

"Only two ways: They go where like-minded people are, to the S/M clubs and support groups or to the pages of newsletters aimed at fetishists. Or they keep quiet about their desires and go into the world at large, find someone to love, then hope they can persuade that person to accept their desires. It's risky."

It's sad. No one I've interviewed uses the word *sad* to describe this state of affairs. Is *sad* a judgment call?

Aren't we talking about men when we talk about kink? "No," she says, which surprises me, because it is practically an article of faith with the experts that deviant sexual behavior is stamped with the male gender symbol. Who, us, women, kinky? You don't find women paying men in a mask to spank them.

"I think you would if it were safer for women to do that," she says, smiling at my disbelief. "There isn't a pro-vision for women to get these things safely. Men aren't as much at risk of being raped or physically overcome. Yes, there is some physical risk for men, but not nearly as much. Safety is an enormous factor. Even if she has a desire to be spanked or tied up, a woman has to be really careful about sharing this desire with a man.

"Women need the safety of an ongoing relationship

with someone they trust before they can explore their 'kinkier' sides, if you will. When a woman is feeling safe in a relationship, you see the flowering of her sexuality, whatever form the flowering takes.''

But, I persist, women aren't fetishists. How does she explain that? The cat, bored with us, swats at the tape recorder.

''Men are more used to thinking about their specific sexual requirements,'' she says, admonishing the cat with a frown, which he ignores. ''A typical man will say, 'I want a set of breasts, thirty-four-C with a pinkish aureole.' Or 'I want a woman with long legs.' The person attached is secondary to the desired characteristics.

''Women are eroticized to preferring a certain body part or activity because someone who elicits their erotic feelings has that body part or likes that activity. They move from the person to the part or the behavior. You said you like large penises. Did you like them before you experienced sex with a man who had one?''

''Well, how would I know I liked them before I had one?''

She laughs.

''I like medium-sized ones, too. A small one on an excellent lover is good, too.''

''You see,'' she says. ''Women see the person first, the part second.''

''So. Men make women kinky. Isn't that what you're saying?''

''No, that's not what I'm saying.''

* * *

Is this behavior healthy or not? We have danced around the question without addressing it head-on. Can fetishism be healthy? Group sex? Crossdressing? Piercing? Is there a standard of mental or sexual health that can be applied to any of these behaviors?

"On a professional level, I use the word *atypical* rather than *healthy*," she says. "I will say a behavior is 'not as popular,' which is not judgmental. But on a personal level, I have really strong feelings about what I like and don't like.

"It can be hard for me around S/M issues to maintain that detached, nonjudgmental stance. I do have a lot of judgments about people who do this sort of thing. They are really prejudices."

"I am having those same prejudices."

"I'm sure you are. I'm picking that up from you," she says kindly. "There's some wonderful people whom I admire on many levels, in San Francisco particularly, people who play in the S/M arena. What they do is inexplicable to me. I also know people who really enjoy skiing. I don't understand why people would spend pots of money on bulky equipment they have to carry around and store, freeze their asses off in nasty weather, and call that fun. I don't understand how people could be spanked or pierced or humiliated and call that fun. I can say, 'You like to ski. I find that weird, but I love you anyway.' I can say, 'You like to have your penis tortured. I find that weird. But I don't know if I love you anyway. It's *harder* to love you anyway.'

"That's my personal prejudice," she says.

* * *

Why? I always come back to why.

"I try not to grapple with why," she says.

"I'm still grappling with why, how, what does it mean," I say in some exasperation. I feel like she is my therapist now. It's okay to express frustration to your therapist. "Why do they do these hurtful things to themselves and others? Why would a beautiful young woman want to have her body pierced in numerous and painful ways? How can someone bear the humiliation, not to mention the physical discomfort, of being another person's submissive? What does their behavior say about these people and their families and, perhaps, our society?"

"I don't grapple with the why," she repeats. "It isn't useful."

"I have trouble not grappling with it when, for example, I talk to a couple like the one I saw before coming here. They are in an S/M relationship—"

"In an S/M relationship, or do they just practice S/M?"

"They describe it as 'an S/M relationship.' He said to me, 'She will tell you how she feels about an experience. That's just her feeling. I will tell you how it *is*.' "

"I would have been tempted to kick him in the balls."

"Yes. That journalistic distance is difficult to maintain sometimes."

I tell her about a couple I interviewed who said that on a typical weekend, she, naked except for her harnesses and nipple clamps, endures three or four "discipline sessions." Will that escalate to four or five sessions, then more? Could the relationship ever change so that she is disciplined less or not at all? Is it possible for her to regain the ground she has lost, *lost* being my word?

Like other therapists, Isadora says there is no set pattern. She might get tired and leave—or he might. One of them may fall in love with someone else. Or the behavior may escalate. Most often, she says, it doesn't. She compares light S/M to marijuana use. The majority of people who smoke occasionally will continue to smoke occasionally— or stop using. How many marijuana users move on to heroin?

"Taking carefully into consideration your judgments and mine, one of them might get into therapy and outgrow this," she says. "You and I might say in a private conversation without a tape recorder, 'She's getting healthier and didn't need this kind of mischegoss [crazy madness] in her life anymore.' "

"I would say, 'She finally got rid of this asshole.' "

"Privately, I would say, too, that a woman who decided she would no longer tolerate this kind of relationship was making a healthy step forward. I would support that as a healthy step forward. He would simply say they were not compatible, and look for another broken woman who was willing to put up with this kind of nonsense.

"Or he might be the one to decide he wants out. He might want a more egalitarian relationship and lose her to another master. Or he might decide he's been topping because he's really a bottom."

"I interviewed a man who topped with women," I say. "Now he thinks he's found himself bottoming with men."

"Maybe he has found himself for the moment; and maybe he will go through another metamorphosis. Sexual predilections are more fluid than people think they are.

Even one's orientation is somewhat open to change. But I've been accused of being an optimist in a lot of ways.''

Now that we're getting down, I have to find out what she thinks of these S/M support groups. Is this behavior that should be supported by groups? They sit around all evening talking about the way they have sex and the issues surrounding the way they have sex. Is all this support necessary?

"I can't imagine a group of vanilla people sitting around talking about the way they have sex all night," I say. "Does that mean sex dominates the lives of lifestylers more than it does ours?"

"Yes, and that may not be a matter of choice. Fat women in support groups talk about how it is to be fat. You won't see blond women sitting around talking about how it is to be blond. Fat is created as a problem by our society. Blond isn't. Blond women have no need to form groups to discuss their hair.

"People who are into S/M talk about what they do because they are labeled constantly as 'weird, sick, disturbed.' To get support and feel validated, they join groups of like-minded people. Maybe they don't define themselves by sexual expression. Maybe it's how they're defined. Gay people say this all the time. They say there is much more to being gay than sex, but people think of them only as 'cocksuckers.' When lifestylers get together with social friends, S/M is probably not the only topic.

"Outlaws are defined and created by the society in which they live."

The cat knocks the recorder over, and Isadora pauses

while I pick it up from the floor and reposition it on safer ground, a nearby table.

"I agree with you that it sounds odd to hear people identify themselves so strongly by the way they have sex," she says. "I have friends into S/M who say they practice an S/M lifestyle. I am a heterosexual, but I don't say I practice a penis/vagina lifestyle."

For me, female submission is the most troublesome aspect of consensual sadomasochism. S/M is scary to me as a woman. I am concerned for the safety and well-being of some of the women I've met. I don't like to see male submissives, either. It bothers me to see anyone consent to humiliation or to call pain something that is "lovingly administered." But the male submissives don't seem as endangered to me as the women. Men have more power in society than women do.

"The other scary aspect of female submission for some women is the political incorrectness of it," Isadora points out. "I can't tell you how many letters I get from women who have S/M fantasies. This is very common. When a woman has fantasies that don't fit her political ideology, she's scared or feels guilty. In today's column, there's a letter from a woman who gets hot being wrestled into submission. She loves to be wrestled knowing she's going to lose."

She reaches over, picks up a copy of the column from her big oak desk, and hands it to me. The letter writer felt embarrassed and guilty about her desires. Isadora reassured her.

A fantasy is not a desire. Most of us have all fantasized

about being raped. Even men fantasize that. I wouldn't worry about a submissive fantasy. Actually putting on the nipple clamps is something else, though. I would worry about where that could take me.

Since she won't go into the why, I try to get Isadora to set some limits. How far is too far? When do you know you've gone that far? But she is an adept verbal dodger. We have no problem condemning clitoridectomies, removal of the clitoris and often surrounding tissues, a custom still practiced in Africa, the Far East, and other parts of the world. Why are we determinedly neutral on clitoral piercings, which, doctors have told me, can lead to infection and scarring that results in loss of sexual feeling and disfigurement?

"There is pain involved in our culture in being female, in being a sex object," she says, citing corsets, underwire bras, and plastic surgery.

Finally, she says, "You wear high heels. I never wear anything but flats because heels are painful. Don't they hurt your feet?"

"I love high heels."

"Why do you love them?"

"They make me feel sexy. Taller. More powerful."

"But they hurt."

"Sometimes."

I look down at my shoes, lying sideways on the floor. They are Italian leather slingbacks, in black with a small platform and green heels. I love them. They hurt sometimes. Are my shoes a symbol of female submission that I willingly accept? Where are the limits?

She has another appointment in ten minutes. I turn off

the tape recorder and pet the cat, who purrs gratefully. We exchange cat anecdotes. My grandson, Opus, is a cat. I put my heels back on, gather my things, and hug Isadora good-bye.

Chapter 17

The Dysfunctional Perspective

BALTIMORE

"I was actively involved in S/M for almost five years," Linda says, "but S/M colored my life from earliest childhood. I put my Barbie dolls in bondage and sought out the books in the library that featured spanking, whipping, caning, books like *David Copperfield*. My mother dressed me in frills and ruffles and people said I looked like a little doll; and in my canopied bed at night I lifted my baby-doll pajama top and pinched my own nipples to feel the pain. I have been free of the behavior for two years, but I still feel like S/M colors my life. It owns my memories and still touches some of my fantasies.

"S/M isn't something you decide to do or something you become after being exposed to it. S/M is stamped on you."

Linda, a petite brunette in her late thirties, agreed to meet me at Baltimore's Inner Harbour when she was in the city on business. A Midwestern attorney, she has lived in several major cities and participated in S/M social-group activities in two of them. Because she fears reprisals from former associates, she does not want to be any more specific than that.

"I don't think any of them will do me physical harm," she says, lighting a cigarette.

We are seated in the light-flooded food court in the mall's upper level on a weekday afternoon. Two young women with toddlers in strollers occupy a table several feet away from us. I can't help looking at them and wondering if either of those innocent babes will be trussing their Barbies in a few years.

"Those people are not above causing me other kinds of problems, like making sure my partners or my big clients know about my past," she says, smoking furiously. "No one except my husband knows I was once an active sexual masochist.

"The S/M crowd is very tight, very smug that what they do is great. There is one kind of support you can't get within an S/M support group—and that's help in getting better. They think they are fine. Once I asked a group of submissive women and dominant men if they thought there was anything potentially dangerous or maybe sick about what we were doing. They went off on me. That night, my master tied me to the hook in our bedroom, blindfolded and gagged me, and gave me fifty strokes with the whip. Then he performed cunnilingus on me, while I was still tied up, until I came, to prove to me this was what I wanted, this was who I was.

"They make fun of vanilla people," she says, biting her

lower lip and looking quickly away as if she fears I'll be offended to hear the S/M crowd might be making fun of my way of having sex. "Thank God, I am a vanilla person now. When I fall asleep next to my husband, after having shared loving sex, I say a little prayer of thanks that I have found a way to have an orgasm without getting the shit beat out of me first."

Two of the nation's foremost authorities on paraphilias and their treatment say Linda is right when she claims, "S/M is stamped on you." Dr. Fred Berlin, M.D., Ph.D., director of the National Institute for the Study, Prevention, and Treatment of Sexual Trauma at Johns Hopkins University in Baltimore, is considered by many to be the successor to John Money, M.D., Ph.D., the internationally renowned therapist who established the research department at Johns Hopkins that led to this institute. Though officially "semiretired" from his position at Johns Hopkins, Money lectures extensively in this country and throughout the world on paraphilias, their causes, and treatments. Both Money and Berlin agree that S/M interests, fetishism, and other paraphilias are probably imprinted in childhood.

Money coined the term "lovemap" to describe the imprinting process that determines what our adult sexual preferences and predilections will be. The lovemap is "a personalized representation or template in the mind and in the brain that depicts the idealized lover and the idealized program of sexuoerotic activity with that lover." Everyone has a lovemap, as personalized as a fingerprint. Money calls it "both a repository and a readout of your sexuoerotic agenda." He says the lovemaps of paraphiliacs have been "vandalized" in some way in very early childhood.

No one fully understands how the imprinting process works. But no one fully understands how and why we become sexual beings in exactly the way we do. Because funds for sex research are limited in this country, we know less than we probably should at this point in human history.

Most researchers believe that people with S/M interests grew up with extremely negative attitudes about sex. They were taught that sex is bad, sinful, dirty. Maybe they were punished for their developing sexuality. Yet not every child who was disciplined for masturbating or grew up in a sex-negative family becomes a masochist or sadist or fetishist. Why would one in a family of abused children become a sadist or masochist while the others do not? The experts do not know. Nor can they explain how some paraphiliacs have no memory of childhood abuse or sex negativism in their parents.

Many of my interviewees described early childhood feelings of lust associated with the giving or receiving of pain, with feet or leather, satin or rubber. Some of them have erotic memories going back to the cradle, which I do not find entirely credible. One diaper wearer claims he can recall the erections he had as an infant in diapers.

His confession prompted one of my friends, to whom I'd told his story, to say, "Now we're reading that memories of child abuse may be false memories, sometimes put there by therapists. Do you think that Diaper Man really remembers his baby erections, or that he thinks he does because the guys in his diaper support group have put them in his mind?"

* * *

304

"I have been aroused by women's feet for as long as I can remember," says Bob, who, like Linda, agreed to meet me in Baltimore to discuss what he terms his "recovery" from foot fetishism. "I remember little girls in Mary Janes and white socks with ruffled tops and high school girls in loafers with no socks and flat shoes with stockings. Heels, oh, God, I remember when girls began wearing heels."

Baltimore is a significant city for both Linda and Bob, who do not know each other, because each received treatment through Johns Hopkins for what they label their "sexual dysfunctions."

Bob, who recently celebrated his fortieth birthday, sought help two years ago because he and his wife wanted a child. His story differed from others I'd heard in a very striking way. They met on a red-eye flight from Los Angeles to New York, had a whirlwind two-week courtship conducted in both cities, a courtship that did not include sex, and got married in San Diego. On the honeymoon in Cabos San Lucas, she discovered he was a foot fetishist.

"Wasn't the fact that you didn't have sex during this very brief courtship a clue to her that something might be wrong?" I ask him.

"We were both involved in high-stakes negotiations for our respective companies, which meant we were stressed out and overscheduled," he says. "We also both agreed we wanted to save sex for our wedding day. We came from strong Christian backgrounds. It seemed the right thing to do."

"Still," I persist, "if a mature man proposes marriage without ever having made love to a woman, doesn't he have his reasons for rushing?"

"You're right," he concedes. "I had my reasons. To be perfectly honest, she has some problems with sex, too. Maybe she had her own reasons. We were both happy to tell ourselves we were too moral to jump into bed at the time."

Kelly, his wife, age thirty-nine when they wed, had never had an orgasm during lovemaking. No man had ever performed cunnilingus on her. Nor had she performed fellatio. Her sexual insecurity and lack of experience for a woman her age probably contributed to her eagerness to wed.

"We were a dysfunctional unit waiting to connect," he says, laughing. "The honeymoon was a disaster. She expected all of her romantic fantasies to come true. Suddenly I would be a prince who awakened her sleeping desire. I don't know what I thought she would be. I'd had a few partners, enough women to know how they feel about foot worship. Why did I think this would be different?

"I told her I wanted to bathe her, shampoo her hair, and give her a pedicure before we made love. She was delighted, until the pedicure took too long. I spent an hour bathing, exfoliating, creaming, and perfuming her perfect little feet. She was trying to pull me up to hold her and kiss her, and I kept making love to her feet." He stops. A blush creeps up from his neck into his cheeks. Bob is a fair-skinned redhead of Irish descent who blushes easily. "I had my penis between her toes, like I was fucking her, and she began screaming.

"After I'd calmed her down, I told her I didn't think of sex the way other men did. She slept on the chaise longue for the entire week we were in Cabos."

They did progress to kissing and fondling during the week, but the marriage was not consummated because Kelly refused to take off her socks and shoes. Bob couldn't get an erection without seeing her feet. She threatened an annulment. He begged her not to leave him. They went back home to Los Angeles to their separate condos and a negotiated truce: She gave him six months to get help. He came to Baltimore, because he'd read about the institute.

There are two general theories held by psychiatric researchers about why a person, usually a man, develops a paraphilia:

Premature and traumatic exposure to sex, often in the form of child sex abuse. Some studies estimate that as many as one in four boys is sexually abused by men as well as women. According to Fred Berlin, 75 percent of the men who are treated at the institute were victims of child sex abuse. For reasons researchers don't fully understand, when girls are abused they are more likely to become inhibited sexually, while abused boys are more likely to become paraphiliacs.

Girls, however, may become sexual masochists.

"Masochism is one of the very few paraphilias in which female cases are often seen," Berlin says. "There are almost no female compulsive voyeurs, exhibitionists, sadists, serial rapists. Masochism is the exception."

But what about all those female dominants? I wonder. Berlin reminds me he does not treat people who merely play at dominance and submission or professional dominants, who, he believes, have honed their particular skills in response to the demands of the marketplace, a surfeit of men seeking submissive experiences.

An overzealous suppression of natural curiosity about sex, for religious or other reasons. Little boys who are taught that sex is dirty and are punished for their interest in it may become men with fetishes or obsessions. Little girls may become masochists. If the antisex messages children hear when growing up have religious overtones, they may begin to associate sexual urges with religious feelings, such as worship, guilt, and punishment. Perhaps this explains why some sadomasochists talk about "the spiritual journey" of pain leading to sexual ecstasy—or why some fetishists perform ritualistic acts of worship toward feet.

Many paraphiliacs are outwardly pious, devout men. While secretly acting out behaviors they profess to condemn, they portray themselves in public as models of rectitude. Both Money and Berlin refuse to label such stances "hypocritical." This public propriety may be a manifestation of the "atonement" phase of a paraphiliac's behavior cycle after he has been repeatedly compelled to act out behaviors that he finds morally repugnant yet sexually thrilling.

"We don't think of severe repression as a form of sexual abuse, but it can be," Berlin says.

Using case studies of men from repressive religious backgrounds, Money connected perverse male sexual behavior with outwardly devout and self-righteous personalities. Because of their backgrounds, these men feel intense guilt over their hidden "sin," the way they behave sexually. To atone for the "sin" of fetishism or another "sin," they publicly exhort morality. (Consider the Reverend

Jimmy Swaggart, the evangelist caught with a prostitute he paid to masturbate for him.)

"When I see somebody who carries self-righteousness to an excess, I automatically say that if I scratch the surface on this one, I'll find the sin," Money says.

Linda, the sexual masochist, and Bob, the foot fetishist, both come from religious families, hers Catholic, his Methodist. They do not believe their siblings have the same "sexual dysfunctions" as they have had, but they admit they can't be sure.

"My four older brothers were supposed to be priests, and I, the only girl, was supposed to be a nun," Linda says. "None of us has a religious vocation. My mother made countless novenas for our 'vocations.' Her prayers were not answered. I do remember romanticizing the suffering of the saints in childhood. My mother is from South America, and I was also fascinated by the flagellants, who whipped themselves bloody and into religious frenzies on Good Friday. I don't remember my brothers ever having much interest in saints or flagellants.

"If men are supposed to be perverts, why did they turn out okay and I didn't?"

Researchers speculate that men may be more prone to paraphilias for two reasons: Male sexuality in childhood is somehow more fragile—or likely to be damaged—than female sexuality; and adult male sex drives are stronger than female. Why more fragile? No one really knows. The experts point to the animal kingdom for proof of the powerful male sex drive. Female animals are interested in sexual contact with males when they are in heat—and thus fertile—while males are always interested in sexual contact with females. Biology dictates that men who are capable of reproduction at any time must be likewise ready for intercourse at any time.

In an interview I conducted with him many years ago, Money put forth the theory that men may have more paraphilias, because they have the biological imperative to become erect and ejaculate in order to reproduce and find a way to do this at almost any cost. He suggested that their paraphilias may be the small openings through which they must somehow fit, the only passages to their sexuality—and the fulfillment of their biological imperative. (For more information, read *Vandalized Lovemaps*.)

A woman damaged in childhood may simply retreat sexually, he explained, because her biological imperative only requires that she be available for fertilization. As far as nature is concerned, inorgasmia isn't a problem. Impotence is.

"Perhaps," a therapist told Linda in answer to her question about why she, and not her brothers, was sexually outside the limits, "your sex drive was too strong to be shut down. When your sexuality was somehow damaged, you became a masochist because that was the only way you could retain sexual feeling."

Like the heroine of the novel *9 1/2 Weeks*, Linda's masochism put her in the hospital, in a state of emotional and physical collapse.

"I read that book," Linda says, "and found myself saying, 'That's nothing. What she endured was nothing.' I ended up in the hospital with an infection so bad it nearly killed me. The infection began in my nipples. My master had hung weights on the rings through my nipples and hung them there until they bled. The blood and the pus kept coming for days. I had swollen breasts. I was feverish. I was dizzy and too weak to get out of bed.

"The people from my support group came over to take care of me, but nobody thought of taking me to a doctor or a hospital. It's such an article of faith with them that S/M is not dangerous, nobody really gets hurt bad, they couldn't see how bad I was," she speaks in an angry rush, the words tumbling like hot coals from her mouth. "They're in denial when they see something bad happen. They refuse to see it.

"Finally, a neighbor came to look in on me. She saw red streaks running up my neck, and she said I had blood poisoning. When she pulled my gown away and looked at my breasts, she was horrified. She called an ambulance. I almost lost my nipples. I almost lost my *life*."

Berlin only sees "the bad cases," people who were sex offenders, including serial rapists, or their victims, people whose S/M activities were "disruptive and problematic." He has treated female masochists who were afraid their masochism would lead to permanent disability, disfigurement, even death.

"Fetishism can be very destructive in relationships," he says, "but it is benign. Extreme forms of sadism or masochism are very dangerous."

The basic method of treatment for a fetishist like Bob or a masochist like Linda is the same: a combination of counseling and medication, typically medroxyprogesterone acetate, to decrease the sex drive and eliminate obsessive fantasies.

"Drug therapy can help the patient to gain control of the fetish behavior," Berlin says.

A female masochist he treated this way came to him because she was appalled at her own behavior and fearful of what she might do next. She sought out abusive men, had allowed them to cut her, and had even cut her own breasts with a razor blade. When she was not in a state of arousal, she hated what she was doing to herself. Aroused, she continued to do it.

"Medication put her in control of her sex drive," he says. "At last, her sex drive wasn't controlling her. In a calmer state, she was able to work through a lot of her issues in counseling. When she was able to change her sexual pattern, we took her off the medication."

Linda was treated in a similar way. In her case, however, some kind of treatment was mandatory, not elective. When she was admitted to the hospital, she was put in a psychiatric ward. A condition of release from the hospital was that she receive treatment for her masochism.

"The admitting physician took one look at my body and knew I was crazy," she says ruefully. "He was right."

Linda was in group and individual counseling and, later, in sex therapy, where she learned how to replace masochistic fantasies with fantasies of kinder, gentler forms of lovemaking.

"My therapist told me that fantasies of rape and submission and of being swept away are common for women," she says, "because they signify the release of guilt or emotional restraints. They free a woman to enjoy her sexuality. I learned to have more romantic fantasies of being swept away. I pictured myself as Scarlett O'Hara being carried to the bedroom in Rhett's strong arms. It was a slow process. I still sometimes find myself fantasizing the whip when my husband is caressing me. But I stop it. I replace the fantasy with something better."

Bob also received a combination of drug therapy and counseling. Like Linda, he learned gradually to replace the arousing fantasies of feet with other fantasies.

"The problem for the fetishist and his partner is that he has no other way to be aroused," says therapist Bernie Zilbergeld, who has also had success with treating fetishists. "Once a man is aroused by feet, he will always be aroused by feet. But he can expand his sexual repertoire—if he is motivated to change."

Over time, he can learn to become aroused in other ways, through a combination of controlling his fantasies—gradually replacing images of the fetish with more conventional ones—and practicing standard sex-therapy techniques with his partner, which include focused erotic touching, stroking, and kissing. Eventually, he can become aroused and ejaculate without the fetish.

Bob says, "I will always find feet sexually exciting. Now I have learned to find other parts of my wife's body exciting, too."

Unlike most therapists, Dr. Fred Berlin has seen the very dark side of sexual obsession.

"I've seen marriages ruined, careers destroyed, families thrown into bankruptcy," he says. "And I have seen the medical consequences of prolonged heavy S/M activity. I am sure there are couples who enjoy these activities in a less intense way. They have found each other, and they're happy together. I don't see those couples. Obviously, I have a skewed view of sexually obsessive behavior.''

Because he is familiar with the risks, he is ''uncomfortable'' with books and articles that describe obsessive or dangerous activities as simply ''sexual variations.''

''The risk needs to be addressed,'' he says. ''I compare it to drinking. Some people are social drinkers. They will never have a problem with alcohol. Other people are going to drink and become alcoholics. We address that risk in our society.''

Is there a psychological profile—some way of predicting who, like Linda, will be seriously hurt by such behaviors?

Other than a likelihood of abusive or repressive childhood backgrounds, sadists, masochists, fetishists, and other paraphiliacs have little in common, according to Berlin.

''There is no typical profile,'' he says. ''The diversity is really quite surprising. People like this come from all socioeconomic backgrounds. Many are educated, intelligent. Many are not. Their only commonality is what they find sexually arousing.''

Will the behavior necessarily escalate with time?

''Not necessarily. There is no reason to believe an S/M couple will get into trouble if a stable pattern of behavior has been sustained over years. These people are probably keeping their behavior more in the realm of fantasy than physical reality.

''Should a pattern of escalation exist, however, the couple needs to step back and look at what they're doing. If it takes more and more abuse to satisfy one or both of them, they are like drug addicts, needing more and more to get high. They can be on dangerous turf.''

He believes people in the S/M culture who don't admit the risks are "in denial."

"I was definitely in denial for most of the time I was involved in S/M," Linda says, crushing the seventh cigarette she's smoked in the hour we've been sitting in the Inner Harbour food court. "The social groups are designed to keep people in denial. No one is allowed to express doubts about their behavior.''

She excuses herself to buy another cup of coffee from one of the vendors. As she walks toward the coffee shop, I notice her posture—shoulders forward, back hunched, chin down. She walks like a submissive. On the way back with coffee in hand, she has pulled back the shoulders, straightened up.

"Talking about it puts me back into it," she says when she sits down. She lights another cigarette and asks, "What did you think of the people you met in the groups?"

"I liked some and didn't like others. I thought they shared some common traits," I say, resisting the temptation to speak in neutral therapeutic tones, "but the experts say there is no psychological profile of the typical paraphiliac.''

"Traits such as?" she asks, leaning forward intently.

"A coldness, not a meanness, but an inability to be genuinely warm. An inability to connect, somehow. They talked a lot about intimacy and claimed that S/M sex is more intimate than vanilla sex, but I didn't believe them.

Like the fetishists, they go to elaborate lengths to keep distance between themselves and the objects of their lust or love." I pause, sip my coffee. Should I really be saying these things to her? "Some people, both dominants and submissives, told me that they felt intensely close to their partners during a scene. I wonder if they need the intensity of pain and the emotion surrounding it to break through their barriers."

"Aberrant sex is all about the performing of rituals to keep you at a distance from each other," she says, wiping a tear from the corner of one eye. "You are right about the failure to connect. I am learning how to connect my feelings of love and warmth and desire to my sexuality. I couldn't do it before. Love was separate from lust. I lusted for the whip.

"I thought I felt love when the whippings were over and my master held me and stroked me."

"Do you think that was love now?" I ask.

"No, oh, no, oh, God, no. I think that was pathetic."

I call Dr. Berlin to check some details. His call-waiting clicks in every few minutes, but he ignores the beep, generously giving his time to me as he has on many occasions. He tells me about an article he's recently read on S/M in the mainstream press that presents "this basically happy collection of people talking about how much fun it is to hurt each other.

"I am cautious about presenting S/M as benign," he muses. "There is a risk in saying, 'This is fun and nobody's business but our own.' It's too easy to miscalculate, to inflict more pain and damage than you mean.

"The issue is more complicated than a matter of individ-

316

ual liberty. Sometimes the political views of therapists, journalists, and other individuals blind them to the dangers. We deny, rationalize, kid ourselves about how risky this is, because we don't want to sound moralistic. We don't know how to analyze the risks without sounding like we're condemning people.

"Piercings, for example, are dangerous. There's a terrible risk of infection. Piercing one's genitals could put one's sexuality in jeopardy. Why are we glamorizing this kind of behavior in the media?"

"Maybe all S/M articles should come with a warning label," I say.

"Talk to Tipper Gore about that," he says, laughing.

As soon as I hang up, a friend calls to ask if I saw *Murphy Brown* the night before. There was a throwaway line from Corky about Murphy's mail: "You got two letters from men who wanted pictures of your feet. I didn't know what to do with them."

"Sexual deviants are out of the closet," my friend says, "when they're mentioned on prime-time sitcoms."

I organize my desk while we chat.

On top of a stack of mail piled in a basket is a press release about the making of the movie *Exit to Eden*. Dana Delaney stars in this film version of the S/M love story, based on Anne Rice's novel of the same name. Girl whips boy, girl falls in love with boy, boy and girl run away from S/M fantasy island together.

Under that is a flier from Jan at Briar Rose, the lesbian S/M support group in Columbus, Ohio. "Domestic Violence in the S/M Community," a workshop. A reality check?

Conclusion:
How Far Will It Go?

When you write about sex, you think about sex. You probably think about sex more than the average person does. People have asked me, "Doesn't writing about sex turn you on?" Yes, it often does. Writing about sex has fueled my fantasies and sometimes expanded them.

Writing much of this book did not turn me on.

In the beginning, I was titillated by what I saw and heard. People shared their experiences, sometimes in vivid detail. Women leaned close over glasses of wine or cups of coffee, their voices lowered to husky levels as they recounted the experiences they considered "kinky." Men looked in my eyes as they talked, watching to see if their words were turning me on, too. And sometimes when the eye contact was broken, I glanced quickly at their crotches to satisfy my curiosity about whether or not they had become erect retelling their own erotic moments. Later, especially if I was alone in a hotel room, I often became aroused listening to those conversations again on tape.

In San Diego, a woman described in a breathy voice how she thrilled to her lover's light slaps across her buttocks before intercourse: "His hands on my flesh feel warm at first. The slaps make my skin tingle and gradually grow warm. Suddenly I notice that his hand caressing my chastened ass feels deliciously cool."

A Chicago artist told me how he liked to perform cunnilingus for long periods of time on his wife when she was tied to the bed: "I lose myself in her, in lapping her juices. Then I pull back and make her come up to me. Seeing her straining to reach my tongue with her arched body is a powerful turn-on for me."

I had never seen two women make love, except on videotape, until I attended the party of swingers in Texas. The sight of a female mouth, slick with lip gloss, pressed against the moist labia of another woman was unexpectedly exciting. Uninhibited women caressing each other's breasts and genitals and rubbing against each other inflamed their male partners—and turned them, for a few minutes at least, into the bull studs they imagine they are.

When I began interviewing people who participate in more strenuous and public forms of S/M and other disturbing—to me—behaviors, I stopped getting excited by my research.

I have some strong opinions about what I have seen and the stories and confessions I've heard. I have drawn some conclusions about what people do and why. These are not *expert* conclusions. (Haven't we all heard enough *expert* opinions?) They are mine, the observations of someone who has stood on the sidelines and watched some remarkable scenes—a view seldom afforded the vanilla curious, people like you and me. Had you been there, you would have formed some strong opinions, too.

LIGHT KINK IS SEXY. HEAVY KINK IS NOT

The "kinky sensualists"—people who enjoy experiencing strong sexual sensations—include those who like anal sex, "tie and tease" bondage, a little S/M. They may have a greater need for sexual variety than the average person. Their more exotic forms of sex play are incorporated into erotic lives that include tender, gentle, and emotional episodes of lovemaking. Some kinky sensualists also have exhibitionistic streaks. They are the couple who used to do it in the bathroom at parties in college.

A very attractive husband and wife recently profiled on a segment of HBO's *Real Sex* played S/M games for the camera. In one scene, she led him up to the bedroom by a leash attached to his slave collar. She turned him over her knee across the bed and lightly spanked him with a shoe tree. In the next scene, he fastened her wrists over her head into a bondage bar, which resembles a trapeze. Dressed in a leather corset leaving breasts and buttocks exposed, she obviously enjoyed displaying her lush body to public view. He whipped her a few times with a thin cane, pausing between strokes to rub her glowing ass cheeks and ask her if she was all right. Both were clearly aroused in each scene. Their excitement was contagious. It was a sexy piece of film.

Once you go beyond anal sex, tie and tease, and fantasy S/M games—which are more about costumes than implements of torture—it isn't about sex anymore. The practitioners of heavy kink are troubled people, and this is one problem you can't blame on the breakup of the nuclear family. Their sex negativism was very likely nourished in the bosom of a nuclear family.

I found the interviews and the research material focusing on the lifestylers—the people whose lives are defined by S/M or fetishism—to be fascinating, sometimes appalling, often riveting. Erotic? No.

Fetishists and those heavily involved in S/M or bondage do not have passionate, wild, out-of-control sex. They act out rituals centered around pain and/or worship and humiliation, punishment and redemption, sacrifice and reward. These people have more in common with Christian fundamentalists than they do with true sexual adventurers. They are, above all else, *rigid,* a quality I never seek in a lover.

If S/M is more than an occasional form of play that doesn't leave marks, you're in trouble. Get help. I don't care what nine out of ten therapists say while a tape recorder is running, you're in trouble.

THERAPISTS ARE TOO POLITICALLY CORRECT

The "I'm Okay, You're Okay, Too, Even If You Like to Be Called Names and Lashed Across Your Butt While Sucking Toes" school of thought annoys me. No, I do not want to see therapists chastising their fetishistic or sadistic or masochistic patients. But isn't there a way of saying "Being a submissive is not a healthy, happy way for you to live" without morally condemning the submissive or the dominant? Shouldn't professionals have the obligation of suggesting there is more to sex than the limited little dried slice of it these people have on their plates?

"Therapists dare not be quoted saying something that

isn't politically correct,'' a Boston psychotherapist told me. ''Seldom is an honest evaluation of the pros and cons of a behavioral situation considered PC. Political correctness permeates the intellectual atmosphere. There is a PC way of viewing everything from crossdressing to race relations. PC thinking can be as rigid and moralistic in its own way as the rhetoric of the Christian right.''

Political correctness is a white liberal construct, the left wing's version of the Puritan code, the Nineties method of expiating our guilt for wrongs done to ''minorities.'' It's also boring, confining, and truly condescending to the ''minorities'' supposedly protected by its guidelines for acceptable speech, behavior, and thought. When you put the language of therapy through the further refinement of the PC filter, you are left with stultifying blather. And few experts dare to suggest that smacking your partner in the name of love or eros may not be such a good thing.

SWINGERS ARE BORING, ESPECIALLY THE MEN

They are also woefully ignorant about STDs and how they are spread, but so are most adults who have multiple partners.

The majority of swingers I interviewed have been swinging for years, decades, even. They often seem like people stuck in a time warp. You expect the men to be wearing polyester leisure suits and to have big droopy mustaches. Their cavalier attitude toward their risk of contracting disease dates them, but so does their prevailing ideology: *Swinging is good for marriages. Swinging keeps couples together. Swingers aren't jealous or possessive of their mates.*

Men who couldn't sell me a used car kept pressing those statements on me like business cards. Male swingers were far more likely than their female counterparts to engage in recruitment tactics. Some women are undoubtedly participating because they accept their husbands' swinging philosophy. Yet other women appear to be having more fun than anyone.

Swinging does seem to be a good way for bisexual women to have affairs with other women. Their husbands approve because they get to watch. Two women together is still a top fantasy for the average man. And maybe the women wouldn't feel comfortable about having sex together without their husbands present.

FETISHISTS, MASOCHISTS, SADISTS, SWINGERS, AND HEAVY-BONDAGE DEVOTEES ALL HAVE PROBLEMS WITH INTIMACY

They're just like everybody else in need of pop-psych guidance on how to relate, only more so. I thought I had problems with intimacy until I met these people. The energy they put into making sure they do not forge one strong truly intimate bond with a sexual partner is astonishing. Haven't they ever seen *Oprah*?

Serious practitioners of S/M do talk about intimacy. They claim they have more intimate relationships than the rest of us do. This is a claim not supported by scientific research. If you have to endure a heavy whipping to be granted the comfort of your lover's arms, you are better off alone with a devoted pet and a good book.

THE MEDIA PORTRAYALS OF S/M AND OTHER ASSORTED KINK ARE FANTASY TRIPS

Spend an evening curled up in bed with your favorite magazines and the remote control, particularly if you have cable. Beautiful women in print layouts assume the postures of dominance and submission. Flip to MTV and see the same women, wearing less clothing, in more active poses. Bodies in exquisite shape are being erotically tormented on The Movie Channel, Showtime, Cinemax, and HBO.

The average sadomasochist does not look like an extra in a Madonna video. He is the geek with stringy hair at the Eulenspiegel Society meeting, the guy you wouldn't sit down next to on a subway train unless there was room for another person in between. She may not look so great, either, unless she spends a lot of time on her makeup before donning the leather gear. They have a look in their eyes you don't want to understand.

Serious sadomasochists are to film stars in bondage as the alcoholic in the gutter is to the elegant couple who only imbibe sips of champagne.

PIERCING, BRANDING, AND SCARRING ARE DANGEROUS, FRIGHTENING PRACTICES

Articles in the mainstream press on piercing have focused on what the young people have to say about why they're doing it. *Sexy. Fun. I'm owning my body. Marking my claim on myself.* When is a journalist going to ask the larger question: Why are our young people mutilating themselves? When is a journalist going to interview a doctor?

My doctor, the highly respected Manhattan internist and Executive Director of the Institute for Sexual Health, Sue DeCotiis, M.D., says of clitoral piercing, "The risk of heavy bleeding is significant. So is the risk of infection and eventual loss of sexual feeling."

I predict that in ten years a *Donahue* show will be devoted to "Piercing Victims." Guests will include men and women left sexually impaired by genital piercings, the parents of a girl who bled to death during a clitoral piercing, the piercer on live satellite feed from his prison cell, a plastic surgeon who specializes in restoring damaged pierced parts, and, of course, a therapist.

CROSSDRESSERS ARE FUN

Being with a crossdresser is like going back in time to a high school slumber party. You and your best girlfriend talking about makeup, clothes, stockings versus panty hose, attracting boys. Crossdressers are fun. And who else will envy your breasts even if they're small and a bit saggy?

But I wouldn't wan~~t~~ ~~it with~~ one.

How far will it go?

Twenty-five years ago, admitting to masturbation was kinky. A man who said he enjoyed performing cunnilingus was kinky. A woman admitting she liked to perform fellatio was kinky. Heterosexual anal sex was beyond kinky. The definition of *kink* has certainly expanded since the baby boomers, my generation, were coming of age. How much further will it go?

Most experts believe that hardcore S/M activity has not increased with the growing acceptability of kink. Such behavior is more open, more freely acknowledged by participants, but not more frequent. More couples do feel they have social permission to explore alternate forms of erotic play, and that's good.

Will this increased openness lead to more of the kinds of behavior that are potentially harmful? Probably not.

Will an increasingly violent, sexually repressive society continue to breed fetishists, masochists, sadists—perhaps an increasingly violent and alienated group of sadomasochists? Probably so.

Do most paraphiliacs represent a threat to society? No. Only to themselves and possibly their consenting partners.

What will be "kinky" twenty-five years from now, then? I'm betting on the missionary position.

- *Should women draw a line between love and sex?*

- 306 ... are
  t...

- *Is "sex addiction" truly a sickness?*

Bakos ... with prescriptive advice that any woman can use to enjoy fulfilling sex and lasting relationships. In the author's singularly personal style, and in the words of hundreds of women from around the U.S., *Sexual Pleasures* brings wisdom, comfort, and sound counsel *to* women, *from* women.

SEXUAL PLEASURES

What Women Really Want,
What Women Really Need

SUSAN CRAIN BAKOS